Uncle John's BATHROOM READER®

TALES TO INSPIRE

By the
Bathroom Readers'
Institute

Bathroom Readers
Ashland, Oreg

D1022590

Uncle John's Tales to Inspire®

For information, write:
The Bathroom Readers' Institute,
P.O. Box 1117, Ashland, OR 97520
www.bathroomreader.com
888-488-4642

Cover design by Michael Brunsfeld,
San Rafael, CA (*Brunsfeldo@comcast.net*)

Cover photos by Jay Newman
(*www.NewmanImages.com*)

Uncle John's Tales to Inspire®
by the Bathroom Readers' Institute
ISBN-13: 978-1592-23604-6
ISBN-10: 1-59223-604-9

Library of Congress Catalog Card Number:
2006923859

Printed in the United States of America
First Printing
06 07 08 09 10   10 9 8 7 6 5 4 3 2 1

THANK YOU!

The Bathroom Readers' Institute sincerely thanks the people whose advice and assistance made this book possible.

Gordon Javna
Thom Little
Jay Newman
Brian Boone
Amy Miller
Julia Papps
John Dollison
Jahnna Beecham
Malcolm Hillgartner
Angela Kern
Jef Fretwell
Michael Brunsfeld
Sharilyn Hovind
Jolly Jeff Cheek
John Gaffey
Sydney Stanley
Allen Orso
JoAnn Padgett
Laurel, Mana, Dylan, and Chandra
Nancy Toeppler

Rad Welles
Connie Vazquez
Matthew Furber
Kristine Hemp
Raincoast Books
Dan Schmitz
Shobha Grace
Jennifer Thornton
(Mr.) Mustard Press
Steven Style Group
Weifeng Ben Liang
Keziah Veres
Shannon Kehle
Michelle Sedgwick
Jennifer P. & Melinda A.
Banta Book Group
Scarab Media
Marley J. Pratt
(our #1 inspiration)
Porter the Wonder Dog
Thomas Crapper

CONTENTS

Because the BRI understands your reading needs, we've
divided the contents by length as well as subject.
Short—a quick read
Medium—2 pages
Long—3 pages or more

AGAINST ALL ODDS

DREAM BUILDERS

LATE BLOOMERS

INTRODUCTION

WELCOME to this very special edition of *Uncle John's Bathroom Reader.*

If you're new to our series, then allow us to introduce ourselves. The Bathroom Readers' Institute is a group of dedicated trivia nuts living in the small mountain town of Ashland, Oregon. Over the two decades that we've been bringing you *Bathroom Readers*, we've uncovered many uplifting stories. That gave us the idea of creating an entire book that celebrates incredible people and achievements.

Just look around you; there are so many. For example...

• **Everyday folks who do extraordinary things,** such as the mysterious driver who always pays the toll for the five cars behind her, the man who sold his house and then used the money to buy a community hall for the Girl Scouts, and the city bus driver who conducts sing-alongs with his passengers.

• **Disabled people who refuse to be limited by their physical limitations,** like the blind man who helped millions learn how to read and write, the high school wrestler who figured out how to win even though he has no arms, and the scientist who can't move or talk, but changed the way we view the universe.

• **Wealthy people who give back,** such as the hockey star who donated his entire salary to help troubled teens, the doctor in India who invented a simple toilet that saved millions of lives, and the robber baron who gave away his entire fortune to promote literacy.

• **Kids who notice a problem and then get to work trying to fix it.** There's the group of high school students who dress up as superheroes and help out their neighbors, the boy who rescued hundreds of old computers from the landfill and placed them into schools, and the little girl whose big idea led to the planting of a million trees.

• **This book is more than just amazing people.** We show you natural wonders, like the tortoise who adopted the hippo, our intricate relationship to the universe, and the lessons that ants can teach us. You'll find architectural achievements, like the village made out of bottles and the castle that took one man 70 years to build (all by himself). And then there are fables, proverbs, jokes, and words of wisdom from the likes of the Buddha, Einstein, Helen Keller, and P-Funk.

While we're talking about inspirational people, here's a great big THANK YOU to the writers and researchers at the Bathroom Readers' Institute who poured their hearts into making this book: Jay, Brian, Thom, John, Amy, Jahnna, Malcolm, Angie, Jef F., and Jolly Jeff Cheek.

And finally...thank *you*. We know we say this in every book, but we can't help it. The love and enthusiasm you've shown for this quirky book series has inspired us to keep doing the very best we can to keep you entertained. Here's to many more years of bathroom reading bliss.

So, until next time,

Go with the Flow!

Uncle John, the BRI staff, and Porter the Wonder Dog

YOU'RE MY INSPIRATION

Everybody is inspired by someone. Who inspires you?

STEVE MARTIN. As a boy in the 1950s, Martin loved watching *The Red Skelton Show* on TV. Amazed by Skelton's power to make people laugh, he wanted that power, too. How'd he get it? By learning every Skelton skit word for word and then performing them for his schoolmates.

CORETTA SCOTT KING. King was inspired by Eleanor Roosevelt's campaign for global human rights. The First Lady once said, "No one can make you feel inferior without your consent." Those words stayed with King her whole life, and reminded her to never be afraid to stand up for what she believed.

HENRY FORD completed his first self-propelled vehicle, the gas-engine powered *Quadricycle*, in 1896. That same year he met his boyhood hero, Thomas Edison, and told him about the Quad. Edison, who was working on an electric vehicle, banged his fist on the table and said, "Young man, you have it! Your car is self contained and carries its own power plant." Years later Ford said, "That bang on the table was worth worlds to me."

STEVIE RAY VAUGHAN. One of Vaughan's first influences was blues guitarist Buddy Guy. Yet while Vaughan went on to fame in the 1980s, Guy fell on hard times and nearly quit the business. Until one day when Guy heard Vaughan's playing. He was so amazed that he decided to pick up his own guitar again...unaware that the man who inspired him to return to music was the same man that he inspired to start playing in the first place.

RYAN'S WELL

"Every individual matters. Every individual has a role to play. Every individual makes a difference." —Jane Goodall

ALL WELL AND GOOD

Ryan Hreljac of Kemptville, Ontario, says he's just a normal kid, but those who know him consider him to be remarkable. In 1998, when Ryan was six years old, he learned from his first-grade teacher that hundreds of thousands of African children die every year from drinking contaminated water. His teacher further explained that in Africa a single penny would buy a pencil, 25 cents would cover the cost of 175 vitamins, 60 cents would supply two months' worth of medicine, and $70 would pay for a well.

Determined to help, Ryan worked for four months doing household chores to earn the money to buy a well, but found that $70 would only pay for a small hand pump. He'd have to raise $2,000 to buy a real well. That didn't stop Ryan; he continued to raise money—from neighbors, other children, and foundations. By the time he was seven, not only had Ryan raised the $2,000 for a hand-dug well, he'd promised the Canadian Physicians for Aid and Relief that he would raise another $25,000 to buy the drilling equipment needed to build more wells in Africa. And he kept his promise.

In 2001 Ryan funded his own charitable organization, Ryan's Well Foundation. "One of the most important things we do," he says, "is talk about the role each of us must play, no matter who we are or how old we are, in making the world a better place." Since then the foundation has raised more than $1 million and funded the building of 197 wells.

LOCAL HEROES

*Here are three stories of ordinary people
who did extraordinary things.*

WE DELIVER
Barely a week into his new job as a cab driver, 37-year-old Nedal Haddad of Chicago got a passenger he'll never forget. A woman and her two daughters climbed in, saying that they needed to get to the hospital fast—one of the daughters was very pregnant. But as they were zipping through traffic, Haddad heard the words every cabbie dreads: "I think I'm going to have the baby!" He immediately pulled over to the side of the road. The woman's mother and sister were too panicked to assist, so Haddad climbed into the backseat and took over. Without any medical training whatsoever (except for watching a show about childbirth on the Discovery Channel), he then proceeded to deliver the baby. Paramedics arrived soon after and took the new mom and her healthy baby girl to the hospital. Birthday gift: In addition to delivering the child, Haddad waived the $60 cab fare.

GOOD CALL
Telemarketers may annoy you at dinnertime, but one man was glad to get the call. Crystal Rozell, who works for Consumer Direct Marketing in Saratoga Springs, New York, made a random sales call to Stanley Bauch, an 85-year-old man in Ridott, Illinois. Bauch was somewhat incoherent, but Rozell could make out enough of what he was saying to understand that he was in serious trouble, and she alerted police. Apparently Bauch had fallen near his rural home and, after spending a freezing December night outside, had

crawled back to his living room. He could reach the phone but couldn't make an outgoing call. The next day, after he'd spent 17 hours without food or water, Rozell was the first person to call him. She kept him talking until paramedics arrived to take him to the hospital. Bauch was dehydrated but otherwise okay. The telemarketing company did one more good deed: They gave Bauch a free subscription to a medical alert network, in case he falls again.

GREAT CATCH

On a cold December morning in the Bronx, New York, a fire broke out in the kitchen of a third-story apartment. Felix Vasquez, the superintendent of the building, was in the street when he heard screams coming from above. He looked up and saw a woman holding something out the window, but couldn't tell what it was. The woman, Tracinda Foxe, recognized her super 30 feet below and tossed the object to him. It was only when the object was in the air that Vasquez realized what it was: Foxe's three-month-old baby.

"She threw the baby," Vasquez recalled, "and that's when I ran in and caught him just in time, just like a football. I gave him mouth-to-mouth, and he coughed, and then started yelling and crying."

Firefighters rushed into the building and rescued the mother, who was soon reunited with her baby. "It's just a miracle, a miracle," Vasquez said. (It may also have had something to do with the fact that Vasquez's position on his softball team is…catcher.)

*   *   *

Pray indeed, but get to work! —*Mexican proverb*

"TAILS" TO INSPIRE

Animals sometimes teach us what it really means to be human.

BUMPUS TO THE RESCUE
In June 1996, firefighters in the Alaskan wilderness found an orange cat that had been horribly burned by a wildfire and was missing his hind feet. The injured cat, nicknamed Bumpus, wasn't expected to survive...but he did. And not only that, he taught himself to walk again. Eventually Bumpus was adopted by Sharon, a fire-and-rescue volunteer who took him home with her to Missouri, where she worked for the local Humane Society, caring for sick kittens. That's how Bumpus met Cheerio, a kitten who was traumatized by the recent loss of one of his legs. Cheerio couldn't walk, cried constantly, bit anything that came near him, and hid under the bed in a secluded room. Sharon thought Bumpus might help, and sure enough, when she let him into Cheerio's room, he immediately ran to the crying kitten, wrapped his paws around him, and licked his face. The crying soon stopped and Cheerio began to purr. This went on for weeks. Eventually Cheerio regained his strength, learned to walk again, and went to live with a new family. Since then, whenever Sharon gets an especially despondent kitten, she sends in her trusted assistant: Bumpus.

FAIR ELLEN
Fair Ellen was a golden collie, born blind in 1921. Her master, Albert Terhune, was going to "put her out of her misery" until his wife pointed out that Fair Ellen was in no misery at all—she was the liveliest one of the litter. Fair Ellen galloped like the rest of the puppies, but after a few steps she'd run

into something—a food dish or fence wires. Each time, she'd right herself and move on, tail wagging as if it were some kind of game. Amazingly, she never collided with the same obstacle twice. In less than a week, she could run across the yard without hitting anything. And within a few weeks, she could traverse the entire 40-acre property, having run into each tree, rock, and shrub only once. She could run at full speed and then stop six inches from a wall. She even taught herself to swim. In her 12 years, most people who met Fair Ellen didn't even know she was blind.

ROULETTE

In 1970 Joe Fulda was drafted into military service and shipped off to Vietnam. He left behind a wife, a son, and a one-year-old poodle named Roulette. He promised everyone —including the dog—that he'd write often. Joe kept his promise and sent home letters two or three times a week. But his wife, Mycki, complained that weeks would pass without any letters from him. They were puzzled…until Mycki finally realized what was going on.

If she was actually there to catch the mail when it came through the door slot, there was likely to be a letter from Joe. But if she wasn't there and picked it up off the floor later, there was never a letter. And she noticed that Roulette became agitated when Mycki got to the mail slot first.

One day Mycki hid behind a wall when the mail arrived, and watched as Roulette sniffed around the stack of mail, then pulled out a single envelope and dropped it behind the living-room couch. Mycki moved the couch…and discovered a trove of letters from Joe. That's when she realized what had happened to the missing letters: Roulette was keeping them for herself.

OLD MAN HOWARD

For kids in this town, the ultimate dare was to
set foot on the Howard Farm. Old Man
Howard hated kids...or did he?

GRUMPY OLD MAN

Wesley Howard was born and raised in a ramshackle house on a 68-acre farm in Medford, Oregon. After his parents died, he remained there alone and over the decades, earned a reputation as a miser and recluse. He never got a phone or indoor plumbing, never married or had any children. His house became known as "the creepy old Howard place."

Like any "haunted house," the Howard property was irresistible to children. They would poke around his barn and orchards; some would throw rocks or golf balls at his windows. Sometimes they'd sneak into his fields to pick grapes and peaches. But Old Man Howard chased them off. Often he'd run out with his shotgun and shoot rock salt at anyone who wandered onto his property. He particularly seemed to hate kids.

For years, they thought Old Man Howard was the meanest man in Jackson County.

MISUNDERSTOOD?

But others saw a different side of Wesley Howard. Some of his neighbors regarded him as a private man who was constantly harassed by the neighborhood children. Howard had served on the local Citizens Planning Advisory Committee for 20 years and was fiercely concerned about land-use and development issues in the city of Medford. And he'd had a lifelong love of baseball.

SURPRISE ENDING

When 87-year-old Wesley Howard died of a stroke in March 2003, it came as no surprise to anyone that his home was filled with years of accumulated newspapers, toys, and baseball memorabilia. It certainly fit his hermit image. What did come as a surprise was that Old Man Howard was rich—*very* rich. Even more surprising: The reading of his will revealed that he'd left his entire estate—$11 million and his farm—to build a sports park for local children.

The amazing gift (#58 on the list of 100 largest charitable donations of 2003) left local residents baffled, wondering whether anyone had known the real Wesley Howard. An editorial in the Medford *Mail Tribune* noted: "We'll never know if Wes Howard had a Scrooge-like epiphany, or if there was always a charitable soul hidden beneath his gruff exterior."

HAVE A BALL

Scrooge or not, Old Man Howard, who cared about his hometown and loved baseball, ensured that his estate would honor both. The Howard Memorial Sports Park, due to be built on the site of his old farm in 2007, will include fields for Little League baseball, as well as facilities for soccer, basketball, and volleyball. According to Howard's attorney, "He wanted to have his family name on the land, thinking especially of his parents, and to leave it for the benefit of young people." Even those kids he once chased off his property with a blast of rock salt.

*   *   *

"Look at people, recognize them, accept them as they are, without wanting to change them."   **—Helen Beginton**

SOUND ADVICE

Some simple wisdom…so simple that we often overlook it.

"Believe those who are seeking the truth. Doubt those who find it."
—**André Gide**

"Think like a man of action, act like a man of thought."
—**Henri-Louis Bergson**

"Sometimes it's necessary to go a long distance out of the way in order to come back a short distance correctly."
—**Edward Albee**

"We have to do the best we can. This is our sacred human responsibility."
—**Albert Einstein**

"When the student is ready, the master appears."
—**Buddhist proverb**

"Be the change that you want to see in the world."
—**Mahatma Gandhi**

"If we had no winter, the spring would not be so pleasant; if we did not sometimes taste of adversity, prosperity would not be so welcome."
—**Charlotte Brontë**

"The three great essentials to achieving anything worthwhile are: first, hard work; second, stick-to-it-iveness; and third, common sense."
—**Thomas Edison**

"When one door of happiness closes, another opens; but often we look so long at the closed door that we do not see the one which has been opened for us."
—**Helen Keller**

GREAT SECOND ACTS

*"Retirement at 65 is ridiculous. When I was
65 I still had pimples."—George Burns*

BOB UECKER
First Act: Uecker was signed as a catcher with the Milwaukee Braves in 1956 and played for three teams over nine seasons. He retired in 1967 with a career batting average of .200.

Second Act: Since 1971, he's been the play-by-play announcer for the Milwaukee Brewers. On the air he honed the personality of a self-effacing, lovable loser and made fun of his terrible baseball career. He carried on the persona in commercials, nationally broadcast games, and dozens of appearances on *The Tonight Show*. He even starred on the ABC sitcom *Mr. Belvedere* in the 1980s. Uecker was inducted into the Radio Hall of Fame in 2001, and the Milwaukee Brewers retired a Bob Uecker jersey in 2005.

JOSEPH CONRAD
First Act: Born Józef Teodor Konrad Korzeniowski in 1857 in Poland, Conrad spent most of his early life at sea—first in the French merchant marines, then as a British sea captain. He sailed the world, even going up the Congo River in Africa. In 1894 he retired at age 36, married two years later, and had two children.

Second Act: Conrad became a writer. He published his first book, *Almayer's Folly*, at the age of 38. His novels (including *Heart of Darkness*, based on his trip up the Congo) are considered masterpieces of English literature, even though English was Conrad's third language, after Polish and French.

RICHARD FARNSWORTH

First Act: Farnsworth started his career as a cowboy and rodeo rider, and then became a movie stuntman. Over 40 years he appeared in more than 300 films.

Second Act: In midlife, Farnsworth stepped into the limelight as an actor. In 1976 he played the stagecoach driver in *The Duchess and the Dirtwater Fox* and a year later, at the age of 57, he was nominated for a Best Supporting Actor Oscar for his performance in *Comes a Horseman*. After performances in *The Natural* and *The Silver Fox*, at 80 he was nominated for a Best Actor Oscar for his final performance in the 1999 film *The Straight Story*—the oldest actor to get such a nomination.

JIM MORRIS

First Act: In January 1983, pitcher Jim Morris was drafted by the Milwaukee Brewers. He played in the minor leagues for a few seasons, but after suffering multiple injuries to his throwing arm, he retired in 1989. Only 25 years old, Morris returned to his home state of Texas, where he became a high school baseball coach.

Second Act: Morris's team wasn't very good, so to motivate his players, he told them that if they won the district title, he'd try out for the major leagues again. It worked. The team won and Morris tried out for the Tampa Bay Devil Rays. In spite of being 35 and having had so many injuries, he could still throw a 98 MPH fastball. The team signed him, and on September 18, 1999, he pitched against the Texas Rangers, striking out his first batter on four pitches. He played in 25 more games until his old arm injuries caught up with him, and he had to retire for a second time in 2000.

Third Act: His story was made into the 2002 film *The Rookie*.

LADYBUGS

The folks in the previous article prove that you're never too old to do great things. Hannah proves that you've never too young.

IDENTIFYING THE PROBLEM

In 2001, five-year-old Hannah Taylor saw a homeless man eating out of a garbage can on a cold day in Winnipeg, Manitoba, and it made her sick to her stomach. A few weeks later, she saw a woman carrying everything she owned piled in a grocery cart. As she noticed more and more homeless people, she told her mother that it made her sad and asked why people had to live this way.

Colleen Taylor didn't know how to answer, but she gave her daughter some advice—if you do something to help solve the problem, it might make you feel better. Hannah's response: If more people knew about homelessness, and if they shared what they could, it might help.

STARTING SMALL

Hannah got to work. First she composed and delivered a speech on the issue to her first-grade class. Then she started asking her teachers, friends, classmates, and family members for their spare change, which she put in homemade "ladybug jars"—baby food bottles painted red and black. (Hannah says ladybugs are good luck.)

This spare change–collection drive soon turned into a formal organization called the Ladybug Foundation. With the help of her parents, Hannah made more ladybug jars—hundreds of them—and put them in stores around Winnipeg to collect more change. She gave all the money she collected to local shelters and charities that directly fed, clothed, and housed the homeless. The operation expanded: Hannah started selling red-and-black bracelets and fleece scarves to raise more money.

In 2005 Hannah expanded her foundation again, this time to British Columbia, where 2,000 Ladybug jars—all still handmade by volunteers—were distributed with the help of a local company, G.T. Hiring Solutions. At the age of 10—and in less than five years—Hannah has raised half a million dollars for the homeless.

MORE GOOD LUCK

When she's not in school, Hannah now tours Canada, speaking to crowds about how important—and easy—it is to help. And though she may be young and idealistic, she's aware of the many challenges faced by the homeless, including substance abuse and mental illness. "It doesn't exactly matter," she says. "They are great people wrapped in old clothes with sad hearts. Don't be afraid of them, be kind to them. If they're cold, share your mittens. If they're hungry, give them a sandwich. If they're sad, give them a smile."

*   *   *

KEEP SMILIN'

In 2005 researchers in England used brain scans and heart monitors to measure people's reactions to a variety of stimuli. Here's what they found: The test subjects registered more pleasure from seeing a photo of a smiling child than they would have from eating 2,000 chocolate bars or receiving $25,000 in cash.

A GREAT TEACHER

*Not many teachers can motivate their students to come
early and stay late—but this is no ordinary teacher.*

UP TO THE CHALLENGE

Since 1981 Rafe Esquith has taught fifth grade at
Hobart Elementary in inner-city Los Angeles, the
second largest elementary school in the United States. Nearly
all Hobart students live below the poverty level and few are
native English-speakers. But Esquith's kids test in the top 5%
in the country. How? "I put my heart and soul in this,"
Esquith says. "I demand the same from them."

He fosters a "culture of excellence" in his classroom.
Portraits of Shakespeare and pennants from prestigious colleges line the walls. Classical music plays all day. He also
makes it clear that there are no shortcuts to success: Esquith's
students show up at 6:30 a.m. (the rest of the school arrives
at 8:30) to do mental math exercises. He assigns the fifth
graders high school–level books, such as *The Catcher in the
Rye* and *To Kill a Mockingbird*. At the end of the year, the
students perform a full-length Shakespeare play.

While Esquith expects his students to rise to the challenge,
he is patient with them until they "get it." And the students
get it—they usually work through recess and stay until 5 p.m.
As a reward for their hard work, Esquith takes his students on
field trips to Shakespeare festivals and historic sites.

"In our neighborhood, you look outside your window and
you see burned buildings," said one of Esquith's students. "He
teaches us that there is more to life than just what's outside
the window."

SECOND CHANCES

The remarkable story of Victoria Ruvolo.

A TERRIBLE ORDEAL

In November 2004, 45-year-old Victoria Ruvolo was heading home in Lake Ronkonkoma, New York, after hearing her 14-year-old niece sing at a school recital. At the same time, 19-year-old Ryan Cushing was out joyriding with a group of friends, who had just finished a spending spree at a nearby supermarket—with a stolen credit card.

One of the items they bought was a large frozen turkey. As Ruvolo's car passed Cushing's—he was in the back seat—the teen threw the turkey into oncoming traffic. The 20-pound bird crashed through Ruvolo's windshield and struck her in the face. The teens didn't stop, and they didn't call 911. Luckily Ruvolo had a passenger who called emergency services, and Ruvolo was rushed to Stony Brook University Hospital. She was put into a medically induced coma and went through a 10-hour operation to save her from dying. She was kept in the coma for two weeks, and stayed in the hospital for months after that, as doctors reconstructed her shattered face and she went through painful rehabilitation. The doctors said it was miraculous that she survived the ordeal at all.

FACE TO FACE

Nine months later, on August 15, 2005, Ruvolo, having beaten the odds and now even back at her old job, walked into the Suffolk County Court building. She watched silently as Ryan Cushing admitted that he had thrown the frozen bird from the car. When the proceeding ended, Ruvolo waited as the teen walked toward the door. He stopped when he got to her. He began to apologize but broke into sobs before he could get the words out. Ruvolo took Cushing in her arms and for the next few minutes held him as she stroked his hair. "I'm so sorry," the teen sobbed over and over. "It's okay, it's okay," responded Ruvolo. "I just want you to make your life the best it can be." Most of the people in the room were in tears as the scene unfolded before them.

VENGEANCE IS NOT MINE

The five other teens who had been with Cushing that night all pleaded guilty to lesser charges and were each sentenced to five years' probation. But Cushing had been indicted on much more serious charges, including first-degree assault. He was facing 25 years in prison. But Ruvolo intervened, secretly meeting with the prosecutor to ask for leniency. At the sentencing hearing in October, Ruvolo spoke before the court. While she made it clear that she had not completely forgiven him, she said to Cushing, "There is no room for vengeance in my life, and I do not believe a long, hard prison term would do you, me, or society any good."

Ryan Cushing was sentenced to six months in prison and five years probation. Ruvolo's compassion for her would-be-killer stunned the court, and the story made the news all over the world. William Keahon, Cushing's lawyer, said, "I've never seen this in 32 years of practicing law."

Ruvolo explained her extraordinary act simply: "God gave me a second chance," she said, "so I passed it on."

*   *   *

"The weak can never forgive. Forgiveness is an attribute of the strong." —**Mahatma Gandhi**

REJECTED...ALMOST

Thinking about giving up on your big dream? Think again.

Korean War veteran H. Richard Hornberger spent 12 years writing a novel about his war experiences. Seventeen publishers turned it down before it was finally published in 1968. Written under the pseudonym Richard Hooker, the novel—M*A*S*H—became a bestseller.

• Barnstorming pilot Richard Bach received 26 rejection slips for his book about an enlightenment-seeking bird before it was published in 1970. *Jonathan Livingston Seagull* went on to sell more than 30 million copies worldwide.

• Robert M. Pirsig wrote a book about a cross-country motorcycle trip—and the meaning of life. 121 publishers rejected it, but the 122nd didn't. Now there are more than four million copies of *Zen and the Art of Motorcycle Maintenance* in print.

• Jerry Boyd was a boxing "cornerman," one of the people who tend to boxers. He wrote short stories all his life, and for 40 years tried—unsuccessfully—to get them published. Finally, in 1999, one appeared in a small magazine. A literary agent happened to read it, tracked Boyd down, and got *Rope Burns* published. Hollywood later bought the rights. Several of Boyd's stories were combined into the 2004 film *Million Dollar Baby*, which won four Oscars, including Best Picture.

• When poet e. e. cummings couldn't get a collection of poems published in 1935, he published it himself. He titled the book *No Thanks,* and the dedication page read "WITH NO THANKS TO," followed by the names of the 14 publishers who had rejected the work. Cummings became one of the most popular American poets of all time.

A GIFT FROM…?

Somehow, it seems even more special when the source of a big donation remains a mystery.

• In November 2005, a group of wealthy donors from Michigan set up a foundation called the Kalamazoo Promise. Their mission: to provide four years of college tuition for any student who graduates from Kalamazoo's public schools with at least a 2.0 grade average. That's roughly $60,000 per student. It starts with the class of 2006 and continues for the next 13 years, putting more than 10,000 students through college. The donors declined to reveal their identities.

• Thanks to an anonymous donation of $100 million in 2005, the Yale School of Music, one of the most exclusive music colleges in the country, is now the least expensive. Until the money runs out, students no longer have to pay the annual $23,750 tuition.

• In 2005 Indiana University alumnus Jesse Cox donated $15 million to his school to create scholarships for students who, like himself, are the first in their family to attend college and have to work to pay their way through school. But that wasn't the only big news at IU: That same day they also received a $70 million *anonymous* donation—the school's largest ever—which created hundreds more scholarships.

• In 1998 a mystery donor in Tampa, Florida, gave $2 million to set up the country's first elementary school for homeless children. Attached to a shelter, it helps ensure homeless children don't have their education interrupted while facing uncertainty in their family lives. When news of the donation spread, two anonymous donors pledged another $100,000.

DIVORCE ROCK

Here's a love story from the Japanese island of Okinawa. It comes
from Bathroom Reader *contributor Jeff Cheek, who lived*
on the island when he was a secret agent with the CIA.

ONCE UPON A TIME
Japan has contributed many treasures to world
culture. Genka, a village on the island of Okinawa,
may offer yet another one: an alternative to divorce. In the
thousand years that the village has existed, residents say they
have never had a single marriage split up. And it all revolves
around the legend of the Divorce Rock.

This story dates back to when the village, which lies on
the northern coast of the island, was founded. A prominent
family had arranged the marriage of their infant daughter to
the six-year-old son of a friend. The children grew up together
but were never equals. The boy was described as a hard-
working fisherman who was gap-toothed, fat, spoke with a
lisp, and had a drooping left eye.

The girl grew into a great beauty, famed throughout the
island for her charm. She was a *mi-bijin,* or "Snake Year
beauty," the highest compliment a Japanese woman could
earn. Many wealthy suitors made their way to the tiny village
to court her. But her family forced her to uphold their
arrangement and marry the poor, homely fisherman. When
she was 18, the girl went to live in the home of her new
husband and his mother.

Social pressure could force her to marry him and live in
his house, but it could not make her love him or sleep with
him. She sullenly did her assigned chores while bewailing her
misfortune at being forced to marry a man who was not only

poor, but ugly as well. Her husband, as kind and gentle as he was homely, endured her insults—and her refusal to consummate the marriage—for many months.

Finally, the girl's mother-in-law had had enough. One morning she invited the young couple to row out with her to collect bird eggs on a large rock that rose out of the ocean, four miles off shore. When they were safely on the rock, the old woman rowed away. "Wave your scarf when you come to your senses," she called back, "and I will come get you."

ON THE ROCKS

For the rest of the day, the young woman harassed her husband. She compared him to the men she could have married: men who could have provided her with palaces and luxuries instead of a meager diet of rice and fish in a thatched hut. But as night fell, she became silent. A cold rain began to fall and, completely desolate, she started to weep. Her husband took off his heavy fisherman's coat and wrapped it around his wife.

Suddenly she started to wonder: Which was better? To have a rich, handsome paramour who might abandon her when her youth and beauty faded, or a brave and loving husband who battled the sea daily to secure their livelihood? She wisely chose the latter and opened the coat so that he, too, could be sheltered. The next day they returned to Genka village for a long and happy life together.

IT WORKED FOR THEM...

This dramatic change so impressed the villagers that the rock was named *ito-fue iwa*—literally "dislike husband rock," but commonly referred to as "Divorce Rock." And a new social custom was instituted: Any mother-in-law had the authority to send a warring couple out to the rock. (In the absence of a mother-in-law, the village headman could make the decision.) Here, away from interfering neighbors and meddling relatives, a couple could address their problems and solve them. And one important requirement was added: Couples exiled to *ito-fue iwa* were given food and water...but only one blanket.

Since that time, Divorce Rock has been the silent marriage counselor for the couples of Genka. They no longer have arranged marriages, and the rock hasn't been used in a long time. But, say the villagers, the ancient lesson still reverberates, and not a single couple from the village has ever been divorced.

*   *   *

HELLO, PEACE!

The Parent's Circle-Families Forum—a joint group composed of Israelis and Palestinians who have lost a family member to the conflict in their region—devised a way to help spread peace. In 2002 they formed Hello Shalom–Hello Salaam! ("Hello Peace" in Hebrew and Arabic). People can dial *6364, talk with somebody on "the other side" about peace, and the call is free. Sammy Waed, a 20-year-old from Ramallah, started speaking regularly with Arik, a 23-year-old Israeli soldier from Tel Aviv. "Before, I thought Israelis didn't care at all when innocent Palestinians are killed," he says. "But now I know they do care. And now I have hope that there can be peace." More than 400,000 people used the service in its first eight months. For many, it was the first time they had ever spoken to one of their neighbors.

HAPPY ACCIDENTS

Watch out—something wonderful might happen at any time.

• Mary Williamson, a housekeeper at a motel in Oklahoma City, found two rolls of bills totaling $8,000 in a room she was cleaning. She did the right thing and reported it to the motel's manager. But police were unable to track down the owner...so Williamson got to keep the $8,000.

• In the 1950s, an Italian woman gave a painting of a rural landscape to her nephew. He liked it and hung it up in his house. It wasn't until 2005, when he had an art-expert friend over for dinner, that he learned it was an original painting by Vincent van Gogh. It's worth an estimated $45 million.

• Liliana Parodi was eating a pasta dinner at a restaurant in Genoa, Italy, when she bit on a small rock. It lodged in her teeth, and she had to go to a dentist to get it removed. The "rock" turned out to be an uncut diamond worth $5,000.

• In 2004 Tom Dixton took out the garbage after changing the oil in his car. His hands were so greasy, he didn't realize that he'd accidentally tossed out his wedding ring. So he drove to the Los Angeles County Dump and started digging. After four days of sifting through 15 tons of rat-infested garbage, he was ready to give up and admit that the ring was gone. Then he found a $20 bill. Soon, he found a sack filled with $63,000. Then a collection of 2,000 old baseball cards, a box of old gold coins, and a perfectly preserved guitar signed by Jimi Hendrix. Altogether, Dixton's findings were worth $169,000. He turned the cash over to police, but they never found its owner, so he got to keep the $63,000. (He bought a new ring.)

THE MAGIC TOUCH, PART 1

All Louis Braille wanted to do was to read and write, but he couldn't—he was blind. So he poured his life into figuring out a way to do it. It was difficult, but Braille never lost sight of his mission…and he opened up a brand-new world to millions.

BLIND EXISTENCE

Before the 1800s, blind people were effectively doomed to a life of illiteracy, cut off not only from reading and writing but also from all of the learning that comes from books. In an age before television, radio, and tape recorders, the blind were denied access to anything they couldn't hear with their own ears. Living independently was pretty much out of the question; all but a lucky few ended up begging in the streets for their food. Even Dr. Sébastien Guillié, head of the Royal Institute for Blind Youth in Paris—one of only the few schools for the blind in the entire world at that time—believed that the students at his school were "degraded beings, condemned to vegetate on the Earth."

SCHOOL DAYS

One of those "degraded beings" was a 10-year-old French boy named Louis Braille. Louis had been blind since the age of three, when he poked himself in the left eye while playing with his father's tools—the injury caused him to lose his sight in both eyes. But Louis was a bright kid, so he continued to flourish at the village school in spite of his blindness…until the other kids began to learn to read and write. Without sight, Louis could do neither; all he could do was sit in silence.

In 1819 Louis was awarded a scholarship to the Royal

Institute. But if he had hoped for anything better after he arrived, he was soon disappointed. Although attempts had been made to find a way to teach blind people to read and write, no one at the Institute—or anywhere else, for that matter—had figured out a practical way to do it.

A COIN IN THE HAND

Valentin Haüy, the founder of the Royal Institute, may have been the first person to realize where the answer might lie. One day, many years earlier, he'd given a coin to a blind boy who was begging outside a church. Although the boy couldn't see, he correctly identified the denomination of the coin. Inspired by the encounter, Haüy took the boy in as a student and set out to make books that blind people could read...by touch.

He came up with the idea of soaking sheets of paper in water, then pressing them over rows of large raised-block letters. When the paper dried, the imprint of the letters remained. The students could "read" the pages by slowly tracing their fingers over each letter. The system worked, but it had its drawbacks: Deciphering each letter individually was a painstaking process; it might take half an hour to read a single page. And the letters had to be large enough to imprint, which meant the books were huge. Constructing them was a time-consuming and expensive process: In 30 years, the school's instructors managed to produce only 14 books.

Haüy's books did little to solve the problem of teaching the blind to read, and they were no help at all in teaching them how to write. If anything, Haüy's work proved just how monumental of a task this was.

To find out how Louis Braille invented his ingenious writing system, turn to Part 2 of "The Magic Touch" on page 125.

HOLDING UP THE SKY

*Around the world, too many children grow up
in overcrowded orphanages. One woman
made it her mission to help them.*

POPULATION PROBLEM

In 1979 China instituted a "one child per family"
policy. Because of a cultural preference for male children, hundreds of thousands of Chinese girls have been abandoned by their families. Where do all they all end up? In
Chinese orphanages. Result: The understaffed and poorly
funded orphanages can't handle the influx. Too many of
these children spend entire days alone in a crib, with little or
no human interaction. This can lead to serious emotional
and health problems later in life. And while the orphanages
do their best to care for every child, they simply don't have
the means to give them the attention they need.

THE HEALING POWER OF LOVE

In the summer of 1997, one of these Chinese babies, a little
girl named Maya, was fortunate enough to be adopted by
Jenny Bowen of Berkeley, California. Maya was in poor
health and emotionally distant. Bowen's remedy: shower the
girl with love and affection. Slowly but surely, the effects of
isolation began to wear off. A year later, Maya was a healthy
and happy toddler running around and playing with her
friends. It became apparent to Bowen that what had worked
for Maya might work on a larger scale in China.

So, with help from some other adoptive parents, Bowen
formed the Half the Sky Foundation, named for the Chinese
saying, "Women hold up half the sky."

STAYING IN TOUCH

Her first task was to raise money to train special nannies, called *zumu* ("grandmother" in Chinese). Their job is simple: play with the babies. But it makes all of the difference. Providing the children with physical and mental stimulation aids in releasing the hormones the babies need to properly develop their minds and bodies.

Bowen's Berkeley-based group of volunteers keeps growing and growing. They've expanded to 13 orphanages in 11 Chinese provinces, employing 450 nannies. In addition, they've built three preschools in China, employing 108 teachers and blending traditional Chinese and modern Western schooling. Between the orphanages and the schools, Half the Sky has had a positive impact on more than 3,000 infants and toddlers...so far.

Bowen continues to lobby the Chinese government on behalf of the children. They need more orphanages and they need more caregivers. "Once it started happening and the results were so successful, it swallowed up my life," Bowen says. "Once you start, there are thousands of kids out there you can reach, and whose lives you can really change."

*   *   *

THINK TANKS

Recent research shows that 80% of all creative ideas occur in informal settings. The most common: while driving, showering, or jogging. Another survey says the bathroom "throne" is the #1 seat of creativity. (Uncle John agrees.) Both surveys agree, however, on the place that inspires the *least* amount of creativity: the office.

GRAY'S ANATOMY

*Uncle John loves stories about people who focus on
what they do have—not on what they don't.*

NOW BATTING...
At the beginning of the 1945 baseball season, the
most famous rookie in the Major Leagues was St.
Louis Browns outfielder Pete Gray. Playing for the Class AA
Memphis Chicks in 1944, Gray batted .333 with five home
runs and 68 stolen bases, and won the Southern Association
Most Valuable Player award. While this alone would have
been enough to draw the attention of Major League talent
scouts, there was something else that made Gray remarkable:
He only had one arm.

At six years old, Pete had fallen from a farm wagon,
catching his right arm between the spokes of a wheel. The
arm had to be amputated. For most people, that would have
ruled out a career in professional sports, but it didn't stop
Pete Gray.

THE ONE-ARMED WONDER!

Growing up in the 1920s, playing ball on the sandlots of his
native northeast Pennsylvania, Gray developed a fielding
technique that allowed him to compete with his peers.
Catching the ball in a glove on his one hand, he would roll
the ball across his chest, grab his mitt with the stump of his
missing arm, pull his hand out of the glove, grab the ball, and
throw it. He performed this complicated maneuver so quickly
that it appeared to happen in one quick blur of motion. This
talent, coupled with his great speed and strong throwing arm,
made him a defensive star in the outfield.

At the plate, Gray batted from the left side and, using a standard-weight bat, developed into a solid hitter. As he grew up, he became a star in a semi-pro league, traveling a circuit of Pennsylvania coal towns. By the time he was in his mid-20s, he'd made the jump to professional minor-league baseball.

During World War II, with much of baseball's talent pool serving in the military, Major League ball clubs had to hunt high and low for quality players to fill out their rosters. On the strength of his MVP season in Memphis, Pete Gray got to play for the St. Louis Browns. He lasted only one season, with a somewhat disappointing .218 batting average (like a lot of players, he had trouble hitting a curveball). But during those war years, Gray became a hero for his determination and perseverance. He continued to draw crowds in the minor leagues until his retirement in the mid-1950s.

OTHER WONDERS

• Bert Shepard was a promising minor-league pitcher who joined the Army Air Corps when World War II broke out and then lost a leg when his plane was shot down over Germany. While still in a German POW camp, Shepard relearned how to pitch—a difficult accomplishment with an artificial leg. In 1945 he pitched one game for the Washington Senators, and was awarded the Distinguished Flying Cross in a ceremony between games of a doubleheader.

• Pitcher Jim Abbott was born without a right hand. He was lucky to have played during the era of the designated hitter, when pitchers didn't have to bat. Still, he had a career any pitcher would envy: 10 years in the majors. He even threw a no-hitter for the Yankees in 1993.

GREETINGS!

Plan on traveling to a foreign country any time soon? If so, you'll find that the locals appreciate it when you try to communicate in their language. And every conversation starts the same way...with "hello."

Greet a stranger in Greece with *kalimera* (kah-lee-MEH-rah).

Bom dia (bohm DEE-ah) means good day in Portuguese.

Privet (preev-YET) is hello in Russian.

In Japan, the common greeting is *konichiwa* (ko-NEE-che-wa).

Traditional Hebrew and Arabic greetings are similar: *shalom* (shah-LOME) in Hebrew, and *salaam* (sah-LAAM) in Arabic.

The Swiss say *grüetzi* (GROOT-si).

The Hungarian greeting is *szia* (ZEE-yah).

In Korea, *annyong* (AHN-yohng) means hello.

In Chinese, it's *ni hao* (nee-HOW).

The Cherokee greeting is pronounced *oh-see-YOH*.

The Zulus say *sawubona* (saw-oo-BOH-nah).

Hello in Thailand is *sawadti* (sa-wa-DEE)

Jambo (JAHM-boh) is the traditional Swahili greeting.

In Vietnam, say hello with *chào ban* (chow-BON)

The Macedonian hello is *zdravo* (zuh-DRAW-vo).

The Polish hello is *dzien dobry* (JEEN-do-bri).

In Hindi you say *namaste* (nah-MUS-stay), which means "I bow to the light within you."

AMAZING RESCUE

*They risked life and limb to save a trapped whale
and were rewarded with the gift of a lifetime.*

TANGLED WEB

On the brisk Sunday morning of December 11, 2005, a crab fisherman spotted a heartbreaking sight off the coast of San Francisco: a 50-foot humpback whale trapped in a tangle of crab-pot lines. He immediately called for help, and within three hours the Marine Mammal Center had chartered a boat—normally used for whale-watching tours—and assembled a rescue team. As soon as they arrived on the scene, they assessed the situation. It didn't look good.

The female humpback was completely entangled in hundreds of yards of ropes that collectively weighed more than 1,000 pounds. To make matters worse, she'd already been struggling for hours to keep her blowhole above water, and they didn't know how much strength she had left. No whale that had been trapped like this off the west coast had ever survived. With time running out, the rescuers knew there was only one way to save her: dive in and start cutting the ropes one at a time.

INTO THE WATER

Four divers went in: James Moskito, Jason Russey, Ted Vivian, and Tim Young. Moskito was the first to reach the whale, and the first to understand the severity of the situation. More than 20 thick lines were wrapped tightly around her tail, flippers, torso, and mouth, all digging deep into her flesh. So, on top of everything else, the whale was losing blood. "I really didn't think we were going to be able to save her," Moskito told the *San Francisco Chronicle*.

EASY DOES IT

The whale wasn't the only one at risk; her rescuers were in danger as well. They knew that even a small flip of the 50-ton animal's tail could kill any one of them. But once they got to work carefully cutting the ropes with large, curved knives, their fear quickly subsided. The men later said that they could somehow sense the whale knew they were there to help her. While they worked, she barely moved at all, just enough to stay afloat. At one point, Moskito found himself face to face with the animal as he cut the ropes from her mouth. "Her eye was there winking at me, watching me work. It was an epic moment of my life."

Finally, after more than an hour of nonstop cutting, the heavy ropes fell away and the humpback whale was able to move again. She immediately wriggled free of the few remaining lines and started out to sea.

THANK YOU

But then the whale did something unexpected. She swam in circles near the men, completing a few rotations. And then she swam right up to each of them and, one by one, gently nuzzled against them for a moment. "It felt to me like she was thanking us, knowing that she was free and that we'd helped her," Moskito recalled. "She stopped about a foot away from me, pushed me around a little bit and had some fun. It was amazing, unbelievable."

It was also fleeting—because a moment later, the humpback whale dove under the water...and was gone.

THE WATTS TOWERS

When someone finds a way to turn junk into beauty,
don't ask why. Just stand back and admire it.

DEVOTED TO A VISION

Simon Rodia was a failure. Born in Campania, Italy, in 1879, he emigrated to the United States at the age of 12 and spent the next 30 years of his life knocking around from one job to another. He worked in coal mines, rock quarries, logging camps, and railroad work crews. By 1921 he was living alone in a shack in the Watts section of Los Angeles. After three failed marriages, he had a reputation as a boozer, a womanizer, and a loser.

Then something changed.

Over the next 33 years, Rodia devoted his life to building a stunning complex of concrete and steel towers around his house, with the tallest almost 100 feet high. He worked alone, without a scaffold or design, using only a tile setter's tools and a window washer's belt and buckle. Rodia took scrap pieces of steel, including bed frames and plumbing pipe, bent them to shape against some nearby railroad tracks, and coated them with mortar. Then he decorated everything with mosaics—bits of broken glass and pottery, seashells, and anything else he could find. He ended work on his project in 1954. The following year he moved away from Watts and never came back.

The Watts Towers, as they're called today, are considered a masterpiece of vernacular architecture, and are studied and admired by architects and artists alike. They're one of less than a dozen sites in L.A. listed as National Historic Landmarks.

When asked to explain why he built the towers, Rodia replied, "I had in mind to do something big—and I did it."

BACKYARD RAIDERS

*In 1982 three kids decided to film a shot-for-shot remake
of* Raiders of the Lost Ark. *Despite many setbacks,
they managed to finish it—seven years later.*

MISSISSIPPI JONES

In 1982, 11-year-old Chris Strompolos of Gulfport, Mississippi, dealt with the pain of his parents' divorce by escaping into the world of Indiana Jones. More than anything, he wished he could be the daring archaeologist of the 1981 movie *Raiders of the Lost Ark*. He took a *Raiders* comic book everywhere he went. One day on the school bus he showed it to another fan, 12-year-old Eric Zala, a kid who wanted to make movies. A few months later, they found a way to make both of their dreams come true: they would film their own version of *Raiders of the Lost Ark*, shot by shot.

The two boys probably didn't grasp the enormity of the project—the original film had airplanes, submarines, explosions, fights on moving cars, melting faces, a man on fire, giant boulders, and a monkey, not to mention Steven Spielberg and a $26 million budget. Undaunted, Chris and Eric spent their summer vacation collecting every *Raiders* item available—the screenplay, soundtrack album, action figures, and a bootleg audio recording obtained by sneaking a tape recorder into the movie theater (a video version wasn't available until 1985).

HAVING A BALL

Chris and Eric didn't have a movie camera, but that didn't stop them, either. They started building the giant boulder that chases Indiana Jones out of a cave, constructing it out of

43

bamboo sticks and cardboard. The prop ended up so big, they couldn't get it out the door, so they had to take it apart—and then they couldn't get it back together again. Frustrated, they were forced to quit because it was September and school was starting. That year, they met a new friend: Jayson Lamb. He got their attention when he made a realistic and gory haunted house for Halloween. They thought Jayson would be a perfect special effects man.

The following summer, Chris's mom rented a Betamax video camera, and shooting could start. Eric's backyard served as the Peruvian jungle in Scene 1. Jayson held the camera, Chris played Indiana, and Eric directed while also playing Indiana's nemesis, Belloq. Little kids from the neighborhood played spear-toting natives.

That night, the boys went to an editing room at WLOX-TV, a Biloxi station where Chris's mom worked. Most kids would have quit when the footage revealed some cold truths: it looked cheesy and amateurish. Even worse, a camera glitch had left a large letter "A" in the corner of the screen on every shot. So they decided to re-do everything...and try harder.

PRODUCTION OF DOOM

The young filmmakers spent an estimated $3,000 over the course of the production. They put all their allowance money into it and engineered their Christmas gifts to support it as well—Chris asked for a whip and Eric asked for a camera. When they were old enough, they got part-time jobs.

Obviously the production values had to be compromised: A truck stood in for an airplane, and Chris's dog stood in for Indiana Jones's monkey. But the stunts are real, and the boys did them all themselves (Chris really held on to the underside of a speeding truck).

By July 1987, Chris, Eric, and Jayson had started to outgrow the project. Changing interests and a squabble over a girl nearly derailed it. But after a two-year letter-writing campaign by Chris, the Navy allowed them to film scenes on real ships docked in nearby Alabama, so the boys decided to finish the last bits of filming. Finally, after six years, shooting was complete. All that was left was editing 23 hours of film down to two hours.

Eric was a perfectionist, but Chris was anxious to be done. So behind Eric's back, he quickly edited the movie and declared it finished. Eric found out and didn't speak to Chris for a year. They made up in 1989 when they saw *Indiana Jones and the Last Crusade* together. Energized, they dug out their movie and re-edited it. At last, it was done. Eric, Chris, and Jayson premiered the movie in Gulfport to 200 friends and family members. They enjoyed the night, put the movie behind them, and went on with their lives.

ONE LAST CRUSADE

Thirteen years later, a copy of the movie surfaced at a film festival in Austin, Texas, where organizers showed it as filler. The audience loved it. The festival contacted Chris, Eric, and Jayson and flew them to Austin in 2003 for a sold-out run of *Raiders of the Lost Ark—The Adaptation*. When the movie was over, the filmmakers got a four-minute standing ovation. Even better: they got a letter from *Raiders of the Lost Ark* director Steven Spielberg. It read: "I wanted to let you know how impressed I was with your very loving tribute. I appreciated the vast amounts of imagination you put in your film. I'll be waiting to see your names someday on the big screen."

Making the movie was so hard it nearly destroyed the friendships of the three filmmakers. But today, Chris and Eric have formed their own production company to make an adventure movie shot in the South. Its name: Rolling Boulder Films.

NEVER TOO OLD

These people didn't let age stop them from following their dreams.

- **Walt Stack** completed the Ironman Triathlon...at 73.

- **Clara Barton** served as a nurse in the Spanish-American War...at age 76.

- **John Glenn** went into space...at age 77.

- **H.G. Wells** earned his doctorate...at the age of 78.

- **Benjamin Franklin** invented bifocals...when he was 79.

- **Jerry Wehman** of Florida bowled a perfect 300 game...at age 81.

- **Margaret Olivia Slocum Sage** founded the Russell Sage College for Women ...at age 88.

- **Frank Lloyd Wright** completed his architectural design of the Guggenheim Museum...at age 89.

- **Corena Leslie** skydived in Arizona...at age 89.

- **Sophocles** wrote *Oedipus at Colonus*...at age 90.

- **Maude Tull** of California got her first driver's license...at age 91.

- **Strom Thurmond** was elected to his eighth Senate term...at 93.

- **Lillian Gish** starred in *The Whales of August*...at the age of 93.

- Choreographer **Martha Graham** premiered *Maple Leaf Gala*...at age 95.

- **Otto Bucher** scored a hole-in-one on a Spanish golf course...at age 99.

- **Ichijirou Araya** climbed Mount Fuji...at the age of 100.

GRANDMA MOSES

Just because you're over the hill...doesn't mean you're over.

FARMER'S WIFE

Anna Moses was born in 1860, before Lincoln was elected and the Civil War started, and died in 1961, not long after the first American astronaut was launched into space. She spent most of her life as a farmer's wife, raising children and chickens in Virginia. After her husband died, she was unable to care for herself because of her advancing age, so she moved to Eagle Bridge in eastern New York in 1936 to be near her family. When she was 76 her arthritic hands could no longer do the needlework she loved, so she decided to take up painting.

Moses began working with house paint. Then she bought some artist's paints and began a series of works on her favorite subject—scenes from her childhood. She painted sleigh rides in the countryside, Halloween on the farm, quilting bees, and apple picking. Painted on boards and masonite, her scenes of rural life and simpler times were rendered in a clear, colorful style. "I like to paint old-timey things," she said. "I like pretty things best. I look out the window sometimes to seek the color of the shadows and the different greens in the trees, but when I get ready to paint I just close my eyes and imagine a scene."

DISCOVERED

In 1938, when Moses was almost 80, an art collector named Louis J. Caldor spotted her dust-covered work hanging in a drugstore in Hoosick Falls and bought every painting for a few dollars. He then went on a quest to buy more. When

Caldor first arrived at the Moses farm in Eagle Bridge, Anna was out, but her daughter-in-law Dorothy assured him that Moses had 10 more paintings to sell.

That night Moses could hardly sleep. She got up early and searched for the promised paintings. When she could find only nine, she cut one of them in half and put it in two frames. "I did it so it wouldn't get Dorothy in the doghouse," she explained later.

CELEBRITY

After Caldor exhibited Moses's work at New York's Museum of Modern Art in 1939, art dealer Otto Kallir took her under his wing, and "Grandma Moses" became the rage of the art world for her mastery of what critics called the "American primitive" style. Over the next 20 years, she painted 1,600 pieces, which were sought out by collectors all over the world.

The petite white-haired woman charmed everyone with her spritely personality and folksy paintings. Gimbels Department Store did a window display of her work at Thanksgiving, and in 1949 President Harry Truman presented her with the Women's Press Club Award for outstanding accomplishment in Art. In 1960 Governor Nelson Rockefeller declared her 100th birthday "Grandma Moses Day."

Grandma Moses died at the age of 101, having outlived 7 of her 10 children. But she left behind a legacy of art that, as her tombstone reads, "captured the spirit and preserved the scene of a vanishing countryside."

*   *   *

"Life is what we make it, always has been, always will be."

—Grandma Moses

RANDOM ACTS
OF KINDNESS

Recipe for feeling good: Do something nice for someone else.

At a restaurant in Sausalito, California, in 1982, a woman named Anne Herbert was lost in thought and scribbled a few words on her place mat: "Practice random acts of kindness and senseless acts of beauty." Other customers read the phrase on the place mat, then it was published in a health magazine, then in *Reader's Digest*, then someone put it on a bumper sticker. Here are a few tales of regular people who understood what Anne Herbert meant.

• Every Christmas season, a woman in a red Honda (no one knows who she is) pays for the tolls for the six cars behind her on the San Francisco Bay Bridge.

• Helen Tapp of Hudson, Florida, is a single mother raising four kids. After watching a news story in December 2005 about families struggling on the Gulf Coast in the aftermath of Hurricane Katrina, her children put a sign in their front yard saying, "Santa, give our gifts to Katrina kids." In the spirit of the season, Tapp arranged for four children in New Orleans to receive Christmas presents that year.

• Matt Allen bought an old ice cream truck in southern Oregon in 2004. But driving around selling ice cream wasn't as much fun as he thought it would be—until he came up with the idea of giving the ice cream away. Now Allen, with the help of a few sponsors, drives around the country, giving away free ice cream at local fairs and music festivals.

• Steve Cathcart, a successful professional photographer, understands how important pictures are in keeping memories alive. That's why he was upset when he read a story about six couples in Denver who were scammed by a phony photographer and never received their wedding photos. So Cathcart contacted the couples, helped them re-create their nuptials, and photographed them for free. "Through his act of kindness," said Paula Dickerson, one of the brides, "we all regained a sense of trust."

• A Los Angeles woman often kept food in her car to give to homeless people. (She was from Iceland and wasn't accustomed to homelessness, which is virtually unknown in her home country.) One day a man asked her for food, but she didn't have any with her. So the man asked her to wish him a happy birthday instead. Not only did she wish him a happy birthday, she sang "Happy Birthday" to him. Then she went to a store to buy a birthday card, put $30 in it...and drove around for a half hour looking for him. Is kindness contagious? When she found him, he was helping a stranded driver push a broken-down car to a service station.

• When Jay Frankston saw a little girl mailing a letter to Santa Claus in 1982, it got him wondering what *really* happens to all the letters to Santa. Answer: They go to the dead-letter room at the post office. So that's where Frankston went. Postal officials let him read a few of the letters, and he was touched to find that some were from kids who simply asked for a blanket, or wanted to not be lonely on Christmas. Frankston picked out nine letters and sent a telegram to each child that read, "Got your letter. Will be at your house on Christmas Day. Santa." Then, dressed as Santa, he went to every house, bewildering parents and delighting children by giving them exactly what they wanted. Frankston carried on the tradition for 12 years.

MOTHERS OF INVENTION

Who invents the little things we use every day and take for granted? Ordinary people, that's who.

MARGARET KNIGHT, known as the "female Edison," held patents for such diverse items as the window frame and sash, and devices related to rotary engines. As a kid growing up in Maine, she made sleds and kites for her brothers and sisters. When she was only 12, she came up with the idea of a safety device that textile mills could use to shut down machinery quickly, helping prevent terrible accidents. Knight spent nearly 50 years—from the 1860s until her death in 1914—inventing industrial equipment such as shoe-cutting machines and sequential numbering devices. But Mattie Knight's out-of-the-ballpark best idea: the square-bottomed paper bag.

MELITTA BENTZ, a housewife in Dresden, Germany, didn't like the bitter, oily taste of coffee made by boiling loose grounds, the common brewing method in 1900. She wondered if there was a way to filter out the grit and oil, and began testing several kinds of filters. One day the blotter paper from her son's school notebook caught her eye. She carefully cut out a circle of paper and placed it in the bottom of a perforated brass pot, measured in the coffee, and poured hot water over it. Result: the perfect, grit-free coffee she was looking for. Bentz's simple drip method was so successful that she applied for a patent in 1908, and the M Bentz coffee company was born. Now, 100 years later, the family-owned company is still going strong under its new name, Melitta.

They sell coffeemakers, espresso machines—and, of course, the Melitta paper filter.

ANN MOORE went to Togo as a nurse with the Peace Corps in the 1960s. She noticed that the babies there rarely cried, and assumed it was because of the way their mothers carried them: tightly swaddled in slings tied to the mother's back. The babies were always close to mom, she reasoned, which made them feel comfortable and secure. When Moore had kids of her own, she devised a carrier based on the ones she saw in Africa. She wore it constantly and was often stopped by people wondering where they could get one. That inspired her to invent the Snugli, which she patented in 1969. It went on to sell millions.

MARION DONOVAN was the daughter of an inventor whose work inspired her to find solutions for everyday problems. In 1949, when she was a mother with two babies in soggy diapers, Donovan invented the first leak-proof diaper, which she made from cut-up pieces of a plastic shower curtain (and later, parachute nylon). Donovan's "Boaters" were sold by Saks Fifth Avenue and were an instant hit. In the years that followed, Donovan invented DentaLoops, precut circles of dental floss; the Ledger Check, a combined check and record-keeping book; the Big Hang-Up, a closet organizer; and an elasticized zipper pull she dubbed the "Zippity-Do."

GERTRUDE A. MULLER invented the child car seat, which she tested with auto-crash studies. She helped set the standard for crash testing—her extreme regard for safety is one of the reasons we have seat belts and air bags today. And she's also Uncle John's all-time favorite inventor. Why? Toddlers needed a way to use the grown-up-size toilet, so Muller invented the Little Toidey collapsible toilet seat.

A THOUSAND WORDS

*Sometimes from the darkest chapters of human history
come the greatest stories of hope and generosity.*

THE SEARCH

One day in 1995, Vernon Tott, a 70-year-old retiree from Sioux City, Iowa, was reading *The Railsplitter*, the newsletter of the Army's 84th Infantry Division. (Tott had served with the 84th during World War II.) In the paper he saw a letter from a survivor of the Ahlem Nazi slave-labor camp in Germany—Benjamin Sieradzki, who now lived in Berkeley, California. Sieradzki was looking for someone: "a tall, blond fellow" who had been taking photographs on April 10, 1945, the day the Americans liberated the camp in which he'd been held prisoner. "I am trying to put together the story of my survival for my children and grandchildren," he said, "so that they may better understand what happened."

Tott put down the newsletter and went to his basement. After some searching he found a dust-covered shoebox. Inside were the black-and-white photographs he'd taken 50 years earlier, the day he and his unit had stumbled upon the camp—a horrific scene of dead bodies and emaciated Jewish prisoners.

Tott was the "tall, blond fellow" that Sieradzki was trying to find.

FOUND

He contacted Sieradzki, and they arranged a meeting that changed both men's lives. Tott had taken the photos to keep a record of the unimaginable scene. "I had no idea this was taking place in the world," he later said. "I was sick to my stomach." The photos had sat in his basement, untouched, for five decades, but now they had a purpose.

"In a way, I needed them," Sieradzki said of the photos, one of which showed him as a sick, 78-pound 17-year-old. "I needed some kind of legitimacy for what I was telling people about what happened there."

After seeing how much the photographs meant to Sieradzki, Tott wanted to do more. Over the next 10 years, through personal battles with cancer and the effects of a stroke, Tott went on a mission to find the 40 survivors pictured in the 19 photographs he'd taken that fateful day. He searched for clues in Germany and Poland, and ultimately found 30 survivors from the camp. Of those, 13 were able to identify themselves—some with great difficulty because of their youth and terrible health—in the photos.

REUNIONS

In 2003 Tott visited the U.S. Holocaust Memorial Museum in Washington, D.C. As he entered, four elderly men rushed up and embraced him. One was Benjamin Sieradzki; the other three were also Ahlem survivors. And they had a surprise for him.

The four proudly looked on as a museum official unveiled an inscription the men had arranged to be made on a wall in the museum's Donor Room. It read, "In honor of Vernon W. Tott, my liberator & hero."

"Hopefully, as people see Vernon's name inscribed in the walls of this great institution," said Jack Tramiel, founder of Commodore Computers and one of the men that Tott's unit had liberated, "they will get a small sense of it all. Vernon, you are my angel."

HERE COMES "THE RIDE"

If you want to make the world a better place, you can either do it quietly... or with flair—like these folks.

DO-IT-YOURSELF SUPERHEROES
A group of teenagers and their teachers from the Wellsprings Friends School in Eugene, Oregon, have secret identities as a band of "superheroes." Known as The Ride, they wear homemade costumes and ride their bikes from town to town, helping local people in need. (The idea came from one of the teachers, Ethan Hughes, who in his high-school days donned a cape and walked around town picking up litter.)

In December 2005, The Ride traveled in their biodiesel-fueled bus to hurricane-devastated New Orleans. There the superheroes put on their costumes and rode around the neighborhoods, making themselves available to anyone— business owners, government authorities, ordinary citizens— in need of assistance.

One of the team, "Intergalactic Love Lady" (14-year-old Rachel Wolfe-Goldsmith), said of their mission: "It seemed like Hurricane Katrina was a really big deal right after it happened, and then people kind of forgot. I wanted to be one of the people who didn't forget."

"Giving myself," added 15-year-old "Little Peace Riding Hood" (Lotus Brashers), "is, I think, the most powerful thing we can do as humans—and having faith that our intentions are right so things will go right."

After three weeks of building shelters, serving food, and doing odd jobs—all in costume—the superheroes were satisfied that they'd done what they could. But they did one more thing before returning to Oregon: they left their bicycles behind for people who needed them.

Some of the other heroes along for The Ride:
- "Gratitude Gretel"—Anna Scheri, 16
- "Shining Knight"—Stretch Barkley, 17
- "Frilly Lizard"—Helena Marcus, teacher
- "Nameless Wonder"—Tina McMurrin, 17

OTHER REAL-LIFE SUPERHEROES

- In England, a dynamic duo known as "Whitley's Batman and Robin" assist stranded motorists, help elderly ladies cross the street, and perform light crime fighting (they helped chase a streaker off the field at a soccer match).

- The people of Mexico City have a champion: a man wearing cherry-red pants, gold underwear, a red cape, and a red-and-gold face mask who calls himself "Superbarrio." His modest mission: to meet with police and government officials and urge them to find new ways to improve the lives of the poor.

- In New York City, a woman known as "Terrifica," wearing a gold mask, red spandex clothes, red boots, and a red cape, keeps a protective eye on women in the nightclub scene and helps make sure they get home safely.

- If you travel to Iqaluit (pop. 6,000) in Canada's Nunavut Territory, you may meet "Polar Man—Friend of Children, Helper of the Weak, and All-Round Nice Guy!" Dressed in black boots, a wool cap, and black shorts over multiple pairs of white sweatpants (depending on how cold it is), "Polar Man" shovels walks for the elderly, entertains kids, and patrols the neighborhoods at night.

LITTLE BUDDY

Here's a true story from BRI writer Thom Little.

PUPPY POWER

When Thom was about 11, one of his family's dogs, six-month-old Buddy, started barking outside the back door. Thom was eating cereal and ignored the barking pup, but his older sister Nancy became curious and went out to see what was going on.

"What's the matter, Buddy?" she asked.

Buddy turned and ran into the neighbors' yard. Then he turned around and started barking again. Nancy followed Buddy as he ran through the yard and into the woods, continuing to bark wildly. Nancy kept following the pup, eventually walking hundreds of yards into the woods...right to the spot where Buddy's mom, Hilda, was caught in a steel trap.

Nancy ran back home, yelling for help. She attracted the attention of a few neighbors and family members (not Thom, who was still eating cereal), and soon Hilda was freed from the trap and brought back to the house. Her wounded foot eventually recovered, and she went on to live a very long and happy life.

While Nancy was praised by everyone for being so perceptive, Buddy was the real hero of the family. Hilda would almost certainly have died if Buddy hadn't acted. That a six-month-old puppy knew to go back to the house for help—and knew how to get someone to follow him back into the woods to save his mother—is a story the family still tells 30 years later, and one they will never forget. (Especially Thom.)

MOM'S THE WORD

Some thoughts about the mother of all inspiration—mothers.

"Mama exhorted her children at every opportunity to 'jump at de sun.' We might not land on the sun, but at least we would get off the ground."
—**Zora Neale Hurston**

"My mother never gave up on me. I messed up in school so much they were sending me home, but my mother sent me right back."
—**Denzel Washington**

"Mothers have as powerful an influence over the welfare of future generations as all other earthly causes combined."
—**John S. C. Abbott**

"My mother said to me, 'If you become a soldier you'll be a general; if you become a monk you'll end up as the pope.' Instead, I became a painter and wound up as Picasso."
—**Pablo Picasso**

"The mother's heart is the child's schoolroom."
—**Henry Ward Beecher**

"I have met a lot of people in this world, but I have never met a more thoroughly refined woman than my mother. If I have amounted to anything, it is due to her."
—**Charlie Chaplin**

"A mother is not a person to lean on but a person to make leaning unnecessary."
—**Dorothy Canfield Fisher**

"There never was a woman like her. She was gentle as a dove and brave as a lioness. The memory of her was, after all, the only capital I had to start life with, and on that capital I have made my way."
—**Andrew Jackson**

"God cannot be everywhere, so he made mothers."
—**Arab proverb**

ANDY MARTIN'S FIGHT

*Here's a question we hope you'll never have to answer:
What would you do if you found out your days
were numbered? Here's how a medical student
named Andy decided to spend his time.*

BEGINNING
One week before he started medical school at Tulane
University in New Orleans in the fall of 2000, 27-year-old Andy Martin went on a "last hurrah" camping trip with
his girlfriend to Mt. Whitney in southern California. On the
trip, his nose suddenly began bleeding uncontrollably. He and
his girlfriend went to the emergency room, where the nurses
told him the nosebleed was probably due to the altitude.
Doctors packed and bandaged his nose for the drive back to
Los Angeles.

But Andy's nose was still bleeding when he arrived home,
so he went to *another* emergency room and had it examined
again. The L.A. doctors just bandaged his nose a second time
and told him to come back if it didn't stop bleeding. Two
hours later, Andy was back.

BAD NEWS
The following day a surgeon operated on Andy to find out
what was wrong and discovered a tumor in his sinuses about
an inch and a half long. Lab tests confirmed that it was
malignant. Andy decided to delay medical school for a year
while he underwent surgery, radiation, and chemotherapy. The
treatments destroyed every visible trace of the cancer, and in
2001 Andy returned to medical school thinking that he'd
beaten it.

But he hadn't—the following year Andy's nosebleed returned, and he knew the cancer was back. This time the doctors narrowed their diagnosis to a very rare, very deadly form of cancer called *sinonasal undifferentiated carcinoma*, or SNUC for short. Only 100 cases of the disease had been reported in medical literature since it was first described in 1986. The doctors told Andy that his case was probably incurable; most patients with SNUC die within five years of diagnosis.

DECISIONS TO MAKE

Andy considered dropping out and traveling around the world, but ultimately decided he wanted to stay in medical school. Perhaps if he studied his own cancer, he could contribute to finding a cure. "If this cancer's going to get me," he told his sister, "I'm going to go down fighting, and make a difference, so that future victims don't have the same outcome that I had."

But scientists at Tulane weren't studying SNUC, and hardly anyone else was, either: SNUC is so rare and research dollars so limited that very little was being done about it anywhere. That only made Andy's research more important—he figured if he didn't do it, many years might pass before anyone else did, and people would die in the meantime. He had to try.

Andy went to Dr. Tyler Curiel, head of Tulane's cancer research center, and asked for permission to try to culture, or grow, cancer cells from his own body in Curiel's lab, creating what is called a "living cell line." Culturing living tumors is a difficult but critical step in cancer research, because once the cancer is able to survive outside the human body, scientists can test different treatments on it without risking the lives of patients.

ON HIS OWN

Culturing SNUC cells wouldn't be easy—and as far as Andy could tell no one had ever tried it before, so he would have to start from scratch, experimenting with dozens of combinations of chemicals in the hope of finding a mixture that would keep his cancer cells alive outside his body. Dr. Curiel wasn't sure if Andy would succeed—even a healthy person would have faced long odds culturing a living cell line in the time that Andy had left. But Curiel decided to let him try. "If we can't cure his cancer," Curiel told the *Wall Street Journal* in 2004, "why not let him take charge of it?"

After doctors extracted cancer cells from Andy's sinuses, he began the painstaking work of trying to get them to grow. But as one experiment after another ended in failure, the lab's budget for his project—$20,000—began to run out.

To restore the funding, Dr. Curiel's 11-year-old son talked his dad, a marathon runner, into doing a "Bounce for Life." On December 15, 2003, Curiel ran 108 miles on the university's track over the course of 24 hours, all the while bouncing a basketball. Curiel's feat set a world record, but more importantly, the event raised $28,000 for Andy's research.

SLOW AND STEADY

As Andy plowed ahead, his cancer treatments took their toll. His hair fell out. Already slender, he dropped another 40 pounds. He suffered from fevers and chills and napped frequently to restore his flagging energy. Yet he still managed to spend many hours in the lab with his eyes glued to his microscope, carefully studying his samples to see if any of them were still alive. They kept dying.

HOPE

In February 2004, Andy traveled to the University of Chicago for radiation treatment. While he was there he got the news he'd been waiting for: Dr. Curiel called to tell him that one of his cultures was alive...and growing. "It was one of the greatest moments of my scientific career," Dr. Curiel told reporters for the *Wall Street Journal*. "I just sat down on the lab floor next to the microscope, speechless."

Andy knew from the beginning that the SNUC diagnosis was a virtual death sentence, and he lost his battle with cancer on November 19, 2004. But thanks to the SNUC cell line he created—the only one in the world—there is now hope for a cure.

But that's not the end of the story. Andy's cells faced another challenge: Hurricane Katrina. Did they survive? Turn to page 233 to find out.

*   *   *

WHEN IN DOUBT, TRUST YOURSELF

Do not believe in something simply because you have heard it.

Do not believe in something simply because it is found in your religious books.

Do not believe in something merely on the authority of your teachers and elders.

Do not believe in traditions because they have been handed down for many generations.

But when you find something that agrees with reason and is conducive to the good and benefit of one and all, then accept it and live up to it.

—Buddha

AESOP'S FABLES

Sure, everyone knows the stories…
but the lessons are still good ones.

THE GRASSHOPPER AND THE ANT

A grasshopper hopped around a field one warm autumn day, singing happily. His friend the ant walked by, struggling to carry a large kernel of corn.

"Where are you carrying that heavy thing?" the grasshopper asked the ant. Without stopping, the ant grunted, "To the ant hill. This is my fourth one today."

"Why don't you forget about all that?" said the grasshopper. "Come and sing and play with me instead."

"Sorry," the ant replied. "I'm storing food for the winter. Shouldn't you be doing the same?"

"Oh, winter is so far away. I'll worry about it later."

"You'll be sorry," said the ant as he continued on his way.

The very next day, the weather turned cold. All the plants in the field were covered with a thick blanket of snow. The grasshopper couldn't find anything to eat and soon grew desperately hungry. He staggered to the ant hill and saw all the ants handing out corn from their reserve.

Suddenly, the grasshopper understood the ant's advice.

Moral: *Prepare today for what tomorrow might bring.*

SOUR GRAPES

One day, a hungry fox was strolling through an orchard when he spotted a bunch of grapes high upon a branch. They glistened in the sun, perfectly ripe.

"Just the thing to fill my belly," thought the fox. So he

stepped back, got a running start, and jumped as high as he could to reach the vine where the grapes rested. Not high enough, though. He fell to the ground.

The fox got back up, took a few more steps back, ran, and spun in the air as he jumped to get just a little higher. Again, he fell to the ground. He tried again and again, but each time the result was the same: He couldn't quite reach the grapes.

Finally, he gave up and walked away, mumbling to himself, "I didn't want those grapes anyway. I'm sure they were sour."

Moral: Don't despise something because you can't have it.

THE TORTOISE AND THE HARE

A hare loved to brag to the forest animals about how fast he was. One day a tortoise grew tired of his boasts and challenged him to a race. All the animals gathered to watch.

At the beginning of the race, the hare quickly sprinted down the road a ways, then paused. A long way back he saw the tortoise and shouted, "You're never going to win walking *that* slowly!" The hare was so far ahead that he sat down under a tree, thinking, "There's plenty of time to take a break, relax, and still win." And he stretched out and fell asleep.

Meanwhile, the tortoise kept walking, and never stopped until he crossed the finish line. The other animals cheered so loudly for him that they woke up the hare. He jumped up and tried to run again, but it was too late. He had lost.

And the hare never bragged about his speed again.

Moral: Slow and steady wins the race.

*   *   *

"He who begins is half done. Dare to be wise. Begin!"

—**Horace**

KON-TIKI

Imagine building a small, flimsy raft and then sailing it across the Pacific Ocean—just to see if you can. Sounds crazy, doesn't it?

ODD NOTIONS
In the winter of 1946, Thor Heyerdahl was unemployed and growing impatient. For nearly 10 years the amateur anthropologist had been working on a new theory about the original inhabitants of the Polynesian Islands. He believed that South American Indians had sailed west in primitive rafts to settle the islands and hoped to publish an academic paper that would prove his theory. But Heyerdahl had no academic credentials; most experts simply laughed at his ideas.

Anthropologists believed that the islands had been settled from the opposite direction—by travelers sailing east from Asia. When Heyerdahl appeared in their offices with his unpublished manuscript full of "crackpot" notions, they scoffed at him, pointing out that ancient South Americans simply didn't have boats capable of surviving a 4,000-mile ocean journey.

CRAZY PLANS

Frustrated and running out of money, Heyerdahl decided to make a desperate gamble: He would build a balsa-wood raft of the type used by prehistoric coastal Peruvians and sail it across the Pacific. If he could prove the trip was possible, his ideas might catch on.

Heyerdahl soon found that a romantic adventure was easier to sell than an obscure anthropological theory. In just a few short months he was able to secure financial backing for his scheme. By the spring of 1947, he'd found five men who were willing to risk their lives and accompany him on the journey. They all caught the next plane for Peru.

The six adventurers built a raft by lashing giant balsa wood logs together with vines. When it was finished, it measured 18 by 45 feet and was rigged with a primitive sail and rudder. Heyerdahl and his crew were ready to head out to sea in an untested vessel, without any way of knowing if it would hold together on the open ocean.

THEY SAID IT COULDN'T BE DONE

At the raft's formal dedication, Peruvian naval officers who attended the ceremony were horrified. They told Heyerdahl bluntly that he and his crew would certainly die at sea. The logs would soak up water and sink; the lashings would come apart under the strain of the logs grinding against one another as they rolled in the waves. They begged him to reconsider, but Heyerdahl and his companions were undeterred.

They set out at the end of April. For 101 days they drifted with the currents, never so much as sighting another ship. Their only shelter was a tiny bamboo cabin, and their only navigational tools were an old-fashioned sextant and a compass. Somehow they survived…and made it. On August 7, 1947, they crash-landed onto an atoll in the Tuamotu Archipelago in French Polynesia, having drifted 4,300 miles across the Pacific.

The trip made Heyerdahl famous, and now he easily found a publisher. His book about the expedition, *Kon-Tiki*, has since sold 60 million copies, and film footage he shot during the trip won an Oscar for the best documentary of 1951.

Unfortunately, anthropologists are still fairly sure that ancient Peruvians had nothing to do with settling Polynesia. But, even though his theory never caught on, the *Kon-Tiki* adventure did accomplish its goal: It could be done.

LUCKY STARS

*One minute you're going about your daily business;
the next minute you're a movie star. Think it's
impossible? It happened to these folks.*

• Looking for a teenage boy to play a troubled kid, a casting agent went to a Boys Club in Pasadena, California. There she spotted 14-year-old Edward Furlong and thought he'd be perfect for the role. He auditioned for the part and got it, despite never having acted before. The film: *Terminator 2*, the highest-grossing movie of 1991.

• While training Army paratroopers in 1944, Harold Russell's hands were destroyed when some TNT he was holding exploded. He was fitted with hooks and, after learning how to use them, appeared in an Army training film called *Diary of a Sergeant*. Hollywood director William Wyler—who also made Army training films—saw *Diary* while he was preparing to make a movie about soldiers adjusting to postwar life. Wyler changed one character from a paraplegic to a double amputee and asked Russell to star, despite his lack of experience. Russell was so good in the role that he won the Academy Award for Best Supporting Actor in *The Best Years of Our Lives*.

• In 1945 photographer David Conover went to the factory of military supplier Radioplane in Van Nuys, California, to take pictures of women involved in the war effort. He was immediately drawn to a blue-eyed 19-year-old named Norma Jean Dougherty, who was making $20 a week spraying glue on aircraft fabric. Dougherty agreed to pose for more pictures, which soon led to professional modeling work. In 1946 she signed a movie contract with Twentieth Century Fox and changed her name to... Marilyn Monroe.

ST. JOAN OF ARCHES

An incredible story of generosity—super-sized.

R AY AND JOAN
When Ray Kroc, the founder of McDonald's
Corporation and one of the wealthiest people in the
world, died in January 1984, he already had a reputation as a
generous man. He had established the Kroc Foundation in
1969 to support scientific research on diabetes, arthritis, and
multiple sclerosis, and in 1974 had started the Ronald
McDonald Houses to support the families of children with
cancer. But when he died and left his fortune to his wife,
Joan Kroc, she took the giving to another level.

In July 1984, just six months after the death of her husband, a gunman killed 21 people in a McDonald's in San
Ysidro, California, not far from the Kroc home in San Diego.
As the corporation's controlling shareholder, Joan was devastated. By the next day she had established a foundation, with
$100,000 of her own money and $1 million more from
McDonald's, to help the families of the victims. After that
she never looked back.

GIVING, INC.

In 1986 Kroc heard the president of University of Notre
Dame give a speech about the dangers of the arms race. She
walked up to him and said, "I'm going to help you." She did—
by giving him $12 million to create what became Notre
Dame's Joan B. Kroc Institute for International Peace Studies.

Over the years her charitable contributions grew in size
and scope. She doled out millions to causes such as medical
research, drug and alcohol rehabilitation, hospice care

centers, animal shelters, arts programs, and wildlife preservation. And she often did it anonymously. In 1997, when the communities of Grand Forks, North Dakota, and East Grand Forks, Minnesota, were hit with devastating floods, she made an anonymous donation of $15 million so that each affected family would quickly receive $2,000. The townspeople were stunned, and the "Angel Fund" became the stuff of legend. Reporters later tracked down the records of a mysterious private jet that had landed at the local airport. It was registered to "Joan B. Kroc Trustees," and Joan Kroc is still known as "the Angel" there today.

BIG SPENDER

The list of the recipients of Joan Kroc's kindness and the size of the gifts is amazing: In 1995 she donated $50 million to Ronald McDonald Children's Charities; in 1998 she donated $87 million for the 12.5-acre Salvation Army Kroc Center, an education, recreation, and cultural arts facility; in 2001 she gave the University of San Diego $30 million to build what became the Joan B. Kroc Institute for Peace and Justice.

A reporter once asked her to explain her incredible generosity. "Ray was once asked in an interview why he gave so much of his wealth away," she answered. "He said, 'I've never seen a Brinks truck following a hearse. Have you?' I loved that!"

GOOD TO THE LAST

On October 12, 2003, at the age of 75, Joan Kroc died of brain cancer at her home in Rancho Santa Fe near San Diego. But she wasn't quite done with giving.

She had a fortune in the neighborhood of $1.7 billion when she died. Within a few weeks KPBS, a local public radio and TV station in San Diego—she had always been a big supporter—learned that they had been left $5 million. That was nothing. The two peace institutes she had helped create at Notre Dame and the University of San Diego got $50 million...each. That was *still* nothing. National Public Radio was given $200 million, the largest gift in its history by far (the next largest was from the MacArthur Foundation—$14 million). Stunned officials at NPR called it the largest gift to an American cultural institution in history. They may have been right...but not for long.

In January 2004, the Salvation Army received word that Joan Kroc had left them funding to build more centers like the one she had helped create in San Diego. How much funding? The remainder of her estate—about $1.5 billion. Officials at the Salvation Army seemed almost terrified by such a large gift, and said they'd have to talk to their lawyers to see if they could even handle that much money.

"Joan would have gotten such a laugh out of that," one of Kroc's closest friends, Thelma Halbert, said. "She loved to surprise people with her money. It wasn't about fame or glory, or even a sense of mission. It came from the heart. It was just who she was."

*   *   *

GENTLEMEN, START YOUR ENGINES

A study by German scientists found that men who kiss their wives before they leave for work have fewer sick days, fewer car accidents, live five years longer, and earn 25% more money. How do they explain it? They believe that the act of kissing starts each day with a positive attitude.

THE GOOD SISTERS

*Phuket—a small island off the coast of Thailand—has had a
difficult history, most recently from the devastating tsunami of
2004. But that wasn't the first storm the island has faced. A
threat of a different sort approached Phuket more than 200
years ago, and it would take a miracle to hold it off.*

UNDER SIEGE

In February 1785, the Thai province of Phuket had
no leader. Its governor was dead, and his widow,
Kunying Jan, was stricken with grief. In fact, the morale of
the entire island was low, and not just because their governor
was gone—so too, were most of the men. Phuket had been
attacked by neighboring Burma several times, and most of the
island's men had been captured and sold into slavery on the
Asian mainland.

So it came as little surprise when Jan received the news
from a passing British sea captain that a massive fleet of
Burmese ships was sailing toward Phuket once again. Thousands of heavily armed soldiers were on their way to battle
the island's few hundred beleaguered soldiers—this time to
finish off Phuket for good.

BATTLE DRESS

But what the Burmese didn't count on was the resiliency of Jan
and her sister, Mook. Instead of focusing on what they didn't
have enough of—men—the two sisters formed a plan that
would utilize what they had a lot of—women. With the invaders
quickly approaching, Jan and Mook explained to the weary
islanders that there was no time to call for reinforcements from
the mainland—it was up to them if they wished to remain free.

First, Jan and Mook ordered the men to ready themselves for battle. Then they told all the women to disguise themselves as male soldiers. To give the appearance that they were *well-armed* soldiers, the women gathered large palm leaves and held each of them over a flame until they blackened and curled into tubes. From a distance, the leaves looked like sheathed swords.

SHOW OF FORCE

When the Burmese armada approached Phuket the next morning, they saw a daunting sight: nearly 1,000 soldiers lined up and waiting for them on the beach. Convinced that the island had been reinforced by the Thai army, the Burmese called off their full-scale assault and sent in smaller forces instead. This was something the residents of Phuket could handle—they used their knowledge of the island to lure the Burmese into traps.

The two sisters and their "army" held off the invaders for nearly a month, until the Thai army arrived from the mainland and forced the Burmese to retreat. The island was saved.

THE KING'S REWARD

Thai King Rama I bestowed upon Kunying Jan the honorific title *Thao Thepkrasatri*, and Mook became *Thao Srisunthorn*—both titles usually reserved for royalty. Today, a bronze statue of Jan and Mook stands in Phuket's capital, serving as a reminder that bravery—and brains—can overcome even the most overwhelming odds.

* * *

You already possess everything necessary to become great.

—Native American proverb

THE CAN-DO KID

*Don't focus on what this kid doesn't
have—because he sure doesn't.*

BIG HEART
Kyle Maynard was born different: His arms are both
stumps, ending before his elbows. He has no knees,
and his deformed feet are useless. Still, Kyle is a star athlete
(yes, you read that right), excelling in swimming and
wrestling, without prosthetic limbs. And he's not competing
in the Paralympics—this is high school and college sports.

But that's not all. Kyle also excels academically, having
graduated high school with a 3.7 GPA. In fact, Kyle can do
most things that abled people can do: eat with utensils, use a
cell phone, ride a bike. He can even type 50 words a minute.
Obviously, none of these skills came easily. How did he do it?
He has great parents.

Scott and Anita Maynard knew they were in for a tough
time when Kyle was born in 1986 with a rare disorder called
congenital amputation. They spoon-fed him like any child until
he reached the age where kids with hands have to learn to
feed themselves. At that point his father said, "If he doesn't
figure out how to eat on his own, he's going to starve." So
they watched Kyle closely and encouraged him while he
learned to pick up objects with his arms and get around on
his own. From the start, the toddler was determined to do
things himself, and that determination has stayed with him
ever since.

IF AT FIRST YOU DON'T SUCCEED...

Kyle joined the wrestling team in high school—and lost the

first 35 matches he entered. His ego was bruised, but not enough to make him want to quit. So Kyle's wrestling coach, Cliff Ramos, decided to try a different approach: With his arms inside his shirtsleeves, Ramos wrestled some of the better members of the team to give him an idea of what Kyle was facing. After working together in the off-season, Kyle and Coach Ramos capitalized on Kyle's strengths: he's just three feet tall so he has a low center of gravity and great balance; he has speed and agility; he's very strong (he can bench press 250 pounds); and he has a hard head—which he started using as a battering ram.

The following year was much different for Kyle. He won 35 matches while losing only 16, and finished 12th in his weight division for the entire state of Georgia.

TEACHING OTHERS

Kyle is now a student at the University of Georgia, where he still wrestles and is majoring in public speaking. The busy 20-year-old also travels to high schools around the country to give inspirational speeches about having a positive attitude. Kyle's autobiography, *No Excuses*, has become a motivational tool for thousands. Its message is simple: Reasons why you *can't* do something only exist in your mind...and so does the courage to get past those reasons. One of the most poignant parts is where Kyle speaks of his low spirits after losing those 35 wrestling matches in a row—and how he convinced himself to get back out on the mat.

"I knew it didn't matter how much I was afraid, how much I was in pain, or how impossible the situation appeared to me. I knew the obstacles. This was no different from the rest of my life. We all have challenges to face and to overcome. No obstacle would keep me from accomplishing my dreams."

99% PERSPIRATION

You've tried it once, you've tried it twice, and it still won't work. Time to give up? Naahh...

LET THERE BE LIGHT

Thomas Edison was looking for a filament that would glow brightly when an electric current was run through it. He tried everything. First, thin wires of gold, silver, platinum, and nickel. When those didn't work, he tried fishing line, cotton thread, coconut hair, even human hair. He tried hundreds of things, but none of them worked. They either required too much current to run efficiently or burned out too quickly. Finally, after working with a team of scientists for over a year, Edison found the solution with carbonized bamboo. And in 1879 the incandescent lightbulb was born.

CRASHING INSPIRATION

W.S. Gilbert—of Gilbert and Sullivan—was pacing in his study one night when a Japanese sword on the wall crashed to the floor. In a flash of inspiration, Gilbert instantly came up with the idea to write a musical about English bureaucracy in a Japanese setting. It was much harder, however, to come up with an acceptable plot. Still, he never gave up. After 11 complete rewrites, *The Mikado* opened in 1885—and turned out to be the most successful English operetta ever written.

BIG WHEELS KEEP ON TURNING

Charles Goodyear worked for 10 years to find a way to turn raw rubber into something useful. He burned through all of his money and was even thrown in debtor's prison for a while, but that didn't stop him. Finally, in 1838, he heated some rubber and treated it with sulfur. The result was a substance that was pliable, durable, and amazingly adaptable. He called his new process *vulcanization*. Goodyear first used the substance in shoes. It wasn't until after his death, in 1898, that the Goodyear Tire Company was formed to use vulcanization for a new technology: the automobile tire.

CUCKOO

Kirk Douglas performed the role of McMurphy in Ken Kesey's *One Flew Over the Cuckoo's Nest* in 1963. He loved the play so he bought the film rights…but no one in Hollywood was interested in making it. He finally got too old to play the part so he passed the script to his son, Michael Douglas, who finally got the movie made—12 years later. But it was worth the wait: It was the first film since 1934 to take all the major Academy Awards—Best Picture, Best Director, Best Actor, Best Actress, and Best Screenplay.

RAZOR SHARP

King Camp Gillette was determined to invent something that would make him a millionaire, but none of his ideas ever worked out. Gillette's boss at the Crown Cork & Seal Company had invented the disposable bottle cap, and suggested that Gillette "invent something that people can use and throw away." While shaving one morning, Gillette became annoyed that his straight-edged razor had gotten dull again. It gave him an idea: a razor blade so cheap that you could throw it away when it grew dull. He spent the next six years doggedly searching for a way to make the paper-thin steel for his disposable razor blade. When he found it in 1902, he patented his process and within 12 years, the Gillette Company was the leader in the razor business. Gillette was a millionaire at last.

PARENTS...BY LOVE

Here are some stories of people who've cared for so many kids that their extended families are almost as big as their hearts.

• Since they married in 1998, Jim Silcock, a quadriplegic, and Ann Belles have legally adopted 34 children, all of them kids who had fallen through the cracks of the adoption system. Some are severely handicapped, some had been abused, some had just been waiting for years to be adopted. "Family is not about blood," says son Hunter Silcock, who was classified as mentally disabled when he was adopted, but who now tests at a "gifted" level. "Family and home—it's where they love you. No matter what."

• For the past 30 years, Katherine Louise Calder of Portland, Oregon, has been a foster mom. To date, she's mothered more than 400 children. Most of the children she takes in are abandoned or withdrawing from drugs because their mothers are addicts. So Calder has had special medical training to care for them. She spends a lot of her time finding good permanent homes for the kids, since they're with her only temporarily. "I knew that there were children out there that needed a home and that I had a home I could share," she says.

• In 2004 guitarist Brian "Head" Welch suddenly quit the popular rock band Korn because it left him feeling empty. He opened an orphanage in Balligeria, India, and legally adopted 212 kids who were living on the street or had been sold into brothels by their families. The children, age 3 to 16, now live among gardens, a petting zoo, and classrooms. "I wanted to do something with my money other than buy BMWs," Welch says. "I've been selfish my whole life and I want to give back."

YOU'RE MY (WEIRD) INSPIRATION

Proof that inspiration can come from anywhere.

METHOD ACTING

Australian actress Peta Wilson played a vampire in the 2003 film *The League of Extraordinary Gentlemen*. Where'd she get her inspiration for the part? From her infant son. "My three-month-old, Marlowe, was breast-feeding, and I couldn't get that corset off quick enough," she says. "He would scream and be ferocious until he got his milk, and afterwards he had this bliss come over him. I thought, 'Yeah, I could play a vampire.'"

YABBA-DABBA-JUDO

University of Pittsburgh judo star Christina Pro, one of the world's best, is an Olympic hopeful for 2008. And she owes it all to *The Flintstones*. "I was about five years old," she said. "Betty and Wilma took a self-defense class. I thought it was neat and wanted to do it too."

FROSTY THE TOE-MAN

American Rulon Gardner became a star when he won the gold medal in Greco-Roman wrestling in the Sydney Olympics in 2000. In 2002 he was severely frostbitten after a snowmobile accident, and one of his toes had to be amputated. Gardner, who now travels the country as a motivational speaker, still has the toe. "I keep it in my refrigerator," he says. "It reminds me of what I went through and how lucky I am. It reminds me of how life is there to be lived to the fullest."

SEQUOIA AND THE CHEROKEE ALPHABET

*The story of a man who single-handedly brought
the written word to his entire culture.*

THE HEIGHT OF HUMAN ACHIEVEMENT
Most people accept written language as a given, but archaeologists believe writing was invented independently by only a few ancient cultures, and that almost every subsequent writing system was derived from these originals. That writing developed at all is a testament to human ingenuity.

So the fact that one man invented a completely original writing system in the early 19th century is pretty remarkable. What makes it even more remarkable is that he did it without ever having read or written a single word in any preexisting alphabet. The only language he had ever spoken was Cherokee. His name was Sequoia.

TAKING UP THE PEN
Few details of his life are known, but Sequoia is believed to have been born sometime between 1750 and 1775, a time when settlers from the growing region around Georgia, South Carolina, and Tennessee were beginning to threaten Cherokee independence. He was a part of the last generation of Cherokees to live freely in their ancestral homeland, the same generation that was eventually forced west over the infamous Trail of Tears. Recognizing that the European culture had an advantage in being able to communicate through writing, Sequoia became determined to level the playing field by devising a similar system for his own language.

Beginning in 1809, he created an 85-character system of syllables, which differed from the English alphabet in that the characters depicted full syllables instead of individual sounds. It took him 12 years. When he was finished, he had created a writing system still marveled at today for the ease with which it can be learned. Previously illiterate speakers of Cherokee were able to master it within a matter of weeks. And they could teach it to others just as quickly.

POWER OF THE PRESS

Sequoia introduced his syllabary in 1821. Within just five years, the Cherokees were operating what the Boston *Missionary Herald* described as:

> the first printing press ever owned and employed
> by any nation of the Aborigines of this Continent;
> the first effort at writing and printing in characters
> of their own; the first newspaper and the first book
> printed among themselves; the first editor, and the
> first well-organized system for securing a general
> diffusion of knowledge among the people.

But while some white settlers gloried in the "civilized" advancement of the Cherokee nation, others saw it as a threat —Indians who successfully adopted European ways would be more difficult to displace. In 1835, as the Cherokees were waging a legal battle to retain their homes, the state of Georgia seized the presses of their newspaper, *The Cherokee Phoenix.*

The Cherokees were forced west into "Indian Territory" (present-day Oklahoma) in 1838. Sequoia is believed to have moved there sometime before the last holdouts were rounded up. In 1844 the tribal government cast a new set of Cherokee type and began publication of a new newspaper, *The Cherokee Advocate*—which ran until 1906.

A LIVING LANGUAGE

The fact that the displaced Cherokees were able to conduct tribal business and publish information in their own language helped ensure the language's survival into the 21st century. Though classified by linguists as "imperiled," today Cherokee is among the healthiest of Native North American languages. It is still spoken by 22,000 people and is undergoing revitalization efforts aimed at increasing its usage.

Through his solitary efforts, made at a time when his entire culture was threatened with destruction, Sequoia helped his people to survive, and gave them a lasting voice.

Here are some of the Cherokee symbols and their corresponding sounds:

Ꭰ	ah	Ꭿ	hi	Ꮍ	mu	Ꮀ	ho
Ꭱ	ay	Ꮪ	du	Ꮡ	su	Ꮉ	ma
Ꭲ	ee	Ꮈ	lv	Ꮥ	de	Ꮔ	nu
Ꭳ	oh	Ꮅ	li	Ꮆ	lo	Ꮛ	quv
Ꭴ	oo	Ꮎ	na	Ꮴ	tse	Ꮶ	tso
Ꭵ	uh	Ꮫ	dv	Ꮹ	wa	Ꮏ	hna
Ꭶ	ga	Ꮝ	s	Ꮾ	wv	Ꮩ	do
Ꭹ	gi	Ꮤ	ta	Ᏻ	yu	Ꮣ	da
Ꭺ	go	Ꮁ	hu	Ᏼ	yv	Ꮦ	te
Ꭼ	gv	Ꮷ	tsu	Ꮃ	la	Ꮗ	que
Ꭸ	ge	Ꮭ	tla	Ꮿ	ya	Ꮱ	tlu
Ꮧ	di	Ꮢ	sv	Ꮑ	ne	Ꮬ	dla

NATIVE WISDOM

Insight from American Indians.

"What is life? It is the flash of a firefly in the night. It is the breath of a buffalo in the wintertime. It is the little shadow which runs across the grass and loses itself in the sunset."

   —**Crowfoot**

"Everything on the Earth has a purpose, every disease an herb to cure it, and every person a mission."

 —**Mourning Dove Salish**

"From the Indian approach to life there came a love for nature; a respect for life; enriching faith in a supreme power; and principles of truth, honesty, and brotherhood."

 —**Luther Standing Bear**

"When you are in doubt, be still, and wait; when doubt no longer exists, then go forward with courage."

   —**White Eagle**

"It does not require many words to speak the truth."

   —**Chief Joseph**

"This we know. The Earth does not belong to man; man belongs to the Earth."

   —**Chief Seattle**

"When we walk upon Mother Earth, we always plant our feet carefully for we know the faces of our future generations are looking up at us from beneath the ground."

   —**Oren Lyons**

"When you were born, you cried and the world rejoiced. Live your life so that when you die, the world cries and you rejoice."

   —**White Elk**

"The only thing necessary for tranquility in the world is that every child grows up happy."

  —**Chief Dan George**

GERTIE THE GREAT

*A pregnant duck taking up residence in a busy city
isn't that unusual. But the way this city responded—with
overwhelming kindness—is worth remembering.*

MAKING A NEST
In April 1945, a mallard duck nested in downtown
Milwaukee on top of a bridge piling. The bridge
carried Wisconsin Avenue, the city's busiest street. Despite
being adjacent to the oil-infested Milwaukee River and the
traffic of 78,000 daily commuters, the duck made herself a
small nest in the top of a white oak log, lined it with her own
feathers, and laid her eggs.

The *Milwaukee Journal* took pictures and printed them,
nicknaming the duck "Gertie the Great." She quickly
became a local celebrity. Traffic was often blocked as people
leaned over the bridge railing to get a glimpse of her.
Gimbels Department Store, across the street from Gertie's
nest, filled their front window with stuffed ducks. With
bridges, buildings, and pollution as her immediate environment, Gertie had nowhere to get food, so people started
leaving bread, corn, cookies, and lettuce. The Humane
Society stationed a guard, and the Boy Scouts formed a
protective "Gertie Patrol."

HATCHING SOON

By the end of the month, there were six eggs in Gertie's nest.
On May 4, the city announced that the piling around the
nest was scheduled to be replaced. Local authorities put it off
indefinitely, declaring, "It might bother Gertie."

Gertie and her ducklings were destined to face many dangers, but luckily, the city of Milwaukee was there to help them at every turn. For example, Laurence Hautz, president of a local conservation league, presented this sobering reality: when the ducklings hatched and tried to swim, the oil in the river would mat their feathers and they'd sink. So on May 29, the city began to pump clean lake water into the Wisconsin River—at the rate of 2.5 million gallons per hour—to flush out the oil. It was just in time, too, because on May 30 the eggs started to hatch.

A few weeks later, a storm struck. The baby ducks fell into the river (a bridge tender retrieved them with a net). Even worse: Gertie was missing. She was finally found a block away in the middle of the night, safe but shaken.

SWIMMING AWAY

Unfortunately, the storm had destroyed Gertie's nest. The ducks had nowhere to go. But Hautz, the conservationist, had an idea: he asked Gimbels if they'd be willing to empty out their front window display of stuffed ducks and house the real Gertie and her brood instead. Gimbels happily obliged.

They stayed at the department store for just a few days. Once Gertie got her strength back and the chicks learned to walk, Gertie the Great and her family were taken to a clean, safe lagoon on the outskirts of Milwaukee. As crowds cheered, Gertie led her chicks into the water and they all swam away.

*   *   *

"I've got a theory that if you give 100% all of the time, somehow things will work out."

—**Larry Bird**

CARNEGIE'S LIBRARIES

Steel magnate Andrew Carnegie made millions in
industry...then gave it all back to the world.

HUMBLE BEGINNINGS

Andrew Carnegie was born in 1835 in Dunfermline, Scotland. As a child, one of his favorite pastimes was listening to workers discuss books at the Tradesmen's Subscription Library, which his father had helped create as a way to share books and knowledge among the town's working class. When Andrew was 12, the family moved to Allegheny, Pennsylvania, and over the next 50 years, he became one of the world's leading industrialists and one of its richest men. His holdings in telegraphy, railroads, and steel manufacturing earned him more than $250 million by 1901.

That's about when Carnegie started wondering what to do with his money. In 1889 he wrote "The Gospel of Wealth," an essay stating his conclusion that the rich should live modestly and distribute their wealth to benefit common people. True to his own belief, Carnegie devoted the rest of his life—and income—to building libraries.

GENEROUS OFFER

Carnegie put out the word that any town in any English-speaking country could request a grant for a free library. The criteria were minimal: a demonstrated need for a library, an agreement to pay the library's annual upkeep, and a vacant lot. If these requirements were met, Carnegie provided the money for raw materials, design plans, and a building crew. How much money each town got depended on their population—$2 for every citizen.

OPEN STACKS

The first Carnegie library was in Dunfermline, his hometown. The first in America: Braddock, Pennsylvania, the location of one of Carnegie's biggest steel mills. The library buildings were rich, ornate, and imposing—often the largest structure in a community. Several styles were available, but all had several features in common: To symbolize that people were elevating themselves, each library had a grand staircase that ascended to the book collections. And over the doorway of each was written "Let there be light" to symbolize the enlightenment of knowledge.

Carnegie changed the way libraries operated, too. Library patrons had always had to ask a clerk to get books for them. But Carnegie wanted people to feel free to browse and discover new books, so he insisted on "open stacks." And when there weren't enough trained librarians to staff many of these new libraries, Carnegie addressed that problem too. In 1919 he stopped building libraries and instead paid for the education and training of new librarians. Hundreds of new jobs were created in the communities he'd already touched.

FINAL CHAPTER

When Carnegie died in 1919 at age 84, he had given away $350 million—90% of his fortune—mostly to libraries. In all, he funded 2,509: 4 in Australia, 156 in Canada, 660 in Great Britain, and 1,689 in the United States—half of all libraries in America at the time. A century later, some have been converted into museums, community centers, office buildings, and homes. But over half are still libraries, many in middle- to low-income neighborhoods. Carnegie libraries still make up a large portion of the New York City Public Library system —31 of the 39 original libraries are still in operation.

AHMED'S GIFT

From the horrors of war comes an incredible story of giving.

THE LOSS

On Thursday, November 3, 2005, Ahmed Ismail Khatib, a 12-year-old Palestinian boy, was playing near his home in the West Bank town of Jenin. It was Eid al-Fitr, the day of celebration that marks the end of the Muslim holy month of Ramadan. Ahmed had received a toy rifle as a present and had gone out to play with it.

But the day's celebrations were shattered when Israeli soldiers mistook Ahmed's toy for a real rifle and shot him. When the soldiers realized what they had done, they rushed the boy to a hospital in the city of Haifa, but it was too late. Ahmed died there two days later.

THE CHOICE

On the Saturday that Ahmed died, his grieving parents, Ismail and Ablah, told doctors that they wanted their son's organs to be donated to children awaiting transplants. Israel has a chronic shortage of donor organs—largely because of religious taboos against the practice—so it would have been a generous offer from any parents in such a situation. But what made this one so extraordinary was they were in an Israeli hospital...and all of the patients were Israelis. "Whether it goes to Jews or Arabs, it doesn't matter to us," Ismail and Ablah told reporters.

Within 24 hours, Ahmed's kidneys, liver, lungs, and heart were transplanted into six Israelis—three Arabs and three Jews—and five of them were children.

News of the transplants traveled through the region like a

shockwave. "This remarkable gesture," said Reuven Rivlin, a member of the Israeli parliament, "despite the war and conflict without solution for nearly 100 years, must be noted." Some Palestinians questioned the Khatibs' decision: Ahmed had been killed by Israeli bullets, and now his organs would go to save Israeli lives. But Ismail, an auto mechanic, said that everyone he talked to supported the choice. "We're talking about young children," he said. "Their religion doesn't make a difference."

THE GIFT

Ismail said the decision was partially motivated by the memory of his brother, who died at age 24 while waiting for a liver transplant. But he also wanted to send a message: "It was a symbol of peace," he said. "But instead of extending an olive branch, I have sown the seeds of my son's organs inside the children of Israelis."

Just days after the operations, Ismail and Ablah Khatib visited some of the children who were saved. Twelve-year-old Samah Gadban, who had been on a waiting list for five years, received Ahmed's heart. Her father, Riad Gadban, thanked the Khatibs "from the depths of my heart," and said his daughter was doing well after the operation. "We are also her parents now," Ablah told him.

"I feel," said Ismail, "that my son has entered the heart of every Israeli."

*   *   *

PUBLIC SERVANT: When Evo Morales became Bolivia's president in 2006, his first order of business was to cut his own salary by half. Reason: He wanted to free up money to hire more teachers.

ENCORE!

These musicians made amazing comebacks.

• **TINA TURNER** left her abusive husband and musical partner, Ike Turner, in 1976. To get a quick divorce, Turner asked for no money. Nearly broke, she took on a grueling tour of small clubs just to pay the bills. It wasn't until 1984's *What's Love Got to Do with It* that Turner found fame again. The album spawned three Top 10 hits. The title song went to No. 1—her first hit in 16 years—and won three Grammys.

• **JOHNNIE JOHNSON** was Chuck Berry's pianist in the 1950s and 1960s, playing on many classic rock 'n' roll hits. (The song "Johnny B. Goode" is rumored to be about him.) But because of Johnson's severe drinking problem, Berry fired him in 1973. He lived in obscurity (he worked as a bus driver) until the 1987 documentary *Hail! Hail! Rock 'n' Roll*, where Keith Richards praised Johnson as the real genius behind Berry's music. With a new audience for his music, Johnson made his very first solo album, *Blue Hand Johnnie*. In 2001, at age 76, he was inducted into the Rock and Roll Hall of Fame.

• **MEAT LOAF**'s 1977 album *Bat Out of Hell*, with songs written by Jim Steinman, sold 30 million copies worldwide. In 1981 Steinman ended their partnership, frustrated that Meat Loaf got all the attention. That started a downward spiral for Meat Loaf: his albums sold poorly, managers stole his money, and he had to declare bankruptcy. He finally reconciled with Steinman, and their 1993 album *Bat Out of Hell II: Back Into Hell* became a smash hit, selling over 18 million copies. The first single "I'd Do Anything for Love" reached #1 in 28 countries and won a Grammy.

PEACE FROM WITHIN

Buddha (c. 568–488 B.C.) defined enlightenment as "the end of suffering." And he taught that enlightenment isn't reserved for the elite—anyone, anytime, can attain it.

"The secret of health for both mind and body is not to mourn for the past, nor to worry about the future, but to live the present moment wisely."

"For those whose minds are shaped by selfless thoughts, joy follows them like a shadow that never leaves them."

"What we think, we become."

"Nothing ever exists entirely alone; everything is in relation to everything else."

"It is better to travel well than to arrive."

"Hatred does not cease by hatred, but only by love; this is the eternal rule."

"Peace comes from within. Do not seek it without."

"However many holy words you read—or speak—what good will they do you if you do not act upon them?"

"Thousands of candles can be lighted from a single candle, and the life of the candle will not be shortened. Happiness never decreases by being shared."

"You cannot travel the path until you have become the path itself."

"There is only one time when it is essential to awaken. That time is now."

"Look within, thou art the Buddha."

EUNICE'S MISSION

Not long ago, the developmentally disabled members of our society were simply forgotten. Many were placed in asylums; others never left their homes. But that was before one woman became their champion.

SILVER SPOON

Eunice Kennedy had a good childhood. She was, after all, a member of the Kennedy clan—one of the most powerful families in America. While two of her brothers, Jack and Bobby, ascended through the ranks of American politics, Eunice looked after her sister Rosemary, who was mentally retarded. It became obvious to her that with a little encouragement and a lot of love, disabled people could lead fulfilling lives. It was those early experiences that led her into a life dedicated to public service.

After graduating from college, Eunice married Sargent Shriver and became a social worker. She then spent the 1940s and '50s helping underprivileged people: female prisoners, juvenile delinquents, runaways, and abandoned children. Her hard work and compassion so impressed her father that in 1957 he asked to her take over the direction of the Joseph P. Kennedy, Jr. Foundation. Established in 1946, the foundation's mission is "to seek the prevention of mental retardation by identifying its causes, and to improve the means by which society deals with citizens who have mental retardation."

GOOD CONNECTIONS

Shriver's tenure at the foundation showed her the uphill battle that disabled people were facing. Something needed to happen on the national level to change the way they were treated. Using her family connections, Shriver helped establish the National Institute for Child Health and Human Development, which provided—and still provides—government funding for laboratory research and studies "to examine the impact of disabilities, diseases, and defects on the lives of individuals."

Research, however, was only the beginning of the answer. The key was community involvement. "I think that really the only way you change people's attitudes or behavior is to work with them," she said. "Not write papers or serve on committees. Who's going to work with the child to change him—with the juvenile delinquent and the retarded? You have to work *with* the person."

Taking her own advice, in 1963 Shriver turned her Maryland home into a day camp for kids and adults with intellectual disabilities. The focus of the camp was on sports—the idea being that daily exercise, a focus on teamwork, and setting goals would help them to better fit in with society. Over the next few years, dozens more of these summer camps popped up all over the country.

SOMETHING SPECIAL

One of the day camp teachers was a woman from Chicago named Anne Burke. In early 1968, she mentioned to Shriver that it would be rewarding to do something bigger than just the camps: a tournament of sports and games "just like the Olympics, but for handicapped people." Shriver loved the idea and knew that the Kennedy Foundation had the resources to make it happen. So they decided to rent out Soldier Field in Chicago and hoped that maybe a few hundred people would attend.

But on July 20, 1968, more than 1,000 disabled athletes

from 26 states and Canada came to compete in running, floor hockey, and swimming, making the first Special Olympics a huge success. In a speech at the opening ceremonies, Shriver said that the high turnout "proves a very fundamental fact: that exceptional children—children with mental retardation—can be exceptional athletes, that through sports they can realize their potential for growth."

But Shriver knew that the games could be even bigger… *much* bigger. So in 1969 she established Special Olympics, Inc., a non-profit organization staffed mostly by volunteers that would oversee future annual competitions. She has kept an active role in the games ever since.

A LASTING LEGACY

In 1984 Shriver was awarded the Presidential Medal of Freedom, the nation's highest civilian honor. Today, nearly two million athletes from 150 countries compete in Special Olympics events each year. But that's not all. Thanks to Shriver's unrelenting efforts, a much larger disability-rights movement has thrived: Handicapped parking spaces, the Americans with Disabilities Act, and special-ed classes in public schools can largely trace their origins to one woman's belief that every person can succeed if only given the chance.

"When the full judgment of the Kennedy legacy is made," said a *U.S. News & World Report* article in 1993, "the changes wrought by Eunice Kennedy Shriver may well be seen as the most consequential."

* * *

"We cannot lower the mountain; therefore we must elevate ourselves."

—Todd Skinner

UNDERGROUND HEROES

One of the most inspiring episodes in American history is the anti-slavery movement known as the Underground Railroad. It wouldn't have happened without these courageous people.

B ACKGROUND
For nearly 250 years, mainstream America justified the legalized ownership of some human beings by others. But there were always those who opposed slavery, and some of them courageously formed the Underground Railroad, an informal chain of abolitionists who smuggled slaves from the South to freedom in the North. Here we celebrate a few of the people who made the Underground Railroad their life's work.

LEVI COFFIN

Like many of slavery's early opponents, Levi Coffin was born a Quaker. Coffin's family lived in Indiana, where they took escaped slaves into their home, hiding them from the professional slave catchers who were sure to be on their trail. But Coffin took it a step further: He believed that most people outside of the deep South were opposed to slavery but were afraid of joining the movement because of the Fugitive Slave Act, which made aiding runaways punishable by fines and imprisonment.

In a stunning effort to counter such fears, Coffin made no secret of his activities. He would even bring runaways with him to church meetings and community gatherings to show his neighbors that he was harboring the fugitives. Coffin appealed to the compassion of his fellow townspeople, urging them to defy the Fugitive Slave Act by not turning in escaped slaves to the authorities. He was also a leader in the "Free Produce" movement—a network of merchants and consumers who refused to trade in goods produced by slave labor. Coffin helped so many slaves during his lifetime that he was known informally as the "President of the Underground Railroad."

THOMAS GARRETT

Another famous Underground Railroad Quaker, Thomas Garrett is believed to have fed and sheltered more than 3,000 runaways at his home in Wilmington, Delaware, in the years preceding the Civil War. His activities were so well known that the state legislature of neighboring Maryland offered a $10,000 reward to anyone who could catch him in the act of aiding an escaped slave. In 1848 he was bankrupted by legal fees and fines resulting from his work, but he never backed away from his mission, stating, "I haven't a dollar in the world, but if thee knows a fugitive who needs a breakfast, send him to me."

JOHN FAIRFIELD

Not all Underground Railroad workers were Quakers, or even Northerners. John Fairfield was a Virginian, born into a wealthy slave-owning family. The first slave he ever helped to escape was his best friend—a young man he'd grown up with who was owned by his uncle. Posing as his friend's master, Fairfield smuggled him to freedom in Canada.

Returning home, Fairfield learned that his own family was preparing to have him arrested, so he secretly gathered a group of their slaves and headed north again. For the next 12 years, he traveled back and forth, North to South, orchestrating one complicated escape after another. Fairfield specialized in helping the relatives of free blacks he had met in the North.

One of Fairfield's most successful ploys was to pose as a slave trader. Often he would organize an escape, then stay behind to join the slave-catching posse and lead it off course. He was jailed several times but always managed to escape. Eventually, however, his luck ran out, and he was killed by a group of Tennessee vigilantes. No one knows exactly how many slaves Fairfield helped free, but estimates run in the thousands.

HARRIET TUBMAN

Working on the Underground Railroad was a dangerous business. For whites, the risks were fines or possibly prison. But escaped slaves bold enough to help lead other slaves to freedom faced far worse: If caught, they were returned to their former owners, who were then free to punish them in whatever manner they saw fit.

The most famous runaway slave to become an Underground Railroad hero was Harriet Tubman. She escaped from a Maryland plantation in 1849 at the age of 30. Over the next 10 years she returned to the South 19 times and led more than 300 others out of bondage. Her exploits became so well known that the State of Maryland offered a $12,000 bounty for her capture. But she was never caught, and she never lost a single "passenger." Her incredible courage has made her name synonymous with the Underground Railroad.

*   *   *

"Though no one can go back and make a brand-new start, anyone can start from now and make a brand-new ending."

—Carl Bard

A LITTLE GOOD NEWS

With all the bad news that makes the headlines, it's easy to forget that good news happens, too. Here are some unlikely stories—with happy endings.

SOFT LANDING

Early in 2006 a technician was performing repairs on high-voltage power lines in Hallstatt, Austria, by the only means possible: hanging by a rope and harness, suspended from a helicopter. As he was dangling, a knot in one of the ropes came loose, and he fell 130 feet to the ground. Amazingly, he landed in a deep snowdrift...and was completely unharmed.

CALL FROM BEYOND

Friends and family of recently deceased Bogoljub Topalovic of Serbia got a surprise as they were watching his coffin being lowered into the grave: He called his daughter on her cell phone. The 84-year-old's hospital records had been mixed up with those of someone who had died. Topalovic was calling to find out why everyone had stopped visiting him in the hospital.

OUT WITH THE OLD

Sark, a tiny island in the English Channel, is the world's newest democracy. For 450 years Sark had been ruled by a feudal system in which only landowners could be lawmakers. But in 2006 the legislators voted to allow any of the island's 600 residents to hold office. (Some things, however, will not change: Only the head of state—the *seigneur*—is allowed to own pigeons or unspayed female dogs.)

ANNIVERSARY PRESENT

In 1946 Arthur Reis married his sweetheart, Ardell. For their honeymoon, the young couple went to Chicago and stayed at the swanky Drake Hotel, overlooking Lake Michigan. Sixty years later, they went back to the Drake for their diamond anniversary. When Ardell presented the receipt from their first visit, the hotel staff were so charmed that they gave the couple a room at the 1946 price of $7. (Rooms at the Drake today cost between $200 and $1,000 per night.)

HOUSE-RAISING

When a tornado swept through Webster County, Missouri, one night in 2006, it completely destroyed the home of Chris Graber and his family. All that was left behind was the foundation. But soon more than 100 of the Graber's Amish neighbors showed up by horse and buggy. And in less than 15 hours they had built the Grabers a new house. "By 2 p.m., we were mopping the floors," said a dazed and thankful Graber.

FROM THE ASHES

Among the thousands of pieces of debris from the Space Shuttle *Columbia* crash in Texas in 2003 was one small piece of hope—an intact canister containing equipment from the experiment known as GOBB-SS ("Growth of Bacterial Biofilm on Inorganic Surfaces During Spaceflight"). The experiment was designed to investigate the origins of life on Earth and elsewhere in the solar system. More than that, it was the joint project of Israeli and Palestinian scientists, meant to promote peace between the two peoples. The experiment survived and continues today.

MRS. WILDER'S *LITTLE* BOOKS

Want to be a writer? Here's an author who began writing late in life and turned her pioneer childhood into a bestselling series.

A FARMER'S LIFE

At 63 years old, Laura Ingalls Wilder had already endured a lifetime of ups and downs: drought, disease, failed farms, blossoming wealth from the stock market...and financial ruin in the crash of 1929. She and her husband, Almanzo, were barely scraping by in 1930, tending their modest Missouri farm, when her daughter had an idea. Wilder had once been an editor for a rural newspaper, so her daughter encouraged her to try writing a book to bring in a little extra money. She certainly had a lot to write about—the memories of her childhood, growing up in a homesteading family on the Great Plains, were a disappearing piece of Americana. So Wilder wrote a story about a pioneer family like hers—even borrowing her sisters' names, Mary and Carrie, and putting herself—young Laura —in the starring role.

The book, *Little House in the Big Woods*, was an instant success. Wilder followed it up with a series of *Little House* books, and by the early 1940s she was a celebrity, with royalty checks bringing her and Almanzo financial security for the first time in their lives. A stream of dedicated fans visited her at her farm, and her neighbors delighted in how famous their "Mrs. Wilder" had become. Wilder lived to be 90, and died in 1957 in the farmhouse in Mansfield, Missouri, that she and Almanzo had shared for more than 50 years. Her books were made into the TV series *Little House on the Prairie* in the 1970s, and remain popular today.

INSPIRATIONAL FUNK

*Wisdom can be found anywhere—even in funk
and R&B songs from the 1970s. Groovy.*

"Get up offa that thing
and dance 'til you feel better!"
—**James Brown,
"Get Up Offa That Thing"**

"As long as I know how to
love, I know I'll be alive.
I will survive! I will survive!"
—**Gloria Gaynor,
"I Will Survive"**

"So just call on me brother
when you need a hand
We all need somebody to
lean on.
I just might have a problem
that you'd understand
We all need somebody to
lean on."
—**Bill Withers,
"Lean on Me"**

"You're a shining star
No matter who you are."
—**Earth, Wind & Fire,
"Shining Star"**

"Now maybe some day
I'll reach that higher goal
I know that I can make it
With just a little bit of soul."
—**Curtis Mayfield,
"Keep on Pushin'"**

"You know we've got to
find a way
to bring some lovin' here
today."
—**Marvin Gaye,
"What's Goin' On"**

"The color of your skin
don't matter to me
As long as we can live in
harmony."
—**War, "Why Can't
We Be Friends?"**

"Love's in need of love today
Don't delay, send yours in
right away."
—**Stevie Wonder, "Love's
in Need of Love Today"**

J-MAC

There's a good chance you saw this on TV—news outlets ran it about a million times—but it's such a great story that we couldn't leave it out. Whenever you need a pick-me-up, read about this amazing young man.

THE SHORT KID

Jason McElwain was a senior at Greece Athena High School in Rochester, New York. The 17-year-old had autism, which kept him from learning to speak until he was five and inhibited his social skills for many years. But over time he learned to make friends, and became popular at his school. But what Jason loved most was basketball.

When he tried out for the school's varsity team, the Trojans, he didn't make it, but not because of his autism; at 5'6" he was too short. But he was so well liked by the players and coach that he was made team manager. "He became so much a part of us and so much a part of our program that we kind of forgot he was autistic," said teammate Steven Kerr. Jason loved the job. He kept stats, ran the clock, handed out water bottles, and kept the players pumped up.

And on February 15, 2006, he was asked to do a little more.

PUT HIM IN

It was the last home game of the season, and with graduation around the corner, it would be Jason's last game as manager. The coach, Jim Johnson, thought Jason deserved something for his dedication to the team. He called Jason into his office and told him not to wear his trademark suit and tie that evening—he wanted him in uniform. The coach wasn't making any promises, but if things worked out, Jason might get a chance to play.

When students got the news, they rallied behind him. They made posters with his nickname, "J-Mac," on them, fastened cutouts of Jason's face onto popsicle sticks, and showed up for the game en masse.

AND THE CROWD GOES...

Greece Athena easily handled their opponents, Spencerport High. With four minutes left, they were up 59–43, and the crowd, who had been chanting Jason's name the entire game, could feel it coming. Coach Johnson stood up and pointed to the bench, directly at number 52, and Jason leapt up and ran onto the court. The place went crazy. J-Mac posters and Jason's cutout face bounced above the screaming fans in the bleachers. Within seconds, Jason got the ball behind the three-point line and took a shot.

"I said to myself, 'Please, Lord, let him get a basket,'" Coach Johnson later said. But Jason missed by a mile. Moments later, he went in for a layup...and missed that, too. Jason's father, David McElwain, wasn't worried, though. "The thing about Jason," he said, "he isn't afraid of anything."

...WILD!

With just under three minutes remaining, Jason got the ball and launched another three-pointer...and made it. The crowd exploded in cheers. A few moments later, he took another three-point shot...Swish. Then he took another. Swish. Then another. Swish. Before he was done, he'd tied the school record with six three-pointers, and finished with 20 points in just over four minutes of play. When he sank his last shot with two seconds to play and the buzzer went off, the crowd—even the opposing players and cheerleaders—

stormed the court. They hoisted J-Mac over their heads and carried him off in triumph.

"There wasn't a dry eye here," said athletic director Randolph Hutto. "I've coached a lot of wonderful kids," said Coach Johnson, "but I've never experienced such a thrill." But the happiest of all: J-Mac. "I felt like a celebrity," he said.

JUST KEEP DREAMING

Experts who study the condition called Jason's moment in the sun a victory for all people with autism. "A lot of us feel like this is a gift to have this receive so much nationwide publicity," Dr. Catherine Lord of the University of Michigan told ESPN. "There are thousands of Jasons out there, carrying the net for the soccer team, keeping statistics for the baseball team, playing the drum for the school band. This serves as a reminder to give these kids a chance whenever possible."

"I look at autism as the Berlin Wall," said Debbie McElwain, Jason's mom. "And he cracked it."

Jason has his own message about his condition. "I don't care about this autistic situation, really," he said. "It's just the way I am. The advice I'd give to autistic people is just keep working, just keep dreaming. You'll get your chance and you'll do it."

*   *   *

HANDLING ADVERSITY

"Some of the choices in life choose you. How you face these turns in the road, more than the choices themselves, is what will define the context of your life."

—**Dana Reeve**

GOOD KARMA

A lot of people believe in karma—the concept that the universe rewards you for good deeds and punishes you for bad deeds. But is it real? This story might make you think so.

THE LIFE YOU SAVE...
    In 1999 Penny Brown took a rare day off from work so she could watch her son's Little League baseball game in Lancaster, New York. The game came to an abrupt halt when one of the players, 10-year-old Kevin Stephan, accidentally got hit in the chest with a swinging bat. The boy reeled and fell to the ground. Fortunately for Kevin, there was a nurse in the stands: Penny Brown. She ran out onto the field and found that his heart had stopped beating. After performing CPR, she was able to revive Kevin, saving him from permanent brain damage—or perhaps even death.

...MAY BE YOUR OWN
Seven years later, Penny was eating dinner at a restaurant in Depew, New York, when she began to choke on her food. The other patrons panicked and screamed for someone to help her, but no one there knew what to do...except for one of the dishwashers. He bolted out of the kitchen and performed the Heimlich maneuver, saving Penny's life.

That dishwasher was none other than Kevin Stephan, now 17 years old and a volunteer firefighter. If Penny hadn't run out on the field to save his life, he wouldn't have been there seven years later to save hers.

THE EMPEROR
OF ATLANTIS

A musical testament to the strength of the human spirit.

ECLECTIC MIX

In 1943 Viktor Ullmann, a celebrated Czech composer, wrote a one-act opera called *Der Kaiser von Atlantis* ("The Emperor of Atlantis"). His innovative score mixed elements of classical opera with folk music and jazz, to be performed by a 13-piece orchestra that included a harpsichord, banjo, guitar, and saxophone. That in itself made the opera unique, but what made Ullmann's work even more extraordinary was its message—a stinging indictment of the evils of war—and the circumstances under which it was written.

The opera's story has the emperor of Atlantis waging war on such a massive scale that Death itself goes on strike for being too overworked. The emperor's soldiers lie on the battlefield, mortally wounded but unable to die. Death offers to go back to work—but only if the emperor agrees to be his first victim.

THE COMPOSER OF THERESIENSTADT

Ullmann finished the opera in mid-1944, but never got to see it properly performed. He wrote it while imprisoned, along with scores of other Jewish artists, interned in the Theresienstadt concentration camp in Czechoslovakia. As a public relations ploy, the Nazis allowed prisoners at Theresienstadt to put on operas and plays. By doing so, they hoped to fool Red Cross officials —and the outside world—into thinking that Nazi prisons were somewhat humane.

At the opera's dress rehearsal, the camp's German guards were not amused—the score included numerous references to Johann Sebastian Bach, despised by the Nazis, and even a musical parody of the German anthem, "Deutschland Über Alles." Two weeks later, Ullmann was deported to Auschwitz, where he was killed in a gas chamber in October 1944.

BURIED TREASURE

Ullmann's opera was lost to the world until 1975, when it was discovered during an excavation of the Theresienstadt camp. A fellow prisoner had secretly buried the score there after Ullmann was taken away. *The Emperor of Atlantis* was performed for the very first time in Amsterdam in 1975, and since then the "Concentration Camp Opera," as it has come to be known, has continued to play in opera houses world-wide. Viktor Ullmann's personal story ended tragically, but his genius, resilience, humor, passion, and courage live on today in his extraordinary musical creation.

*   *   *

STOP AND SMELL THE LAUGHTER

"They usually have two tellers in my local bank, except when it's very busy, when they have one."   **—Rita Rudner**

"I got my hair highlighted, because I felt some strands were more important than others."   **—Mitch Hedberg**

"In my house there's this light switch that doesn't do any-thing. Every so often I would flick it on and off just to check. Yesterday, I got a call from a woman in Japan. She said, 'Cut it out.'"   **—Steven Wright**

THE COMEBACK KID

*Whether you're a Democrat or a Republican, you've got
to admire this man and his refusal to accept the
picture history was about to paint of him.*

DOWNWARD SPIRAL
In 1981 Jimmy Carter was at the lowest point of his
career. As his presidential term was winding down, so
were his approval ratings. To many Americans, Carter
seemed ineffectual and weak: Iranian militants were holding
52 Americans hostage, and President Carter seemed helpless
to do anything about it. Inflation was at its highest since
World War II. After his devastating loss to Ronald Reagan in
1980, "loser" was added to the list of negatives attached to
Carter's name.

When he retired from politics at the age of 56, Carter
found himself a has-been without a future. He was, as he
wrote years later, facing an "empty life." He didn't know what
to do with himself. At first he did what most ex-presidents
do—worked on his memoirs, raised money for his presidential
library, and indulged hobbies like fishing and woodworking.
But Carter wasn't ready to give up yet.

GOOD WORK
In 1984 he emerged from obscurity in a striking way—
wielding a hammer as he helped construct low-cost housing
with Habitat for Humanity. Something about the sight of a
former president in jeans and a ball cap, driving nails into
lumber, captured the public's imagination. It was one step
toward his rehabilitation as a respected public figure.

Another step was the opening of the Carter Center, his

presidential library outside of Atlanta. From the beginning, he envisioned it as being more than an archive of his presidency; he wanted it to become a "mini–United Nations," a place where nations could meet to "advance human rights and alleviate human suffering." Since its inception, it has helped with food production, disease eradication, and conflict resolution in 65 countries.

GLOBAL INFLUENCE

But it's as an ambassador-at-large that Carter has most distinguished himself since his presidency. He's served every succeeding president except Reagan, monitoring elections around the world and even brokering peace agreements in North Korea, Haiti, and Bosnia. Along the way he's developed a reputation for unshakable honesty and integrity. His tireless efforts to promote fairness and equality culminated in his being awarded the Nobel Peace Prize in 2002.

Carter may not be remembered as a great president, but he will go down in history as a great humanitarian. As his former pollster Patrick Caddell said, "There won't be many American presidents who can walk away saying they accomplished what he's accomplished." Adds former vice president Walter Mondale, "Finally, the American people are seeing all this happen and saying, 'Hey, here's a really good man.'"

* * *

"You can do what you have to do, and sometimes you can do it even better than you think you can."

—Jimmy Carter

BOTTLE VILLAGE

*"Anyone can make anything with a million dollars. Look
at Disney. But it takes more than money to make
something out of nothing. And look at the fun
I have doing it." —Grandma Prisbey*

WHAT SHALL I DO TODAY?
It all started in 1956 with a pencil collection.
Tressa Prisbey of Simi Valley, California, needed a
place to store hers—the 60-year-old grandmother had 17,000
of them. Using discarded bottles as bricks, she built a rectan-
gular hut across from the trailer she lived in with her husband Al. The Pencil Hut inspired her to embark on a building binge that lasted for the next 25 years. She added one
whimsical structure after another to her 1/3-acre lot until she
called it "done" in 1981. She mostly used bottles scavenged
from her daily visits to the local dump, but eventually any
thing and every thing she could scavenge found its way into
her structures. There was the Leaning Tower of Bottle
Village, the Dolls Head Shrine, a birdbath made out of automobile head lights, an intravenous feeding tube fire screen,
and a mosaic walkway bordered by TV picture tubes.

LOCAL COLOR
"Grandma" Prisbey became renowned for her odd sense of
humor and tireless optimism. The curious were charged a
quarter to take a tour, which consisted of following her from
building to building as she regaled her listeners with stories.
The tours always ended in the Meditation Room, where she
would play the piano and sing naughty novelty tunes from
the 1920s.

But what made Tressa special was not *what* she made, but *why* she made it. Her life was full of hardships and heartbreak. Married at 15 to a man three times her age, she endured his abuse through the births of seven children. Finally, she took her kids and fled, supporting her family by waiting tables and various odd jobs. She married her second husband in 1947, but he succumbed to alcoholism. Over the years she endured the deaths of six of her children, both husbands, a fiancé, and all but one of her siblings. Bottle Village became the way Tressa transformed the sorrow in her life into something joyful. In the words of Vera Greenfield, author of the book, *Making Do or Making Art*, "Bottle Village is not only a one of a kind, quirky, fun, and brilliant approach to recycling and shed making, Bottle Village is also a bold and personal statement to the importance of the creative act in everyday life."

Tressa "Grandma" Prisbey died in 1988 at the age of 92. Although Bottle Village was severely damaged in the Northridge earthquake of 1994, the village was added to the Register of National Historic Places in 1996 and is being restored, so you can still visit it today.

✳   ✳   ✳

BRAIN FOOD

According to scientists, some foods can actually make your brain work faster, clearer, better, and longer. Examples:

• Turkey, chicken, and soy are loaded with phytochemicals that regenerate brain tissue, chemicals, and neurotransmitters.

• Beans and whole grains keep blood sugar levels steady. That lets the brain work at high energy levels for longer periods.

• Antioxidants in dark, leafy vegetables, and fruits like grapes and berries, help develop brain tissue and maintain memory.

THE PLANT DOCTOR

The amazing story of George W.....no, the other one.

BACKGROUND
George Washington Carver was born to slave parents in Missouri around 1864 (he was never sure exactly what year). His father died before his birth, and his mother was kidnapped by slave traders and disappeared when he was an infant. He was raised by a German immigrant couple, Moses and Susan Carver, who had owned his mother before the Civil War.

The Carvers encouraged young George to read all he could. But his real gift was in working with his hands—in the soil. He had an uncanny way with plants even as a child, cultivating his own garden and experimenting with different soils and combinations of plants. By the time he was seven, neighbors were asking him for advice on their gardens and trees, already calling him "the plant doctor."

A WEIRD KID

When George was 10, he told the Carvers that he was leaving home so he could go to school. The closest school for black children was 10 miles away, so George packed some food and an extra shirt and walked there. It was closed when he arrived, so he slept in a barn the first night. In the morning he was discovered by a woman named Mariah Watkins. When she asked him who he was, he answered, "Carver's George," the only name he had ever known, and told her he was there to go to school. Mariah and her husband took him in, and he lived with them while he attended school. They also told him that he was never to call himself

"Carver's George" again. From then on, his name was George Carver.

When George graduated from high school, he wanted to go to college but couldn't because of racial barriers. So he traveled all over the Midwest, working odd jobs before he could find a college that would accept him. In 1890 he finally got into Simpson College in Indianola, Iowa. His first classes: painting and piano. Many say Carver could have been successful in either discipline, if he had chosen to. But his art teacher, whose father was head of Iowa State's Department of Horticulture, advised him that his skills with plants offered a better future than the arts. Carver agreed. In 1891 he became the first black student at Iowa State University, and after graduating, became its first black faculty member. It was there that he added "Washington" to his name, to avoid confusion with another George Carver.

THE NUT PROFESSOR

In 1897 Booker T. Washington invited Carver to the school he'd founded, the Tuskegee Normal and Industrial Institute for Negroes in Alabama. He wanted to hire Carver as the school's Director of Agriculture. But Carver had a good future at Iowa State, where they wanted him to stay on as professor, and Tuskegee wasn't offering nearly as much money. But Carver, as he would prove numerous times, wasn't in it for the money. He accepted the Tuskegee job and over the next four decades revolutionized agriculture in the South. Just a few of his accomplishments at Tuskegee:

• Cotton and tobacco had long been the major cash crops in the South. But they both depleted nutrients from the soil, making for declining harvests and poor farmers. Carver found that by rotating crops like peanuts, peas, and soybeans into a field's growing cycle, a farmer could restore nutrients to the soil and bring it back to health.

• Getting farmers to grow these new crops was going to be difficult if there was no market for them, so Carver found profitable uses for them. For example, from the peanut he developed more than 300 different products, including cheese, shampoo, plastics, and printer's ink. Before long, peanuts were a $200 million industry in Alabama alone.

• From the sweet potato and the pecan came more than 100 products, including dyes, paints, and even a material for paving roads. Many of these new products would be used by the Allies in World War I.

MAKING AN IMPACT

Carver's discoveries were so revolutionary that the work of "the Wizard of Tuskegee" spread around the world. In 1916 he was elected a Fellow of the Royal Society of Arts, Manufacturers and Commerce of Britain. It was a rare award for any American, let alone a son of slaves. In 1921 he appeared before the House Ways and Means Committee, arguing for a tariff on cheap imported peanuts. He was supposed to speak for 10 minutes. An hour and 45 minutes later, the spellbound committee members came around to Carver's point of view and passed the tariff.

Over the years, Carver met personally at Tuskegee with presidents Theodore Roosevelt, Calvin Coolidge, and Franklin Roosevelt. The crown prince of Sweden and Mahatma Gandhi both consulted him, and Henry Ford became a friend and collaborator.

Thomas Edison also became Carver's friend, and around 1917 offered to build him his own lab in New Jersey, with a salary of $100,000 a year—unheard of at the time. But

Carver refused the offer. He would stay at the Tuskegee Institute until his death in 1943, and he never allowed them to raise his salary of $125 a month. Of the hundreds of products he developed in his career, he took patents out on only three. A deeply religious man, Carver would say of his ideas and inventions, "God gave them to me. How can I sell them to someone else?"

GIVING BACK

In 1940 he gave his life savings, $33,000, to establish the George Washington Carver Foundation at Tuskegee Institute to continue his research. When he died in 1943, he also left them the rest of his estate, nearly $30,000 more. The epitaph on his grave at Tuskegee says it plainly: "He could have added fortune to fame, but caring for neither, he found happiness and honor in being helpful to the world."

*   *   *

HOW TO THINK LIKE A GENIUS

Anyone can be brilliant, says psychologist Scott Tiler. You just have to exercise your brain regularly. Here are three starters.

1. Look around your office, house, or car and choose a common object, such as a coffee cup, paper clip, pen, or dish towel. Think of five new uses for it.

2. Listen to other people's ideas to find out how they view the world. If you loosen your usual approach to gathering information, you'll find that the world is filled with fresh images that will enhance your thinking skills.

3. Challenge your mind by looking for similarities and links between things that appear unrelated.

PAY IT FORWARD

Here's how a single act of kindness led to countless acts of kindness...and even more that are happening every day.

TO THE RESCUE

Late one night in 1978, Catherine Ryan Hyde was driving her '73 Datsun in Los Angeles when the car suddenly lost power. She hit the brakes at the end of an off-ramp, and the engine, the lights—everything—went dead. Then the passenger compartment started filling with smoke. Hyde jumped out as fast as she could and saw more smoke billowing out from under the hood. That was when she realized she was in one of L.A.'s most dangerous neighborhoods—at night. And to make matters worse, two men were running straight at her. She tensed up, expecting the worst.

But the men ignored Hyde—they had more important matters to attend to. One jumped into the smoke-filled car and opened the hood; the other used a blanket to smother the spreading flames. It all happened so fast.

When emergency crews arrived, firefighters told Hyde that the car could have exploded at any time. She looked around to thank the men who'd put themselves at such great risk to save her. But they were gone.

WRITING IT DOWN

"In the wake of that incident," Hyde recalls, "I had to try to figure out what to do with a favor of that magnitude, that can't be repaid. Over the following months, I started keeping an eye out for someone else who needed help. If I couldn't pay the favor back to the men who helped me, I figured I would have to 'pay it forward' to somebody else. That's how I learned that this brand of caring can be contagious."

The idea stayed with Hyde for years, and she eventually developed it into a novel entitled *Pay It Forward*. Published in 2000, it's about a 12-year-old boy named Trevor whose class is given a unique assignment: "Think of an idea for world change, and put it into action." Trevor comes up with a simple but extraordinary idea:

> You see, I do something real good for three people. And then when they ask how they can pay it back, I say they have to Pay It Forward. To three more people. Each. So nine people get helped. Then those people have to do 27…Then it sort of spreads out, see. To 81. Then 243. Then 729. Then 2,187. See how big it gets?

A MOVEMENT IS BORN

The idea did get big—in the book as well as in real life. *Pay It Forward* became a bestselling novel and was made into a film. In 2000, Hyde created the Pay It Forward Foundation, an organization that supplies schools with materials and ideas "to educate and inspire young students to realize that they can change the world, and provide them with opportunities to do so." And, as Hyde found out, big changes can start with one small act.

The Pay It Forward movement has inspired thousands of people to contribute to their communities and make other people's lives better. Want to see some examples? Turn to the next page.

PAYING IT FORWARD

Here are some real examples of people who read Catherine Ryan Hyde's book, Pay It Forward, *and were inspired to do something good for someone else. (Used by permission of www.payitforwardmovement.org.)*

THE CAR PAYMENT

Melissa Firt had $250—only half the money she needed for her car payment. She decided to send it anyway, but she lost the check somewhere en route to the post office in Buffalo, New York. She searched and searched, but couldn't find it anywhere. The next day she received an anonymous note in her mailbox: Someone had found her check and mailed it. But that's not all—they had added another check for $250 to the payment. They explained that they had recently seen the movie *Pay It Forward* and were wondering what they could do for someone...when the answer appeared right there on the pavement in the post office parking lot. "This is one of the best things that has ever happened to me," says Melissa. "I believe this will change the outcome of my life."

THE OLD COMMUNITY CENTER

In 2002 Andy Mullen was looking to buy a house in Leicestershire, England, when he heard about an old community center that was for sale. The Girl Guides (that's what they call Girl Scouts in England) owned the building, but were forced to sell it because they couldn't afford to pay for its upkeep (the ceilings leaked and the floors flooded). "I saw *Pay It Forward*," he said, "and was inspired by the idea that the whole world could be affected by one person's actions." So Mullen decided to buy the center and give it back to the Guides. Was he rich? No. He sold his house and used the money as a down payment on the community center. Then Mullen, along with a small army of volunteers, spent a year fixing the old building. The Girl Guides still use it, along with other community groups. It also serves as national headquarters for Pay It Forward U.K.

MRS. BURGESS' 6TH-GRADE CLASS

One morning in 2001, Lisa Burgess told her students at Golden Elementary in Placentia, California, some sad news: The home of one of their schoolmates, Kenny Bramber, had burned down. His family had lost everything they owned in the fire...and they had no homeowner's insurance.

Burgess asked her students to brainstorm ways that they could help. Their first idea was to each donate a few dollars, but that wouldn't amount to much. Then one of the kids, Ben Vail, said that he had $250 saved up, and had been waiting to spend it on something special. Other kids offered to donate their savings too. By the next day, the class had raised $1,500 of their own money.

But they weren't done yet. Students went classroom to classroom and raised even more money. Others donated their unused gift certificates, then went to stores and restaurants and asked them to donate clothes and free meal vouchers. Donations continued to pour in: clothes, food, toys, furniture. In just one day, the students had made it possible for the Bramber family to get by until they were back on their feet.

In 2002 Burgess and her class received the first annual Pay It Forward Award. Catherine Ryan Hyde presented it, saying that the kids sent a message of hope: "When people get to the point where the world is too bleak, they can read stories like the one at Golden Elementary."

MARATHON OF HOPE

Terry Fox, Canadian hero.

DETERMINATION

Terry Fox was born in 1958 and grew up in British Columbia. He was an average kid, except for being very athletic—in high school he played hockey, basketball, lacrosse, and ran track. But in 1977, shortly after graduating from high school, he was diagnosed with osteogenic sarcoma: bone cancer. A few months later, his right leg had to be amputated. Fox didn't think he'd ever be able to run or play sports again.

Then something happened. The night before the surgery, Fox read a magazine article about an amputee who'd run in the New York Marathon. The story inspired Fox so much that he determined then and there not to let an artificial leg prevent him from living the life he wanted to live. He would never stop running. In fact, he decided he would raise both awareness and money for the fight against cancer by running his own marathon...all the way across Canada.

THE RACE IS ON

For nearly two years, Fox prepared for his "Marathon of Hope." First he learned to walk with his artificial leg, then he learned to run, then he worked on building up his endurance. Finally, on April 12, 1980, he flew to St. John's, Newfoundland, dipped his prosthetic leg in the Atlantic Ocean, and began his trek west. His mission: to run until he could dip it into the Pacific Ocean.

His run began with almost no fanfare, but then the press picked up the story, detailing his daily progress. Suddenly all of Canada was rooting for him and bombarding his family with letters and donations. Fox's pace was staggering: Every day he ran an average of 26 miles—the length of an entire marathon. Marathon runners typically train for months and require weeks afterward to recuperate. And that's for a single race. Not only was Fox was running a marathon every day for months on end, he was doing it with an artificial leg.

Then, on September 1, 1980, the Marathon of Hope ended abruptly near Thunder Bay, Ontario. Fox's cancer had come back and spread to his lungs. After running for 143 days straight, through Nova Scotia, New Brunswick, Newfoundland, Quebec, and Ontario—more than 3,300 miles—he had to abandon the quest and return home for treatment.

Terry Fox died on June 28, 1981, just shy of his 23rd birthday, but his strength and determination continue to inspire people all over the world.

FOX'S LEGACY

• The day after the run ended, the Four Seasons hotel chain announced plans to sponsor an annual marathon in Fox's honor. Since 1981, annual Terry Fox Runs are held every September in cities across Canada and around the world to raise money for cancer research. As of 2006, the runs have donated $360 million.

• In 1980 the Canadian press named him Canadian of the Year. He was named Canadian athlete of the decade (beating Wayne Gretzky) and in 1999 was voted Canada's greatest national hero of all time in a magazine survey.

• During his actual run, Fox raised $1.7 million for cancer research.

• Four years after Fox's run, 18-year-old Steve Fonyo started a 10-month cross-Canada run to raise money for cancer research. Like Fox, Fonyo had lost a leg to cancer and had a metal limb. But unlike Fox, Fonyo made it all the way from St. John's, Newfoundland, to Victoria, B.C., raising $13 million along the way.

• Rick Hansen was paralyzed from the waist down in a car accident at age 15. After a string of wheelchair-marathon victories, he was inspired by Fox to embark on a wheelchair "run" across Canada to raise funds for spinal cord research. Hansen crossed Canada in 1985...and kept going. He traveled 25,000 miles over 34 countries (including China, Australia, and France) in 26 months. By the time he returned to Canada in May 1987, he had raised $26 million.

*   *   *

WALK FOR LIFE

Steve Vaught weighed 400 pounds—so dangerously obese that he was afraid he'd never survive to see his children grow up. So he decided to do something drastic: he'd lose the weight by walking...across the country. In April 2005, Vaught left San Diego with the intention of reaching New York City within six months. That turned out to be impossible: his size and 80-pound backpack slowed Vaught to a snail's pace. When a sporting-goods company donated new lightweight gear, Vaught picked up the pace, averaging 18 miles a day. By April 2006, he'd walked 2,400 miles—three-quarters of the way to New York—and lost more than 100 pounds. But now his reasons for taking the trip have changed. He doesn't just want to *survive*; he wants to *live*. "It's no longer about the walk," he says. "It's more about the journey."

"Twenty years from now you will be more disappointed by the things that you did not do than by the ones that you did do. So throw off the bowlines. Sail away from the safe harbor. Catch the trade winds in your sails. Explore. Dream. Discover."

—Mark Twain

MARK TWAIN AT 70

*Benjamin Franklin had his apple a day, but here's a
man who had a different formula for longevity.*

BACKGROUND
On February 3, 1905, Mark Twain celebrated his 70th
birthday—quite a feat, considering that the life
expectancy at that time was only 47. At his lavish birthday
party at Delmonico's restaurant in New York City, Twain
gave a raucous speech on his secrets to longevity. Here are a
few excerpts.

ON SLEEPING: "Since 40 I have been regular about going
to bed and getting up. I have made it a rule to go to bed
when there wasn't anybody left to sit up with; and I have
made it a rule to get up when I had to. This has resulted in
an unswerving regularity of irregularity."

ON EATING: "In the matter of diet, I have been persistently
strict in sticking to the things which didn't agree with me
until one or the other of us got the best of it. For 30 years I
have taken coffee and bread at eight in the morning, and no
bite nor sup until seven-thirty in the evening. That is all
right for me, but headachy people would not reach 70 com-
fortably by that road, and they would be foolish to try it. And
I wish to urge upon you this—that if you find you can't make
70 by any but an uncomfortable road, don't you go."

ON SMOKING: "I have made it a rule never to smoke more
than one cigar at a time. As an example to others, it has
always been my rule never to smoke when asleep, and never
to refrain when awake. I have stopped smoking now and

then, for a few months at a time, but it was not on principle, it was only to show off."

ON DRINKING: "When others drink, I like to help."

ON MORALITY: "Morals are an acquirement—like music, like a foreign language, like piety, poker, paralysis—no man is born with them. But if you are careful with a moral, and keep it in a dry place, and disinfect it now and then, and give it a fresh coat of whitewash once in a while, you will be surprised to see how well it will last and how long it will keep sweet, or at least inoffensive."

ON BEING INVITED TO PARTIES: "If you shrink at the thought of night and the late home-coming from the banquet and the lights and the laughter through the deserted streets, you need only reply, 'Your invitation honors me, and pleases me, but I am seventy—*seventy*—and would rather nestle in the chimney-corner, and smoke my pipe, and read my book, and take my rest, wishing you well in all affection.' "

ON REACHING THE BIG SEVEN-O: "The 70th birthday! It is the time of life when you arrive at a new and awful dignity; when you may throw aside the decent reserves which have pressed you for a generation and stand unafraid and unabashed upon your seven-terraced summit and look down and teach—unrebuked. You can tell the world how you got there.

"I have achieved my 70 years in the usual way: by sticking strictly to a scheme of life which would kill anybody else. It sounds like an exaggeration, but that is really the common rule for attaining old age. We can't reach old age by another man's road."

THE MAGIC TOUCH, PART 2

On page 33 we told you Part 1 of Louis Braille's story.
In this part, he invents a writing system for the blind, inspired
by an unlikely source—the Napoleonic Wars.

SPOILS OF WAR

In 1821 a former soldier in Napoleon's army named Charles Barbier de la Serre made a presentation to the Royal Institute for Blind Youth in Paris. During his army days, Barbier had witnessed what happened to some soldiers when they received new orders in the dark of night. When they lit a lantern to read the orders, the light revealed their position to the enemy, and they were blown to bits by cannon fire.

The experience prompted Barbier to invent what he called night writing, or "sonography": a system of dots and dashes pressed into pieces of cardboard that soldiers could read by touch instead of by sight. But the army had rejected the method as too complicated, so now Barbier was offering it to the school as a possible writing system for the blind.

CLOSE, BUT NO CIGAR

Samples of the code were passed around the room, and Louis Braille, one of the smartest kids in the school, knew that Barbier was onto something as soon as his fingers touched the dots. But he also agreed with the army's assessment: sonography was too complicated to be of much use. For starters, its 36 different symbols represented sounds instead of letters of the alphabet. Translating books from French into sonography would have been a nightmare, especially since the system had no punctuation.

Another problem was that the symbols themselves were too complex. Each was constructed of two vertical columns of six dots, so large that readers had to brush their fingertips several times across each symbol to figure out what it was. When the symbols were strung together, a single word might contain as many as 100 dots. Louis realized that Barbier's system wasn't much better than Valentin Haüy's enormous raised-letter books, but it was on the right track—so he decided to try to improve on it.

After months of steady progress, Louis's schoolmasters arranged for him to meet the old soldier. But Barbier was incensed that a 12-year-old kid—and a *blind* one at that—was tinkering with his work. He refused to collaborate with Louis.

THE MAGIC NUMBER

So Braille soldiered on by himself, spending three years perfecting a writing system all his own, based on the letters of the alphabet instead of sounds. His most important breakthrough: He replaced Barbier's system of 12 dots with a 6-dot system—two vertical columns of 3 dots each. As neurologists have since proven scientifically (and Louis Braille appears to have figured out on his own), six dots are about as many as the human brain can process at a single touch. Each of Louis's six-dot symbols was small enough to fit under a fingertip and simple enough for the brain to interpret instantly.

But that's not the end of the story. Like many inventors, Braille had to fight to get his writing system accepted. Meanwhile, the hopes of blind people everywhere were hanging in the balance. To find out what happened next, turn to page 241 for Part 3 of "The Magic Touch."

BACKS TO THE WALL

One of our favorite themes: ordinary people doing extraordinary things.

While waiting at a bus stop in Manchester, England, 60-year-old Gloria Fitton was hit by a bus that pulled up too close, pinning her between the vehicle and a large, wooden wall. Because the driver was on the opposite side, he couldn't see her. Unable to breathe, Fitton quickly lost consciousness. Luckily for her, just as the bus was about to pull away, the driver heard someone shouting, "Don't move the bus! Don't move the bus!"

The shouts came from Graham Bingham, a 31-year-old office worker and father of four who had witnessed the accident. After the driver stopped, Bingham ran over to the woman and, with his back against the bus, pushed on the wall with all of his strength. He was able to move it just enough to ease the pressure on Fitton's chest, allowing her to breathe again. She came to and asked, "Am I dead?"

Bingham told the injured woman that she would be fine, then yelled for more people to help. One by one, shoppers and bystanders came over and added their weight to the wall. They gave Fitton just enough room to keep breathing and stay conscious until firefighters arrived with heavy equipment and freed her. She was taken to the hospital and treated for hip and pelvic injuries.

A spokesperson for the police later said that if Bingham hadn't alerted the driver, the bus would have crushed Fitton as it pulled forward. The *Manchester Evening News* gave Bingham a citizenship award, but he downplayed his heroism. "I don't want thanks," he said. "I just hope that someone in the same position would do the same for me someday if I was ever in an accident."

SOUND ADVICE

"Here's my advice: Read this page." —Uncle John

"First say to yourself what you would be; and then do what you have to do."

—**Epictetus**

"Always listen to experts. They're tell you what can't be done and why. Then do it."

—**Robert Heinlein**

"Be who you are and say what you feel—because those who mind don't matter, and those who matter don't mind."

—**Dr. Seuss**

"I don't believe in adhering to any rules I don't support and I didn't vote for. To hell with what people think. Just be who you are and you'll be happy."

—**Willie Nelson**

"When one tugs at a single thing in nature, he finds it attached to the rest of the world."

—**John Muir**

"The person who is waiting for something to turn up might start with his shirtsleeves."

—**Garth Henrichs**

"When in doubt, make a fool of yourself. There is a microscopically thin line between being brilliantly creative and acting like the most gigantic idiot on earth. So what the hell, leap."

—**Cynthia Heimel**

"A ship in a harbor is safe—but that is not what ships are for."

—**John G. Shedd**

LATE BLOOMERS

*As these people prove, it's never too late
to become a spectacular success.*

LATE BLOOMER: Harlan Sanders
STORY: Sanders was a Kentucky gas-station owner
who started selling fried chicken to his customers. The
chicken became so popular that he opened a restaurant across
the street. When a highway expansion forced him out of business, Sanders was reduced to living on Social Security. But in
1955, at the age of 65, he used his $105-a-month check to
start a restaurant called Kentucky Fried Chicken, which
would serve, as he put it, "Sunday Dinner, Seven Days a
Week." Today, KFC serves nearly 8 million customers a day in
11,000 restaurants worldwide.

LATE BLOOMER: Jacob Cohen
STORY: At the age of 19, Cohen was determined to become
a comedian. But after struggling for nine years, he gave up—
he needed a real job to support his family. He worked odd
jobs (including selling aluminum siding) until his 40s, when
he decided to give show business a second try. Cohen went
on to have a *very* respectable 40-year career in television and
films under the name...Rodney Dangerfield.

LATE BLOOMER: Clara Peller
STORY: Peller was a 74-year-old manicurist when a television crew member plucked her out of her salon and asked her
to appear as an extra in a commercial—as a manicurist. Eight
years later, the commercial's producer remembered Peller
when he was casting a series of ads for Wendy's hamburgers.

He located her—now 82 and retired from her nail salon—and gave her a role as a grumpy old lady with a catchphrase: "Where's the beef?" Peller's one-line performance was a hit. In the final three years of her life, she worked in commercials and movies, and even made an appearance on *Saturday Night Live*.

LATE BLOOMER: Helen Hooven Santmyer
STORY: Santmyer, born in 1895, always wanted to be a writer. By the age of 33 she'd published two novels, but neither was a commercial success. That wouldn't come for another 55 years when, at the age of 88, she published her landmark novel, *…And Ladies of the Club*. The book, which had taken her nearly 10 years to write (and a year and a half to condense down to 1,300 pages) became a runaway success, selling more than a million copies and spending eight months on the *New York Times* bestseller list.

MORE LATE BLOOMERS

• Richard Adams spent most of his life as a British civil servant working in the palace of Whitehall. He was 52 when he wrote and published his first novel, *Watership Down*.

• Classical composer Anton Bruckner didn't start writing music until his 40s.

• Edward Hopper's painting career began at 43.

• Ian Fleming started his series of James Bond novels at 45.

• John Houseman began his acting career at age 71, starring in the 1973 movie *The Paper Chase*. His performance as Professor Kingsfield won an Oscar.

• Julia Child published her first cookbook at 49.

• Anna Sewell wrote *Black Beauty* at age 57.

ALEX'S LEMONADE STAND

"I will never replace her love and spirit, but I do believe that it lives on in all of us who were inspired by her. We remain grateful for her life and legacy." —Liz Scott

FIFTY CENTS A CUP

Alexandra Scott had never known life without cancer and painful medical treatments. In 1997, at age one, she was diagnosed with neuroblastoma—pediatric brain cancer—and spent the next several years in and out of Connecticut Children's Medical Center. It was while lying in her hospital bed that four-year-old Alex decided she wanted to do something to help cure the disease, because, as she said, "all kids want their tumors to just go away."

So, in July 2000, Alex asked her mother, Liz, if she could set up a lemonade stand and donate the profits to her hospital. Liz replied that a lemonade stand charging 50¢ a cup wouldn't earn much money. But Alex didn't care. With her older brother Patrick's help, she set up a stand in the front yard of their home in Wynnewood, Pennsylvania.

The stubborn girl proved her mother wrong. Because of the youngster's cause, the local newsmedia paid attention to her efforts and hundreds of people came to buy lemonade. Alex raised $2,000 for her hospital in one day.

A BIGGER STAND

In early 2001, Alex's family moved to Philadelphia so she could receive experimental cancer treatments. Word of her "lemonade crusade" spread. She held another lemonade-stand event, raising $600 for the Children's Hospital of Philadelphia. A 2002 stand raised $18,000, which Alex donated to the hospital in the name of a friend she'd recently lost to pediatric cancer.

Alex's story was now being covered by the world press, and lemonade stands held in her name began popping up throughout the United States, Canada, and France. She was featured on *Oprah* and in *Time*, *People*, *The New York Times*, and *USA Today*. The surge of international attention helped make Alex's 2003 lemonade stand another huge success. Despite a massive rainstorm, thousands of people (and the *Today* show) came to buy lemonade, and Alex raised $14,000. But at the same time, her health was deteriorating. In spite of the treatments, the cancer had not gone away.

In 2004 individual stands banded together to form a national Alex's Lemonade Stand. On June 12, more than 1,000 stands opened simultaneously (including Alex's); they raised $220,000. By the end of the year, numerous stands—staffed by kids, senior citizens, college students, and even a group of homeless people—had raised $1.5 million.

CARRYING ON

On August 1, 2004, eight-year-old Alex Scott lost her long battle with cancer. But her legacy remains strong. Three thousand stands staffed by 25,000 volunteers have brought Alex's total amount raised for cancer research to $5 million. Her parents, who now run the Alex's Lemonade Stand Foundation for Childhood Cancer, still get reports from children who've been inspired by Alex—kids who hold their own lemonade stands, or turn down birthday presents to donate money to Alex's cause.

"Alex taught lessons it takes many people a lifetime to learn," says an avid supporter. "One person can make a difference, and even the smallest donation helps—even if it's only 50 cents."

THE ODD COUPLE

*The next time you think you can't get along with
someone because your differences seem greater
than your similarities...think of these guys.*

HUNGRY HUNGRY HIPPO
On December 27, 2004, a baby hippopotamus was
found wandering on a beach in the East African
nation of Kenya. The hippo, estimated to be about four
months old, had probably been separated from his family a
day earlier, when devastating waves from a tsunami struck the
coast. Local townspeople captured the hippo—it took hours
because the "baby" weighed about 600 pounds—and trans-
ported him to Haller Park, a wild animal sanctuary in nearby
Mombasa. Upon arrival, the hippo, given the name Owen,
immediately ran up to one the park's longtime residents—a
130-year-old tortoise named Mzee—and started following
him around.

ARE YOU MY MAMA?

The tortoise, who also weighs 600 pounds, didn't know what
to make of this new intruder. "Mzee hissed, lifted himself up
off the ground, and tried to run," said park ecologist Paula
Kahumbu. "But by the next morning, they were together."
Apparently Owen had adopted Mzee as his new mom...and
Mzee had accepted the position.

After that the two were inseparable. They wallowed in
the water together during the day, woke each other up at
feeding times, and even slept snuggled next to each other at
night. Park workers had never seen anything like it. Some
surmised that the hippo may have been attracted to Mzee

because of the familiarity of the tortoise's grayish color and round shape, but no one could really explain it.

On December 28, 2005, Owen and Mzee marked their first year together, and were still inseparable. The odd couple has received so much attention that the park now keeps an ongoing daily diary about them on the Internet. Owen, the park reports, was recently introduced to Cleo, a female hippo who also lives at the park. But, says Kahumbu, so far he prefers to spend his days with Mzee.

*   *   *

NATURAL WONDERS

Frustrated by a setback? Take a moment to consider the amazing natural world around you.

• Salmon have been known to swim more than 1,000 miles —upstream—to get to their mating grounds.

• If African termites were human-size, the colonies they build would be nearly 2,000 feet tall—the size of a 200-story skyscraper.

• The oxpecker, an African bird, gets all of its food (ticks and mites) from the back of the zebra. The zebra, in return, is continually cleaned of parasites by the oxpecker. In addition, the oxpecker flies into the air and screams a warning to the zebra when danger approaches.

• When a giant redwood falls at the end of its long life, it provides nutrients and shelter for hundreds of species of plants and animals, becoming one of the world's most dense ecosystems.

WHOA, NELLIE

Here's the story of Nellie Bly, a woman who fled an abusive home, pioneered investigative journalism, and helped the world realize that women weren't second-class citizens.

LONELY ORPHAN GIRL

In 1882 the *Pittsburgh Dispatch* ran a column called "What Girls Are Good For." It argued that women should neither vote nor hold jobs, but rather make their home "a little paradise" for the men in their lives. Eighteen-year-old Elizabeth Cochrane was outraged. She'd quit school and left her family at the age of 16 to escape an abusive step-father. Then she'd worked a succession of dead-end, low-paying jobs to support herself. So she wrote an angry letter to the *Dispatch* under the name "Lonely Orphan Girl."

The editor was impressed and ran a classified ad to find Cochrane. When she showed up, he offered her a job—an opportunity to provide a more realistic women's voice for his newspaper. Taking the pen name Nellie Bly (from a Stephen Foster song of the same name), she wrote two articles: "The Girl Puzzle," about the difficulty of being a poor, self-sufficient woman, and "Mad Marriage," condemning Pennsylvania's tough divorce laws.

UNDERCOVER

Bly's column became successful, and soon she found herself working on hard-hitting news stories. Her first one focused on unsafe working conditions in the sweatshops and factories of Pittsburgh. She went undercover and actually worked in a sweatshop under an assumed name. But there was a conflict: the businesses she exposed were advertisers in the *Dispatch*.

Not wanting to lose ad revenue, Bly's editors banished her to fashion articles and homemaking tips—exactly the kind of stereotyping she had protested in her letter to the newspaper.

Bly's response: She moved to Mexico. Again she went undercover, this time to expose government corruption. When the government discovered her activities, she was deported back to the United States, but published her journals as a book entitled *Six Months in Mexico*.

SHE MUST BE MAD

In 1887, with a book under her belt and having ably proven herself as a reporter, Bly thought getting a job at the *New York World*, the newspaper run by Joseph Pulitzer, would be easy. They turned her down. She kept asking for four months and they kept turning her down. Nearly broke, she finally fast-talked her way into the office of *World* managing editor John Cockerill...and then talked him into hiring her.

Bly's first story for the *World* covered the plight of women in mental institutions. Working undercover again, she had herself committed to New York's Women's Lunatic Asylum. She exposed abuse of patients by staff and the fact that many of the women being held there weren't mentally unbalanced at all—husbands had had their wives committed to get rid of them, and some patients simply couldn't speak English. She called the asylum a "human rat-trap—easy to get in, but impossible to get out." She wrote a book about the experience, called *Ten Days in a Madhouse*. Not only did it lead to asylum reform—it made Bly a celebrity.

AROUND THE WORLD IN 72 DAYS

In 1889 the *World* announced that they would send a reporter around the world in 80 days, a reference to Jules

Verne's popular novel of the time. They wanted to send a male reporter because a woman would need an escort. But Bly, furious, threatened to make the trip for another newspaper if the *World* didn't let her do it. They caved. And—using boats, trains, rickshaws, and hot air balloons—Bly circumnavigated the globe in only 72 days. She became the first woman to travel around the world unaccompanied by a man.

The city of New York gave her a parade and a fireworks display on her return. But the respect she got from the public was not shared by her editors at the *World*, so Bly quit. She went to work as a freelance journalist writing about women's rights and the suffrage movement.

REFORMING FACTORIES

In 1895 Bly retired from journalism and married industrialist Robert Seaman, 40 years her senior. When he died in 1905, she took over his business, the Iron Clad Manufacturing Company. At a time when many factories were unclean and unsafe, Bly radically improved the conditions for her workers, including switching a piecework rate for an hourly wage, paying for health care, and building a company library. But behind her back, the accounting staff was embezzling, and Iron Clad went bankrupt in 1910.

When World War I broke out during her 1914 vacation to Europe, Bly came out of retirement and filed stories from the front lines for American newspapers. She returned to America in 1919 and became a full-time reporter once more, this time for the *New York Evening Journal*. She remained there until her death from pneumonia in 1922 at the age of 56. The *New York World*'s obituary stated, "Nellie Bly was the best reporter in America."

TRY, TRY AGAIN

Abraham Lincoln—the Great Emancipator, savior of the Union, author of the Gettysburg Address—did not sprint up the ladder of success. As you can see, his path to greatness was strewn with hard luck and adversity.

ABRAHAM LINCOLN (1809–1865)
1831—Lost his job as a store clerk.
1832—Was demoted from captain to private in the militia.

1832—Lost first election to Illinois legislature.

1833—Failed in business.

1835—Went bankrupt.

1838—Lost bid for speaker of the state legislature.

1849—Tried to get a job as a land officer, but was rejected.

1856—Was considered for nomination as U.S. vice president, but was rejected.

1858—Lost a race for the U.S. Senate.

• And that's just his professional life. In addition, he was born into poverty, lost his home at age 7, went to work at age 8, lost his mother at age 9, and lost his business partner when he was 24. He spent most of his adult life paying back debts.

• Yet after all of this hardship, pain, and loss, Lincoln didn't dwell on the negative. Instead he focused on his achievements: He was elected to the state legislature three times, became a prominent lawyer, and served in the U.S. House of Representatives. In 1860, at age 52, he ran for president of the United States...and you know the rest.

WHAT A NICE SURPRISE

You never know what may be around the corner...

YOU DON'T SAY?
In January 2006, 72-year-old Derek Glover of
Lincolnshire, England, was on a skiing vacation in
the Italian Alps when he started hearing things...for the
first time in 15 years. Glover's hearing was damaged when
he was a soldier 50 years earlier and had continued to dete-
riorate until he'd become completely deaf in 1990. But now
at 7,000 feet he could hear the voices of the people standing next to him. "It was unbelievable," he said. "All of a
sudden my ears went pop, and their voices were dead clear."
Doctors were unable to explain the recovery.

LITTLE HOT CORVETTE

In January 2006, Alan Poster, a 63-year-old man from
Northern California, got a call from two police detectives:
They had found his stolen car in Southern California. And
the detectives were calling from Queens, New York. Confused?
So was Poster. What confused him even more was that his
1968 Corvette had been stolen...in 1969.

The detectives explained that his car was found on a ship
sailing out of Long Beach, bound for Sweden. A routine
check revealed that it had been reported stolen in the late
'60s, and the car's owner was traced to Queens—Poster's
home at the time of the theft. The two New York detectives
had spent a month tracking him down. "To have this come
full circle after 37 years is absolutely amazing," Poster said.
"I'm pinching myself." Another nice surprise: Poster had paid
$6,000 for the car. Now a collector's item—and still in perfect
condition—it's now worth an estimated $60,000.

THE ANONYMOUS VANDAL

In 2005 Principal Chris Ann Horsley of Shull Elementary School in San Dimas, California, received an anonymous gift with the following note:

> Approximately 32 years ago myself and a group of local kids broke into a classroom and vandalized the room terribly. I have felt guilty for far too long and want to give something back to the school that I personally took from. I am sorry for any grief that I caused anyone at that time.
>
> —A Regretful Baby-Boomer

Enclosed with the note was a cashier's check for $2,500.

GOOD FOR WHAT ALES YOU

Haldis Gundersen of Kristiandsund, Norway, was getting ready to wash the dishes when she turned on her kitchen faucet...and got a surprise. "I turned on the tap to clean some knives and forks, and beer came out," Ms. Gundersen said. "We thought we'd died and gone to heaven."

And in the pub two floors below, bartenders couldn't figure out why water was flowing from their beer taps. They soon discovered that a bartender had caused the mix-up. "I was changing beer tanks and I guess I connected them wrongly," said bartender Ann-Mari Rande.

"Maybe it would be easier," reflected Gundersen, "if they just invited me down for a beer."

*　　　*　　　*

One joy scatters a hundred griefs. —*Chinese proverb*

THE HEROINE OF BASRA

"In the Koran, the first thing God said to Muhammad was 'Read.'" —Alia Muhammad Baker

HISTORY REPEATS ITSELF

When the Mongols invaded Iraq in the 13th century, they burned down Baghdad's library and threw all the books in the Tigris River, turning the water a fierce inky blue. Eight hundred years later, during the 2003 invasion of Iraq, the Central Library in Basra went up in flames. But this time the books—which included irreplaceable ancient Arabic texts—were saved through the heroic efforts of one librarian.

When the Iraqi army abandoned the town, the library was quickly overrun by looters. Alia Muhammad Baker, Basra's chief librarian, had to work fast: With the help of friends and neighbors, she labored through the night to move the books, and was able to hide 70% of the library's collection—nearly 30,000 volumes—in a nearby restaurant. Nine days later, the library burned down and the fire threatened the restaurant as well. So Baker moved the books again—this time to her own house. Books filled closets, cupboards, and even an old refrigerator.

Sadly, locals accused Baker of looting the books for her own profit. Anxiety over their suspicions (on top of the herculean effort of moving thousands of books and seeing her own town become a war zone) caused Baker to suffer a stroke. But when she recovered, she found that word of her daring rescue had spread far and wide. An account of her heroics has already inspired two children's books...so maybe someday her library will carry the story of *The Heroine of Basra*.

OUR AMAZING UNIVERSE

*So much is going on every single second that we rarely
pause to reflect on how incredible this existence
really is. For example, isn't it amazing that...*

• **The most complex machine in the known universe is
right between your ears.** Weighing in at only three and a
half pounds, your brain can outperform even the largest
supercomputers when it comes to something as seemingly
simple as recognizing a face—which only takes it a fraction
of a second. Right now, as you're reading this, billions of
neurons are firing in your head, allowing you to process this
information and store it for future use. Your brain is also
sensing the world around you: the air, the temperature, the
ambient noise, and everything in your field of vision. But
instead of bombarding you with this information, your brain
filters through it all and allows you to concentrate only on
what you can handle. At the same time, it's also sending and
receiving signals, keeping tabs on everything from your heart
to your lungs to your toes—keeping you alive.

*So if you think you're just sitting there, you're actually pretty
busy. But even if you are just sitting there...*

• **Every second, you travel thousands of miles.** In the time
it takes you to read this sentence, you've traveled thousands
more. Here's the breakdown: Planet Earth is spinning at
1,040 m.p.h. at the equator. At the same time, it's traveling
around the sun at 67,000 m.p.h. And our sun is moving
through our local star cluster at 45,000 m.p.h. Our local star
cluster rides on the outer spiral arm of our galaxy, which is
rotating at another 500,000 m.p.h. Our galaxy is moving

through what we call the Local Group of galaxies at about 180,000 m.p.h. And the Local Group is moving through the universe at an estimated 540,000 m.p.h.

So Earth is carrying you through the cosmos at breakneck speeds. And thanks to a very thin—yet very strong—atmosphere, you're protected from the cold and radiation of space, which lets you admire…

• **Total solar eclipses.** Few people understand how incredibly rare this phenomenon actually is. The sun is 400 times larger than the moon, but it is also 400 times farther away. So even though these two celestial bodies are vastly different in size, they appear to be almost the *exact same size* from our point of view. The chances of that happening are…astronomical. None of the other planets in our solar system—along with their hundreds of moons—share this one-to-one ratio.

It's also amazing that something so tiny can completely block out something so big, proving that even the smallest of things can live large. Just look at atoms and consider that…

• **You are mostly empty space.** You are made of atoms. What are atoms? Basically, hollow balls. Inside each ball lives a tiny nucleus. If the nucleus were the size of a marble, the ball would be the size of Yankee Stadium. And the distance *between* each atom is also vast (atomically speaking). So what holds us together? Good question. Physicists, theologians, and philosophers are still trying to figure that out.

*   *   *

One more thing: Over your entire lifetime, you'll spend about six months on the toilet. (Now that's what *we* call inspiring.)

NOT YOUR
TYPICAL POP STAR

Harry Chapin is best known for his 1974 song "Cat's in the Cradle," a cautionary tale about a father more interested in success than in his own son. But his legacy goes far beyond just singing songs.

RISING STAR
Harry Chapin started making a name for himself as a singer-songwriter in the late 1960s. In 1972 he got his big break with the hit single "Taxi." Several hit albums followed, and Chapin seemed headed for stardom.

As he was becoming more and more successful, Chapin's wife, Sandy, urged him to take a different route than that of the typical self-serving pop star. He could use his fame, she told him, to help people less fortunate than himself. He had already developed an interest in doing something for the world's hungry, dating from a trip to Ethiopia in the 1960s. So he took Sandy's advice to heart…and decided to dedicate the rest of his career to eradicating world hunger.

Chapin was a man of enormous energy. "The credo of my life is, very simply, when in doubt, do something," he explained. And he lived up to his credo. Between 1972 and 1981, Chapin released 11 acclaimed albums and wrote and produced a Tony-nominated musical, while averaging 200 concerts a year all over the world.

And still he found enough time to set up several organizations to fight hunger, both domestic and international. The largest was World Hunger Year (WHY), which he used to lobby Congress. Between concert tours and recording sessions,

Chapin constantly pestered politicians to raise awareness about the issue. In 1978 his persistence paid off when President Carter created the Presidential Commission on World Hunger—and appointed Chapin to it.

Chapin's personal generosity was also legendary. "A dollar for me," he used to say, "and a dollar for the other guy." Of the more than 2,000 concerts he performed during his career, more than half were benefits for which he received no pay at all. In just eight years, he personally raised $6 million for more than 100 different charities.

GONE TOO SOON

On July 16, 1981, Harry Chapin was killed in a car accident on New York's Long Island Expressway. He was only 38 years old. At the time, he was on his way to perform a benefit concert not far from his lifelong suburban home. In his typical non-pop star way, he was driving a 1975 VW Rabbit.

Nine senators and 30 representatives—Democrats and Republicans—paid tribute to the generous and energetic songwriter. Senator Robert Dole of Kansas gave an emotional speech lauding Chapin, saying, "What he was really committed to was decency and dignity."

That wasn't the only tribute. Elektra Records set up the Harry Chapin Memorial Fund "to keep his work going and to accomplish some of the goals he set." The fund is still running, and has given away more than $5 million to Chapin's causes. In 1987 President Ronald Reagan posthumously awarded Chapin the Congressional Gold Medal of Honor. Chapin's daughter Jen, also a songwriter, is on the board of World Hunger Year. Every year the organization gives an award for outstanding work on issues of hunger and poverty. It is called, appropriately, the Harry Chapin Award.

VIDEO TREASURES

*The next time you're feeling down, try renting
one of these great inspirational movies.*

OCTOBER SKY (1999) *Drama*

Review: "Heartwarming drama based on the true story of
Homer Hickam, Jr., who grew up in a West Virginia mining
town. When he sees Sputnik soaring across the nighttime sky
in 1957, he enlists his friends to share the dream of building
his own rocket. An old-fashioned sense of can-do American
spirit makes this movie something special." (*Leonard Maltin's
Film and Video Guide*)

KOYAANISQATSI (1983) *Documentary*

Review: "Using aerial, slow-motion, and fast-motion photography, the camera glides across the American landscape,
revealing an astonishing panorama of natural and manmade
wonders. Set to a hypnotic score by Philip Glass, with no
dialogue, this mesmerizing and gloriously beautiful film is a
stunning sight and sound experience." (*Great Movies You've
Probably Missed*, by Ardis Sillick and Michael McCormick)

BILLY ELLIOT (2000) *Comedy/Drama*

Review: "Living in working-class England, Billy is allowed to
take boxing as a sport but his eyes are on the dance class next
door. The dance instructor notices his interest and invites
him to dance. He does—quite badly—but over time he
improves. This film does well in showing a young man's
enthusiasm for dance and how he's able to win acceptance
through perseverance." (*Scarecrow Video Movie Guide*)

BABE (1995) *Family*

Review: "An orphaned piglet is adopted by a sheepdog and decides that he wants to grow up and follow in his mother's pawprints. Delightful, witty, clever and almost irresistible children's tale with a wide appeal. A pleasure all the way." *(Halliwell's Film and Video Guide)*

SULLIVAN'S TRAVELS (1941) *Comedy*

Review: "Pure genius produced this social comedy, a witty and knowing spoof of Hollywood. A film director decides to find out what life outside the Tinseltown fantasyland is really like. A genuine Hollywood classic." *(Video Movie Guide)*

MR. HOLLAND'S OPUS (1995) *Drama*

Review: "Well-done tearjerker begins in 1965 as musician Glenn Holland takes a music teaching job to support his wife and their deaf son. Spanning three decades, Holland sets aside his dream of composing a great symphony and finds his true calling—mentoring and inspiring young minds." *(Videohound's Golden Movie Retriever)*

HOOSIERS (1986) *Drama*

Review: "A tiny Indiana high school sends a team all the way to the state basketball finals. *Hoosiers* is a "comeback" movie, but what makes it special is not its story—it works a magic in getting us to really care about the fate of the team and the people depending on it. It's all heart." (Roger Ebert)

Other movies you might like: *Lilies of the Field, The Right Stuff, Cool Runnings, Cry Freedom, Sounder, Working Girl, Norma Rae, About a Boy, The Day the Earth Stood Still.*

REJECTED!

If you gave up every time you failed, you'd never succeed. These people got rejected, but they didn't give up—and the rest of us benefited.

W ho wants to copy a document on plain paper?" This was included in one of the 20 rejection letters Chester Carlson received for his invention—the Xerox machine. After six years of rejections, the Haloid Company bought his idea in 1944. The first copier was sold in 1950, and Carlson made over $150 million in his lifetime.

"A cookie store is a bad idea. America likes crispy cookies, not soft and chewy cookies like you make."
Debbi Fields ignored this investor's advice and started Mrs. Fields' Cookies in 1977. There are now more than 400 of her cookie stands around the world.

"We don't like their sound and guitar music is on the way out."
Dick Rowe of the British music label Decca Records said this in 1962 to a young rock group. The group signed with EMI Records instead. The band? The Beatles.

"The girl doesn't have a special perception or feeling which would lift that book above the 'curiosity' level."
A book editor said that about *The Diary of Anne Frank*. Since 1952, the book has sold 25 million copies and has been translated into 60 languages.

"The product is worthless."
Bayer pharmaceuticals' 1897 rejection of Felix Hoffman's formula for aspirin. (They eventually accepted it in 1899.)

"Too different from other juvenile titles on the market to warrant its selling."
One book publisher said this in 1937 about *And to Think That I Saw It on Mulberry Street*, the first children's book by Dr. Seuss. In fact, 27 publishers rejected it before Vanguard Press accepted. Dr. Seuss went on to write over 40 children's books that sold nearly half a billion copies.

"The most insipid, ridiculous play that I ever saw in my life."
Member of Parliament Samuel Pepys wrote this diary entry after seeing William Shakespeare's *A Midsummer Night's Dream* in 1662.

"We are not interested in science fiction which deals with negative utopias. They do not sell."
This was said to Stephen King in the early 1970s about his first novel, *Carrie*. The book went on to become the first of dozens of bestsellers for King, the top-selling horror author of all time.

"Balding, skinny, can dance a little."
Paramount Pictures made this assessment after an early audition by Fred Astaire. He signed with RKO Studios instead.

"Hopeless."
A music teacher's opinion of his student's composing ability. The student: Ludwig van Beethoven.

FOR THE AGES

Wisdom from the senior circuit.

"Sure, I'm for helping the elderly. I'm going to be old myself some day."

—**Lillian Carter, in her 80s**

"I am long on ideas, but short on time. I expect to live to be only about a hundred."

—**Thomas Alva Edison**

"Wisdom doesn't necessarily come with age. Sometimes age just shows up all by itself."

—**Tom Wilson**

"A man is not old until regrets take the place of dreams."

—**John Barrymore**

"If I'd known I was going to live this long, I'd have taken better care of myself."

—**Eubie Blake, on his 96th birthday**

"The longer I live the more beautiful life becomes."

—**Frank Lloyd Wright**

"How old would you be if you didn't know how old you were?"

—**Satchel Paige**

"I have enjoyed greatly the second blooming that comes when you finish the life of the emotions and of personal relations; and suddenly find—at the age of fifty, say—that a whole new life has opened before you, filled with things you can think about, study, or read about. It is as if a fresh sap of ideas and thoughts was rising in you."

—**Agatha Christie**

"Age is something that doesn't matter, unless you are a cheese."

—**Billie Burke**

THE SIXTH PASSENGER

The harrowing tale of a man who made the ultimate sacrifice.

DISASTER
A horrific scene unfolded on one frigid January day in 1982. In the midst of a snowstorm, a passenger jet carrying 79 people crashed into Washington D.C.'s 14th Street bridge. The plane hit seven cars, then ripped through 20 feet of guardrail before plunging into the icy waters of the Potomac River. Yet amid all the sorrow and chaos that resulted from this terrible accident was an incredible story of selflessness.

Because of the severity of the storm, it took rescue teams nearly 30 minutes to get to the scene. When they arrived, only the tail of the plane remained above water—and six survivors were clinging to it for their lives. As the news cameras rolled, the heavy snowfall and blustery winds made the rescue attempt difficult for the police helicopter, but the skilled pilot was able to keep the aircraft steady enough to start sending down lifelines.

THE RESCUE BEGINS

The first man to grab the rope seemed more alert than the others, and instead of taking the line for himself, he helped secure it to a badly injured woman who was then carried to shore. A few minutes later the helicopter returned, lowering the line again. And again the man passed the line to someone more in need. When the chopper next returned, two lines were lowered, along with a shout from one of the rescuers: "We need all of you on these lines *now*—the tail is sinking fast!"

The "sixth passenger," as the press would later call him, helped secure two people to the first line, then tied the other line around the last injured survivor. But there was no room left on the line for him. Once again he waved for the helicopter to go on without him. It had nearly reached the riverbank when the two people on the single line lost their grip and fell back into the water. It took an agonizing few minutes for rescuers to get them to shore, but with the help of a bystander who jumped into the water, they did. Sadly, by the time the helicopter was able to get back to the downed plane, it was too late—both the tail section and the sixth passenger had been swallowed by the icy river.

REMEMBERING A HERO

The "sixth passenger" was later identified as Arland Williams, a 46-year-old bank examiner from Atlanta. Many paid tribute to his selfless act—saving five lives at the cost of his own. Williams was posthumously awarded the U.S. Coast Guard's Gold Lifesaving Medal. Williams's alma mater, The Citadel in South Carolina, created the Arland D. Williams Society "to recognize graduates who distinguish themselves through community service." And the 14th Street bridge—up until then called the Rochambeau Bridge—was renamed the Arland D. Williams, Jr. Memorial Bridge. But the most apt tribute came from the pastor at Williams's funeral:

> His heroism was not rash. Aware that his own strength was fading, he deliberately handed hope to someone else, and he did so repeatedly. On that cold and tragic day, Arland D. Williams, Jr., exemplified one of the best attributes of human nature, specifically that some people are capable of doing anything for total strangers.

STEPHEN HAWKING

This groundbreaking scientist overcame incredible physical adversity to become the greatest mind of his generation.

SMART KID

Stephen Hawking was born in England on January 8, 1942—exactly 300 years after the death of the astronomer Galileo. That's just a coincidence, but like Galileo, Stephen showed a great talent for math and science at a young age. He never had to study much, even to understand his favorite subjects: thermodynamics and quantum mechanics. In 1959 he applied to Oxford University. He didn't try very hard on the entrance exam and thought he did poorly, but Oxford admitted him with a scholarship.

Undergraduate work came easily—Hawking claims he barely studied and he even graduated a year early. In 1962 he was accepted by University of Cambridge to pursue a doctorate in cosmology, well on his way to a career as a research scientist.

SICKNESS

Then something happened. Hawking suddenly grew extremely clumsy. He would stumble unexpectedly and some mornings he couldn't even stand up. He ignored the problems for a year, but in 1963, he was diagnosed with *amyotrophic lateral sclerosis* (ALS, also known as Lou Gehrig's disease), a severe disorder that slowly robs the body of all muscle control, speech, and the ability to breathe. He was given two years to live.

But Hawking—known as much for his arrogance as for his brilliance—didn't resign himself to this fate. He knew he couldn't take his talents, or his time, for granted ever again. He was engaged to marry a fellow Cambridge student named Jane Wilde. In order to support her, he'd have to get a job, and in order to get a job, he'd have to get his doctorate. So he did all three. "Although there was a cloud hanging over my future," he says, "I found to my surprise that I was enjoying life in the present more than I had before."

ASTRONOMICAL SUCCESS

Only 10% of ALS patients live over 10 years. Hawking has survived for over 40. Despite his being confined to a wheelchair and losing the use of his arms, the disorder didn't slow his career as a research scientist. Among his discoveries and achievements:

• In 1971 Hawking provided a mathematical basis for the Big Bang theory of the universe's origin.

• He discovered in 1974 that black holes emit subatomic particles, contrary to the widely held theory that nothing could escape a black hole.

• Also in 1974, he connected gravity directly to the behavior of atoms, contributing to the development of a Grand Unified Theory that would help explain how and why everything in the universe functions.

• Since 1979 he's held the mathematics chair at University of Cambridge, a post once held by Sir Isaac Newton.

In 1985 Hawking decided to write a book that would make his work easier for non-scientists to understand. But while writing it, he contracted pneumonia and had to be hospitalized. When his breathing became severely impaired, doctors suggested that life support be removed, but Jane Hawking refused. Hawking got a tracheotomy instead. It worked. He recovered but permanently lost his voice. He finished his book, *A Brief History of Time*, in 1988. In May 1995, it was still on the *New York Times* bestseller list, a record 237 weeks.

EVER-EXPANDING UNIVERSE

Hawking is now completely paralyzed except for a few facial muscles. He communicates with a high-tech computer: He scrunches up his cheeks and blinks into a sensor embedded in his glasses. It controls a cursor that scrolls through a list of words, which Hawking compiles to form sentences which are sent through a voice synthesizer. Hawking also uses his computer to write, browse the Internet, and control the doors, lights, and lifts in his home and office. However, the computer is limited—Hawking still has to figure out the complex astronomical equations in his head.

Hawking looks at life philosophically: "We are just monkeys on a minor planet of a very average star," he says. "But we can understand the universe. That makes us something very special. To confine our attention to terrestrial matters would be to limit the human spirit."

*   *   *

WISE WORDS FROM THE IDIOT BOX

Claire: Why do people have to die?
Nate: To make life important.   —*Six Feet Under*

"You know, Wally, shaving is just one of the outward signs of being a man. It's more important to try to be a man inside first."
            —Ward Cleaver, *Leave it To Beaver*

"He who chickens out and runs away will chicken out another day."   —Robot, *Lost in Space*

FAMILY REUNIONS

Many people take their families for granted. If you lost your family, how far would you go to find them?

Michael Drennen, who was given up for adoption when he was six, spent years searching for his biological mother after he became an adult. He didn't know much about her; all he knew was that her last name was "Keener." In 1992 he was in a video store in the small town of York, Nebraska, and overheard a woman tell the clerk that her maiden name was Keener. Could it be? Yes, incredibly, it was Shirley Keener, Drennen's natural mother. They had both been living in York for two years.

• Two-year-old Tammy Harris was taken away from her alcoholic mother in 1971 and adopted by another family. When she turned 21 in 1990, she began looking for her birth mother. In 1991 she was working at a convenience store in Roanoke, Virginia, and mentioned her unsuccessful search to her co-worker Virginia Schultz, who coincidentally had been looking for 20 years for the daughter she'd given up. You can guess the rest: Mother and daughter had worked together for six months...and lived two streets apart.

• All Vivien Fletoridis knew of her birth was that she was the child of a wartime love affair. She was adopted as a baby in 1941 and moved from England to Australia in 1954. In her 40s she decided to track down her parents and flew back to England, only to learn that her mother had died in 1983. Still searching for her father, Fletoridis was looking at an election log in a library in Southport, England, when an elderly man asked her if she was going to be long. She told him she was looking for her birth father, whose name was Hewitt. The man turned out to be none other than Wilf Hewitt, the father Fletoridis hadn't seen in 46 years.

• Two college students, Janelle Eaton and Julius Melton, met and fell in love in Arizona in 1969. When they broke up a few years later, Eaton was pregnant...but she never told Melton. She had the baby (it was a girl) and then put it up for adoption. In 1998 that girl, Laura BlackFeather, tracked down her birth mother, who was living in Springfield, Missouri. Once they met, both BlackFeather and Eaton wanted to find Julius Melton. Here's the good part: It was easier than they thought—he was living right there in Springfield, Missouri. But it gets better: In 2005, 36 years after they split up, Eaton and Melton renewed their romance...and got married.

• In 1943 Dorothea Kowalski, 18, gave birth to a daughter named Renate in Berlin. As Germany made one last push at the end of the war, Dorothea was drafted to serve at an anti-aircraft battery site. The baby's father was on the front lines, so Renate was moved from one foster home to another before finally being evacuated to a farm in Pomerania, north of Berlin. By 1944 Dorothea had lost track of her daughter. Unsuccessful searches through the Red Cross led her to believe that Renate had been killed. But she hadn't; she was actually living in northern Germany. When she was 16, Renate set out to find her mother. She searched for decades, but nothing turned up. Finally, in 2005—60 years after they'd been separated—Renate got a call from a search agency saying that they'd found Dorothea, living in Australia. A few weeks later, the 62-year-old daughter and her 81-year-old mother were reunited.

TWO WOLVES

*Here's an old Cherokee folk tale about a universal lesson
that was handed down from the old to the young.*

CAMPFIRE STORY
One snowy morning a young boy was huddled in the
cold, waiting for his grandfather to build a fire. The
old man tried and tried, but every time the flames started to
rise, the wind whipped up and blew the fire out. The boy
grew impatient. "Please hurry, Grandfather! I'm freezing!"
But his grandfather remained calm.

"The fire will light when the wind allows it to."

Sure enough, a few minutes later, the wind let up enough
for the fire to take hold. While warming their hands, the boy
said, "Grandfather, I do not understand how you could have
remained so calm every time the flames were blown out. If it
were me, I would have surely gotten frustrated and thrown
the sticks in anger."

Grandfather smiled, then asked his grandson, "Did you
know that there are two wolves living inside me?" The boy
shook his head. "One is Fear. He is angry, jealous, greedy,
arrogant, and very frustrated. The other is Love. He is joyful,
peaceful, generous, truthful, and very, very patient. And do
you know what else?"

Again, the boy shook his head.

"The two wolves are fighting a war against each other.
They are always engaged in fierce battle."

"Which wolf will win?" asked the boy.

Grandfather answered, "Whichever one I feed."

PICTURE THIS

We tend to think of wealthy industrialists as pictures of pure greed. But here's a man who changed the world twice, once in how he created his fortune, and once in how he gave it away.

EARLY DEVELOPMENTS

George Eastman, founder of the Eastman Kodak Company, was born in 1854 in Waterville, New York. His family moved to Rochester, the town he would later put on the map, when he was five. Two years later his father died. George managed to stay in school until he was 14, but then he had to go to work to help support his mother and two sisters.

Eastman was incredibly driven. He got his first job as a messenger boy for an insurance company, and within a year was writing insurance policies. His $5-a-week salary wasn't enough for the family, so he studied accounting in the evenings and got a job as a bank clerk. By 23 he'd saved enough money to consider going into real estate, and he'd heard there were good deals down south—in the Dominican Republic.

GETTING THE PICTURE

When Eastman started planning a trip to the tropics, a friend suggested he keep a record of it. That prompted him to buy some photographic equipment—"a pack-horse load," as he later put it. In those days, photography used the "wet plate" process, which required immediate developing, so photographers had to carry portable darkrooms everywhere they went. The trip to the West Indies fell through, but Eastman's fate was sealed: He'd fallen in love with photography, and he wanted to simplify it.

In 1878 he started experimenting with a new "dry plate" process being developed in Europe. By 1879 he'd patented a machine that could mass-produce dry plates, and the following year he started the Eastman Dry Plate Company. But his biggest inventions were still to come.

In 1885 Eastman invented the first transparent photographic film. Then in 1888 he introduced the revolutionary Kodak handheld camera, which came preloaded with film. After the film was exposed, the camera could be sent back to the company, where the film was developed and the camera was then returned to the customer with new film inserted. With the slogan, "You press the button—we do the rest," the camera changed the world of photography forever. In 1889 he invented the flexible "roll" of film, which would make Edison's invention of the motion picture camera possible just three years later. His company, now called the Eastman Kodak Company, would soon become a hugely successful international corporation, and would make Eastman one of the richest people on Earth.

GIVING BACK

But Eastman's innovations weren't limited to photography. While other successful business owners sought ways to wring everything they could from their employees for as little pay as possible, Eastman saw his employees as the very reason for his success and thought they should get a share of the profits. In 1899 he began paying employees sizable bonuses out of his own pocket.

In 1912 he shocked the industrial world when he set up a "wage dividend" program, through which each employee would receive a share of the company's profits. In 1919 he went further, giving a third of his company holdings—worth about $10 million—to his employees. He also started retirement, life insurance, and disability-benefit programs. Such benefits were virtually unheard of at the time.

But Eastman's generosity didn't stop there.

• In 1901 he gave the Mechanics Institute (now known as the Rochester Institute of Technology), a gift of $625,000—$13.9 million in today's dollars.

• Over the years he donated more than $20 million to the Massachusetts Institute of Technology—because some of his most valuable assistants were MIT graduates. He insisted the donations be attributed to a "Mr. Smith."

• Eastman had trouble with his teeth when he was young and he didn't want other kids to endure what he did. So in 1917 he donated $2.5 million to create a free dental clinic in Rochester. He would go on to fund similar clinics in New York, London, Paris, Rome, Brussels, and Stockholm.

• Eastman was also a huge supporter of the arts. In 1921 he set up what became the Eastman School of Music, still one of the most respected music schools in the country, and helped to create the Rochester Philharmonic Orchestra (now the Eastman Rochester Philharmonic).

• In 1924 he decided to make donations to four colleges: the Hampton and Tuskegee Institutes—both African-American colleges in the South—as well as the University of Rochester and MIT. The four checks totaled $30 million. He is said to have laid his pen down afterwards and said, "Now I feel better."

THE END OF THE PICTURE
It is estimated that he gave away, with little fanfare, more than $100 million in his lifetime—billions in today's dollars.

But perhaps the most remarkable thing is that it was his *entire* fortune; he never married and had no children. And even if he had had children, he probably wouldn't have left them any money; he once quipped that those who passed wealth to children created "whoremongers of their sons and gilded parasites of their daughters."

George Eastman took his own life on March 14, 1932, at the age of 77. He had been suffering from hardening of the cells in his lower spinal cord, and the inability to remain as active as he had grown accustomed to was apparently too much for him. He left a simple note: "To my friends; My work is done. Why wait? G.E."

*   *   *

INSPIRING ANAGRAMS

Uncle John loves anagrams—words or phrases whose letters can be arranged to form new words or phrases. That someone has the patience and perseverance to craft these amazing word puzzles is...inspiring.

STATUE OF LIBERTY
*becomes...***BUILT TO STAY FREE**

WILLIAM SHAKESPEARE
becomes...
I'LL MAKE A WISE PHRASE

VALENTINE POEMS
*becomes...***PEN MATES IN LOVE**

THE UNITED STATES OF AMERICA
becomes...
THE DREAM: FINE CAUSE—TOAST IT

THE ART OF GIVING

Have you ever heard the phrase "give until it hurts"? Well, guess what—giving actually hurts a lot less than you might think. In fact, it can make you feel better.

"If you knew what I know about the power of giving, you would not let a single meal pass without sharing it in some way."
—**Buddha**

"The best way to find yourself is to lose yourself in the service of others."
—**Mahatma Gandhi**

"We get to make a living; we give to make a life."
—**Winston Churchill**

"I have found that among its other benefits, giving liberates the soul of the giver."
—**Maya Angelou**

"The only gift is a portion of thyself."
—**Ralph Waldo Emerson**

"No one has ever become poor by giving."
—**Anne Frank**

"A person's true wealth is the good he or she does in the world."
—**Mohammed**

"Think of giving not as a duty but as a privilege."
—**John D. Rockefeller Jr.**

"Charity should begin at home, but should not stay there."
—**Philip Brooks**

"Believe, when you are most unhappy, that there is something for you to do in the world. So long as you can sweeten another's pain, life is not in vain."
—**Helen Keller**

ONE GOOD TURN DESERVES ANOTHER

*If not for a single act of kindness, the Boy Scouts
of America might never have been created.*

L ONDON FOG

One dreary August day in London in 1909, the fog was so thick that it was difficult to see from one side of the street to the other. And William Dickson Boyce was hopelessly lost. Boyce, a rich American publisher in London on business, desperately needed to get to his appointment on time. He was standing on a street corner, looking bewildered, when a boy of about 12 walked up and saluted him. "May I be of service to you?" asked the boy.

"If you can show me how to get this address, then you will have done me a very great service," replied Boyce as he handed the boy a slip of paper with the address on it.

The boy looked at the address and said, "Follow me, sir." He then led the businessman through a maze of streets and alleys and finally to his destination. Upon arriving, Boyce took out his change purse and offered the lad a shilling.

"Sir, I am a Scout. Scouts do not accept tips for good turns," said the boy.

"You're a...what?"

"Sir, do you not know who the Scouts are?"

"No, but I would like to. Tell you what, let me attend to my business here and then you can tell me all about it."

The boy agreed, and Boyce hurried through his appointment. When he came back out to the sidewalk, the Scout was there waiting for him. "Follow me," he said, as he led Boyce through the fog for the second time that day.

STORY TIME

The boy took Boyce to the local scouting office, where he was introduced to Lord Robert Baden-Powell, the man who had founded the Boy Scouts two years earlier. Boyce listened eagerly as Baden-Powell told his account: He was a major-general fighting for the British in South Africa in 1899 when he noticed that the youngest soldiers were in poor physical shape and knew very little about how to survive in the wilderness. So he wrote an outdoor-skills manual to assist them called *Aids to Scouting*, which detailed survival techniques and guidelines to proper behavior. When Baden-Powell arrived back in England, he rewrote the manual, calling it *Scouting for Boys*. Troops soon popped up all over Great Britain.

Inspired by the story, Boyce went to Washington, D.C. after he returned home and filed incorporation papers for the Boy Scouts of America. He wrote that the mission of the BSA "shall be to promote, through organization and cooperation with other agencies, the ability of boys to do things for themselves and others, to train them in Scoutcraft, and to teach them patriotism, courage, self-reliance, and kindred virtues, using the methods which are in common use by Boy Scouts."

Today there are more than three million Boy Scouts in the United States.

Note: No one knows the identity of the boy who helped Boyce (he never gave his name), but Boy Scouts from the United States erected a statue of an American buffalo—representing the Boy Scouts' Silver Buffalo Award, the highest award in scouting—in his honor. It stands proudly in the British Scout Training Center at Gilwell Park, England.

SAVING THE BEACH

*Here's a David and Goliath story about some little folks
who took on a corporate giant...and won.*

GAS ATTACK

Saro Rizzo was barely out of law school in 1992 when he took on the case of a lifetime. The town he lived in, Avila Beach, California, was being polluted by a century-old Unocal petroleum plant located high on a bluff just outside town. For two decades, evidence of contamination had been mounting. First, a business owner had his property tested, and the ground was so saturated with gasoline that the testers advised him to put up "No Smoking" signs. Later, two college students were blown out of their apartment window when the furnace pilot light ignited gas fumes in the air. Then things got even worse: Crude oil started showing up on the beach and in the ocean.

Rizzo complained to Unocal. He was ignored, so he complained again. And again. The company's official response was that the problem "would be looked into." But nothing happened. Scientists and government experts were brought in to assess the damage, but they all seemed to have different political agendas, submitting a staggering number of conflicting cleanup recommendations. Still, nothing happened. All the while, the town of Avila Beach was steadily becoming uninhabitable.

ARMED WITH KNOWLEDGE

Frustrated but unwilling to give up, Rizzo—now working side by side with two other concerned citizens, county planner David Church and geologist Gerhardt Hubner—urged residents to join together and fight Unocal. Their first order of business: learn as much as possible. They studied past cases of corporate pollution, went over the finer details of zoning ordinances, and deciphered confusing government regulations. Now the crusaders were able to communicate with Unocal officials in their language, and it became harder and harder for Unocal to keep stalling with corporate doublespeak and bureaucratic red tape.

It took nearly 10 years—and 60 lawsuits—but Unocal finally ran out of stall tactics. In 1998 the company's lead attorney, Mark Smith, sent his entire law team off on a skiing trip (to get rid of them) and held a private face-to-face meeting with Rizzo and Hubner. Result: Unocal agreed to spend $100 million to clean up Avila Beach, and to pay another $18 million to the town's residents.

A MAMMOTH CLEANUP

Decades of gas leakage had caused extensive damage. It was so bad that most of the town—five city blocks—had to be bulldozed. Then the petroleum-laden soil needed to be removed and properly disposed of. Then the town had to be put back together again. The project, which took more than five years to complete, was one of the largest environmental cleanups in history. Today Avila Beach is once again the sunny coastal town that it once was.

"You *can* make a difference," says Hubner, "and truth will prevail...eventually."

*　　*　　*

"Knowing is not enough; we must apply. Willing is not enough; we must do."

—Goethe

5 IN 6

*People often focus on the negative to address a problem. Here's the story
of a man who looked for positives—and found a lot of them.*

NEW APPROACH

In South Africa—as in many developing nations—
domestic abuse is a major issue. Charles Maisel, a
social worker in Cape Town, counseled families facing this
problem but was frustrated with his lack of success. The women
were too scared to confront the men, and the men weren't
ready to confront themselves. Something else was needed.

In 1998 Maisel found that "something else" when he read
an alarming statistic: one in six South African men are domestic abusers. But to Maisel that meant five in six are *not* abusers.
Those men, he believed, could become part of the solution.

Creating a new program called "5 in 6," Maisel traveled
across South Africa and went door to door asking women to
identify the "good" men in their neighborhoods. Whereas few
women were willing to identify abusers, most were eager to
praise those who didn't abuse. Maisel then invited these men
to participate in workshops, teaching them positive ways to
deal with difficult domestic situations and showing them how
to act as role models in their communities.

From those workshops came the Everyday Hero campaign,
which asks women to nominate the best men in their towns.
Maisel calls the program a success because attitudes are defi-
nitely changing. Everyday Hero now includes more than
50,000 participants. Similar programs have since begun in
Nicaragua, Canada, and Nigeria, proving that positive people, when given the opportunity, can bring about positive
change.

"CHICAGO SHALL RISE AGAIN"

When fire destroyed most of their city in 1871, Chicagoans banded together and built a new city from the ashes.

MRS. O'LEARY'S COW

On the night of October 8, 1871, a fire broke out in Southeast Chicago. Legend has it the blaze started when a cow belonging to one Mrs. O'Leary kicked a kerosene lantern into a pile of hay. However it started, the fire quickly grew out of control. In just 24 hours, it consumed over 200,000 acres of the city and killed more than 300 people.

Chicago was ripe for such a disaster. It had grown from a frontier trading post to a bustling transportation hub of more than 300,000 residents in less than 50 years. The city grew so fast that its buildings went up haphazardly without any real safety or building code regulations. When the ashes of the Great Fire had cooled, 18,000 buildings had burned to the ground, leaving a third of the population homeless.

IN THE ASHES

In the aftermath of the fire, Chicagoans refused to give up on their city. The *Chicago Tribune* headline, just two days after the fire, screamed the message: "CHICAGO SHALL RISE AGAIN." Before the fire had even stopped burning, donations were pouring into the city government from all across the country.

• The first item of business was to establish order out of the chaos. Civil War hero and Chicago resident Lt. General Phillip Sheridan was put in charge of a citizen militia that patrolled the streets for several weeks.

• The Chicago Relief and Aid Society was put in charge of all of the donated funds. Within days of the disaster, they were hard at work building temporary housing and distributing food, clothing, and water to the city's dispossessed.

• They also organized a Public Health effort to prevent disease spreading among the refugees. In addition to making sure that conditions in the shelters were sanitary, they inoculated 64,000 homeless people against smallpox.

• And that *Chicago Tribune* headline? It's amazing they got a paper out at all, considering their offices had burned to the ground. But within two days they were up and running again, disseminating urgent information, such as news of missing people and where to get donated supplies.

REBUILDING

Meanwhile, the city's financial leaders were determined to turn the fire into an opportunity. They embarked on a program of civic planning designed to improve upon pre-fire conditions. Rubble was pushed into Lake Michigan and used as fill to extend the land out into the water. Eventually, the business district would be twice as large as it had been before the fire.

Over the following months Chicagoans of all classes worked seven days a week on rebuilding. Within a year more than $50 million worth of new construction was complete or underway. Within three years no trace of the fire could be seen. By 1880 the population had nearly doubled to more than 500,000 and the city had far surpassed its former prosperity.

By 1890, the city—little more than a smoking pile of ashes just 19 years earlier—was a thriving metropolis of more than a million people, the second-largest city in the United States. Chicago had, indeed, risen again.

LITTLE THINGS

These people took it upon themselves to make their corner of the world a better place. They started small and made big changes.

NEIGHBORHOOD PRIDE

In the late 1980s, an inner-city neighborhood in Rotterdam, the Netherlands, was going to seed. The streets were lined with litter and there were so few streetlights that citizens worried about their safety. Most local residents blamed the government, but one man, J.L. Hooymayers, had another approach: he would improve the neighborhood himself. In 1989 Hooymayers bought a couple of brooms, enlisted some neighbors, and started sweeping. Next they tackled the safety issue. They asked the city for more streetlamps, but Rotterdam refused—each new light would cost $2,000. So Hooymayers bought some extra-large halogen lights and a long industrial extension cord, and rigged up his own streetlamp. Then they began to plant flowers along the sidewalk. Inspired by Hooymayers and frustrated by a lack of government help, more than 100 neighborhoods in Rotterdam organized their own street-improvement plans. With Hooymayers leading the way, once-seedy streets are now trash-free, crime-free...and even pretty.

HAIL TO THE BUS DRIVER

For 20 years, Seattle bus driver Reggie Wilson has lived his mother's advice: take pride in your work and always enjoy yourself. So Wilson hides candy under seats, gives toys to crying children, and leads his passengers in sing-alongs, like "If You're Happy That It's Friday, Say Uh-Huh."

Participation is *not* optional, but that's just fine with the passengers. People take Wilson's bus even if it's not on their direct route to work. Why? Wilson's songs, candies, poems, jokes, and smiley-face decorated bus make them feel good. When he first started, Wilson's bosses told him to stop his antics—they thought he wasn't taking the job seriously. But that same day, a passenger told Wilson that she'd just been diagnosed with cancer and Wilson's ride had made her laugh. So Wilson resumed the jokes and songs. "I love being a bus driver," he says. "Do you know how great it is to see a busload of smiling people? When I see that I feel like I've found my glory."

GARDEN PARTY

In the spring of 1999, John T. Young was living in a concrete apartment building on Chicago's Brompton Avenue. The view out his back door: another concrete apartment building. So he put some potted geraniums and a wicker chair outside. "It gave me a whole new outlook," Young says. Then he figured that if such a little bit of effort made him feel so much better, what if all 27 families in his building got involved? He went door to door and proposed his plan. By 2003 vines, potted plants, and flowers covered every inch of the complex where there was room. Young coordinated it all and tends to plants in the common areas. "You don't have to be a flower expert," he says. "The focus is on building a community." On summer nights, residents gather to weed and plant. Children and pets help, too. In 2004 Brompton Garden won a beautification award from Mayor Richard Daley and Young was named Chicago Gardener of the Year. Says Marcia Jimenez of Chicago's Department of Environment, "His garden makes it impossible for people to be strangers."

SIMPLE SOLUTIONS

Many of us take clean water for granted—just turn on the faucet, and there it is. But in many parts of the world, it's not that easy. These brilliant yet simple inventions have solved this problem for thousands of people who really needed it.

SAFE WATER

Problem: Arsenic in drinking water. Scientists say that naturally occurring contamination of groundwater in developing countries causes as many as 200,000 deaths a year. How can people without high-tech filters or water-treatment plants make their water safe to drink?

Solution: In 2001 Xiaoguangc Meng and George Korfiatis, scientists at the Stevens Institute of Technology, invented a system that consists of two buckets, some sand, and a tea-bag-sized packet of iron-based powder. Their STAR filtration system reduces arsenic levels in well water from 650 parts per billion (deadly) to 10ppb, the level recommended by the World Health Organization. Cost per family: $2 a year.

PUMPING WATER

Problem: How can people irrigate crops in impoverished parts of the world? With electric pumps? Nope—electricity is often nonexistent, and where it is available, it's too expensive for poor farmers.

Solution: Approtec, a nonprofit company in Nairobi, Kenya, has developed a foot-powered irrigation pump called the MoneyMaker-Plus. Working the pedals like a stair-climbing exercise machine, one person can pull water from a stream, a pond, or a well 20 feet deep, send it to sprinklers, and irrigate up to one and a half acres a day. In underdeveloped countries, such a device can be life-changing. As of 2002, Approtec estimates that 24,000 MoneyMaker-Plus pumps were in use, bringing an average of $1,400 a year to people who previously earned less than $100 a year. The pumps helped create 16,000 new jobs and generate $30 million a year in profits and wages. They're made from local materials (creating more jobs), they're easily repaired without special tools, they're lightweight for easy transport (25 pounds), and most importantly, they're affordable—they cost only $38.

RUNNING WATER

Problem: In South Africa, more than 15 million people have to carry water from wells or rivers to their homes—sometimes as far as six miles away. It's traditionally carried by balancing five-gallon buckets on top of the head, requiring many trips and often leading to neck and back injuries. How can people get water from one place to another without breaking their backs doing it?

Solution: The Hippo Water Roller looks like a lawn roller. Fill the large, barrel-shaped drum with water, screw on the lid, lay it on its side, attach the handles, and then just push or pull it home—the barrel becomes a wheel. It holds 20 gallons of water and weighs 200 pounds when full. But the design makes the weight feel like 22 pounds, so even kids and the elderly can handle it. And it's made of UV-stabilized poly-ethylene, durable enough to ride over roots, rocks, and even broken glass. Cost: about $60. (The manufacturer, Imvubu Projects of Johannesburg, has donated thousands of the rollers to water-needy communities.)

THE SEEKER

Many powerful stories emerged in the wake of the 9/11 tragedy. Here's the tale of a dog who worked to find the missing—and became a symbol of courage to the people of New York.

DOGGEDLY DETERMINED
The 2003 *Guinness Book of World Records* declared him "the world's most celebrated dog." How did Bear, a Golden Retriever, earn the title? Search and rescue.

Bear started his career when, as a puppy, he leapt off the side of a boat to save a boy from drowning. From then on, Bear traveled the world with his human partner, Captain Scott Shields, working search-and-rescue missions. And on September 11, 2001, his skills were really put to the test.

Bear was the first dog to arrive at the World Trade Center, arriving with Shields just 38 minutes after the second plane crashed into the twin towers. For the first six or seven hours following the tragedy, Bear worked on his own, searching through the rubble for survivors. Over the next few days, he worked an exhausting 18 hours a day, often being lowered into holes filled with glass, metal, and debris. It is believed that Bear had the most finds of any rescue worker—human or canine—who searched the area. As expected, most of Bear's finds were fragmented human remains, but he was the only rescue dog to find survivors, even finding the remains of New York City Fire Chief Peter Canci.

TOP DOG

Bear spent nearly a year working at the site, lifting spirits with his wagging tail and unflagging determination. And for his contributions he received numerous awards and honors.

In October 2001, he led the Columbus Day Parade down Fifth Avenue and in November was presented with "The Hero's Award" by the International Cat Society at the Westchester County Cat Show—something that Captain Shields said, "brought the first smile to my face since the incident, just the irony of the cats giving a dog an award."

Sadly, Bear's valiant efforts came at a price. Injured by a jagged piece of metal on his first night working at the site, Bear was treated and went right back to work. But the area around the wound later became cancerous, and Bear passed away on September 23, 2002, two months before his 13th birthday.

After his death, the dog was honored with a funeral as a New York City firefighter. Two weeks later, the state Senate proclaimed October 13 "Captain Scott Shields and Bear Day" in New York. Captain Shields took Bear's ashes home, where he keeps them in a gold box inscribed with the words, "Bear Shields, Hero of the World Trade Center."

A FINAL TRIBUTE

On September 11, 2004, Bear's name was added to the wall of honor for those who died at the World Trade Center. It was a fitting tribute to a hero, but perhaps the best compliment that was paid to Bear was one that came from Paul Augler, a firefighter at Ground Zero. When asked, "How much do you credit Bear with?" he replied, "Everything!"

Here's a happy postscript: Shields has a new partner, a Golden Retriever named Theodore. He's Bear's son. Theodore and Shields spent several weeks on the Gulf Coast after the devastation of Hurricane Katrina, where Theodore helped rescue displaced, stranded, and abandoned animals.

A GOOD BOSS

Proof that "work" and "boss"
don't have to be dirty words.

TRIAL BY FIRE

On December 11, 1995, a boiler exploded in the
Malden Mills textile factory in Lawrence, Massachusetts. The explosion quickly turned into a raging fire.
More than 200 firefighters were needed to control the blaze,
which ended up being the largest in the state of Massachusetts
in the 20th century. By the time it was extinguished, much of
the factory was destroyed.

Roughly 700 people were working at the time, but thank-
fully no one was killed (although 20 were badly burned).
Still, the fire was a devastating blow to the company—as
well as to the towns of Lawrence and nearby Methuen, both
of which were already suffering high unemployment. More
than 3,200 people from the towns worked at the factory,
many of them for decades. And most of them were immediately aware of their fate: not only were they out of work two
weeks before Christmas, but the factory would in all likeli-
hood not be rebuilt in Lawrence. The textile business had
been going elsewhere for decades—mostly overseas. But
Malden Mills had something going for it that other doomed
companies didn't: Aaron Feuerstein.

FAMILY BUSINESS

Feuerstein had been the owner and CEO of Malden Mills
since 1957 and was very proud of his company. His grandfather had opened the factory in 1906, and Feuerstein had
managed to keep it operating through some trying times. In

the 1980s, with the company on the brink of collapse, Feuerstein had personally pushed for the production of a synthetic fabric called Polarfleece. Now known as Polartec, it saved his company, becoming hugely popular with the booming outdoor gear business of companies like The North Face and Patagonia.

By the time of the fire the factory was doing $400 million a year in business, and Feuerstein had developed a reputation as a great employer. Besides paying higher-than-average wages and providing good benefits, he paid for any necessary training and for English classes for the many immigrant workers. "This is not the end," he said while standing in the parking lot with thousands of his employees, watching the factory burn.

TO FLEECE OR NOT TO FLEECE

Sure enough, Feuerstein's advisors wanted him to take the $300 million in insurance money and rebuild his factory overseas. Sure enough, he refused. "It would have been unconscionable," he said, "to put 3,000 people on the streets and deliver a deathblow to the cities of Lawrence and Methuen." The day after the fire, Feuerstein announced that the factory would be rebuilt right where it had stood in Lawrence. "I have a responsibility to the worker," he said. Sure enough, he became an instant local hero—but he wasn't done yet.

Feuerstein also announced that he would continue paying the employees, all 3,200 of them, their full wages—with full benefits—while the factory was being rebuilt. That meant for the next three months. The news instantly spread around the world. "I consider our workers an asset, not an expense," Feuerstein said, seeing nothing special in his actions.

Over the next three months, Feuerstein spent $25 million of his own money paying the employees who had helped his company become a success. By the time the factory reopened, he had used all of the $300 million in insurance money, and borrowed $100 million more to complete the rebuilding.

Unfortunately for Aaron Feuerstein, the story does not have a storybook ending. In 2003, after a two-year struggle to keep control, he lost the company that his grandfather had opened nearly a century earlier. He had never been able to recover from the debts of his kindness. Still, Feuerstein has no regrets. Asked if he'd do the same thing if he knew how it would end, he simply said, "Yes. It was the right thing to do."

*   *   *

DON'T!

"Don't ask what the world needs. Ask what makes you come alive, and go do it. Because what the world needs is people who have come alive."

—Howard Thurman

"Don't confuse fame with success." **—Erma Bombeck**

"Don't just read the easy stuff. You may be entertained by it, but you will never grow from it."

—Jim Rohn

"Don't make excuses. Make things happen. Make changes. Then make history."

—Doug Hall

"Don't eat the yellow snow."

—Frank Zappa

PRESCRIPTION: LAUGHTER

Q: What has four legs and goes "Boo"? A: A cow with a cold.

A COMEDY A DAY KEEPS THE DOCTOR AWAY Researchers at the University of Maryland made an incredible discovery in 2005: Watching a 90-minute comedy is as good for the heart as a run around the block. The study was performed on 20 healthy adults whose hearts and blood flow were monitored as they watched a sad movie (*Saving Private Ryan*) and a funny movie (*There's Something About Mary*). Result: The funny movie increased blood flow; the sad movie decreased it. "The extent of the impact of watching a sad film," explained researcher Dr. Michael Miller, "was of the same magnitude as remembering episodes of anger and doing mental arithmetic, while the impact of watching a funny film was equivalent to a bout of aerobic exercise."

Dr. Uncle John's advice: If you want to give your ticker a well-deserved treat, go to the video store and rent a really funny movie. Here are eight recommendations from your friends at the BRI:

• *Duck Soup* (1933) The Marx Brothers go to war.

• *Best in Show* (2000) A dog-wild mockumentary.

• *Groundhog Day* (1993) Bill Murray gets redundant.

• *Airplane!* (1980) "Surely" *the* classic disaster-movie spoof.

• *The Music Box* (1932) Laurel, Hardy, and one heavy piano.

• *Blazing Saddles* (1974) There's a new sheriff in town.

• *A Shot in the Dark* (1964) Peter Sellers's silliest Pink Panther.

• *Office Space* (1999) The cubicle walls come tumblin' down.

POETIC RESISTANCE

Václav Havel had a hard enough time becoming a writer. But becoming his nation's president was an even rougher road.

APPLICATION DENIED

Growing up in a family of intellectuals and business owners wasn't easy in Czechoslovakia in the 1950s. The Communist government kept close tabs on artists and thinkers—they were seen as a threat to the regime. Václav Havel came a family just like that, which is why he was banned from studying drama or literature at any university. Václav had to make do with what opportunities were open to him in his teens and 20s, so he took a job as a laboratory assistant and studied economics. But one day he found work as a stagehand at a Prague theater...and that changed everything.

Havel loved the theater so much that he knew he had to find a way to circumvent the restrictions on his education. So he enrolled in correspondence drama courses and began to write plays and literary articles. But the opinions he expressed on human rights and politics drew the attention of the Soviet-backed government—especially when he became an outspoken supporter of the Prague Spring, a hugely popular anti-government movement that was crushed by the Soviet Army in August, 1968. The brutality only strengthened Havel's resolve.

WRITTEN INTO A CORNER

Now chair of the Czech Circle of Independent Writers, Havel used his position to express—and publish—his opposition to government repression via plays, poetry, and essays. In retaliation, the government banned his writing in

1969 and confiscated his passport. Havel was forced to leave Prague and move to the countryside, where he kept a low profile. But he still would not stay quiet.

In 1975 he wrote an "open letter" to Czech President Gustáv Husák, warning him of a deep dissatisfaction that threatened the nation. That letter led to his first arrest. In 1977 the hard-line Communist regime arrested the members of the Czechoslovakian rock band Plastic People of the Universe (named for a Frank Zappa lyric) and a group of Czech artists and intellectuals signed a manifesto—Charter 77—protesting the arrest. Havel, one of the founders of the group, was arrested again. In 1979 Havel was tried for sedition, and spent the next four years in prison.

FROM PLAYWRIGHT TO POLITICIAN

When he was released in 1981, Havel went right back to civil rights activism. When the Soviet Union broke up in 1989, Czechoslovakia gained its independence and hundreds of thousands of Czechs took to the streets in peaceful protest against their own Communist government. The movement came to be known as the Velvet Revolution—and Havel emerged as one of its leaders. That year he was arrested again, spending another nine months in prison.

In December 1989, under the weight of protests growing to millions of people, the Czech Communist government finally fell. On December 29, in a turn both surprising and poetic, Vaclav Havel became the first democratically elected president of Czechoslovakia, and then served as president of the Czech Republic until 2003.

The writer-turned-politician summed up up his story in 2002: "People saw the Velvet Revolution as heralding hope for a more humane world, one in which poets might have as powerful a voice as bankers."

CHÂTEAU LAROCHE

*When we searched for great human achievements to include in
this book, we were amazed by what we found—but nothing
can compare to the man who built his own castle.*

INSPIRED CONSTRUCTION

Harry Andrews was not your average scoutmaster. A
veteran of World War I, he returned home to southern
Ohio completely disenchanted with the modern world.
Inspired by the old ideals of knighthood from the days of
chivalry, he named his Boy Scout troop the Knights of the
Golden Trail. After building two small stone structures for
storing tents and other gear between camping trips, Andrews
decided his young "knights" deserved a real castle, so he built
one—by himself.

He got to work in 1929, hauling wheelbarrows full of
rocks from the nearby Little Miami River up to the site. He
mixed the rocks with cement to create stone-shaped blocks,
which he used to construct a full-size replica of the 11th-
century Norman castle he was stationed in during the war.
The 17-room structure, 96 feet long and 65 feet wide, has a
main hall, banquet room, chapel, armory, dungeon, and
master bedroom, all built by Harry Andrews, brick by brick,
stone by stone.

By the time Andrews finished the castle, which he named
Château Laroche, his scouts were old enough to be grandfa-
thers and Harry was in his 90s. By his own estimation, he put
over 50,000 wheelbarrow loads of rocks into the structure. A
lifelong bachelor, Andrews left the castle to the Knights of the
Golden Trail, who use the castle and its grounds to this day.

HERE'S TO MOM

Parenting is one of the most important and most difficult jobs a person can do. That's why it's so nice that we take two days out of the year to honor those amazing folks who brought us up. Here's the origin of Mother's Day.

LIKE MOTHER, LIKE DAUGHTER

You can thank Anna Jarvis for Mother's Day—or, rather, you can thank her mother. In the late 1800s, Anna's mom taught a Bible class. One day she gave a lesson called "Mothers of the Bible" and ended the class with this prayer: "I hope that someone, sometime, will found a memorial mother's day commemorating her for the matchless service she renders to humanity in every field of life. She is entitled to it."

When her mother died in 1905, Anna (now grown up and a schoolteacher herself) vowed at her grave site to carry out her wish. First she persuaded a few local West Virginia churches to hold Mother's Day services in May 1907. The sermons drew so many people—and their mothers—that Jarvis launched a letter-writing campaign, inundating politicians with proposals for the new holiday. It took six years, thousands of letters, and many trips to Washington, but Jarvis's hard work paid off. In 1914 President Woodrow Wilson issued a proclamation establishing Mother's Day as the second Sunday in May.

Want to celebrate Mother's Day the Anna Jarvis way? Forget about candy and flowers. "Any mother would rather have a line of the worst scribble from her son or daughter," she said, "than any fancy greeting card."

HERE'S TO DAD

While Anna Jarvis was working to turn Mother's Day into a holiday (see previous page), someone else was doing the same thing for fathers. One more great example of putting an idea into action.

THE MOTHER OF FATHER'S DAY
One Sunday morning in May 1910, Sonora Smart Dodd was sitting in church, listening to a long sermon about the merits of mothers. The words were all well and good, Sonora thought to herself, but why had she never heard any sermons dedicated to dads? Her own father, William Smart, had raised six children all alone (mom had died when Sonora was a girl). Believing that dads should have their day, the Spokane, Washington, housewife immediately took it upon herself to create Father's Day.

She started locally, proposing that the first Sunday in June—her father's birth month—be set aside to honor fathers. Religious leaders liked the idea but preferred the *third* Sunday (they needed more time to prepare their sermons).

The first Father's Day was celebrated in Spokane on June 19, 1910. Dodd rode down Main Street in a horse-drawn carriage and brought gifts to fathers all over town. Newspapers around the country reported on the day's festivities, and the next year dozens of cities followed suit. President Woodrow Wilson even traveled to Spokane in 1916 specifically to celebrate Father's Day. Unlike Mother's Day, however, Father's Day remained an unofficial holiday for decades. But Sonora Dodd lived long enough to see her wish come true: In 1972 President Nixon finally proclaimed it a national holiday. When she died in 1978 at the age of 96, more than 30 countries were celebrating the holiday she had started.

CONFUCIUS SAID

The famous Chinese philosopher lived 2,500 years ago, but his words still ring true today.

"A journey of a thousand miles begins with a single step."

"Our greatest glory is not in never falling, but in rising every time we fall."

"Everything has its beauty, but not everyone sees it."

"The gem cannot be polished without friction, nor man perfected without trials."

"Forget injuries; never forget kindnesses."

"When you are laboring for others, let it be with the same zeal as if it were for yourself."

"What the small man seeks is in others. What the superior man seeks is in himself."

"When anger rises, think of the consequences."

"What you do not want done to yourself, do not do to others."

"Choose a job you love, and you will never have to work a day in your life."

"I hear and I forget. I see and I remember. I do and I understand."

"They must often change who would be constant in happiness or wisdom."

"Respect yourself, and others will respect you."

"When you have faults, do not fear to abandon them."

"To study and not think is a waste. To think and not study is dangerous."

"Wheresoever you go, go with all your heart."

THE WILL TO LIVE

*These stories remind us that even when all hope seems lost,
there may still be a chance—if you keep your wits about you.*

SHARK ATTACK!

On a chilly day in December 2005, Brian Anderson was surfing off the coast of Oregon, waiting for the next big wave. But what came instead was a great white shark. The 10-foot-long beast attacked, took a huge chunk out of Brian's right leg, and then made a move to get the rest of him. Remarkably, the 36-year-old kept his cool and remembered something he had learned from a TV documentary: A shark's most sensitive area is the tip of its nose. So Brian started punching the shark, and kept punching ferociously until the great white gave up and swam away.

Bleeding profusely from his wound but still strong enough to swim, Brian made his way back to shore. He was hospitalized with severe lacerations on his leg, but was released in time to open Christmas presents with his wife and 11-year-old son. "It was like your worst nightmare," he later said, "but it was also an adventure which has made life that much more precious."

LANDSLIDE!

Stuart Diver, a 27-year-old ski instructor, was staying at a ski resort in Thredbo, Australia, with his wife, Sally, and 17 other people in 1997. In the early hours of a cold winter night, a natural spring on the mountainside above triggered a massive landslide—and several tons of earth and snow came crashing down on the small resort. Diver's wife and the other people were swept away, but Diver found himself lodged inside a small crevice up to his neck in freezing water, barely able to move his arms and legs. He had plenty of water to drink, but if he relaxed even a bit, he would drown. So there he stayed, alone, his body numb, surrounded by darkness, forcing himself to keep his chin above water.

Diver had no choice but to wait, so that's what he did... for 43 hours. Finally, he heard a faint voice. At first he thought he must be hallucinating. But then the voice got clearer: "Is anyone alive in there?" With what little strength he had left, Diver replied, "I can hear you." It took 12 hours of furious digging to free him.

Stuart's inspiring story captivated all of Australia. And though he was devastated by the loss of his wife, Diver credits her with his survival: "When all logic told me hope had vanished, in my heart I know it was Sally's will, her resilience of spirit, that gave me the strength I needed to hold out, to hold on."

TRAPPED!

Eighty-eight-year-old Mary Anderson of Vancouver, Washington, was driving home from the grocery store one cold January day. Suddenly she lost control of her car, veered off the road, and went nose-first down an embankment, landing in a thick patch of blackberry bushes. Though she was within earshot of Interstate 5, her doors were wedged shut and she was trapped and hidden from view. A trunkful of groceries was just a few feet away, but she had no way to reach them.

So how did she survive? By staying calm and using what she did have—a small hand towel. As condensation built up on the windshield, Mary wiped it up with the towel and then sucked it out. As day turned to night and night turned to day—for six days—Mary kept her mind occupied by praying and "counting up to 500 and then back down to 1 again."

Finally, nearly a week later, a truck driver named Andrew Thompson spotted her car in the bushes from the high perch of his cab. He climbed down the embankment—preparing for the worst—but was relieved and surprised to see a smiling woman looking back at him from inside the car. Thompson called paramedics, who came and freed Anderson. She was treated for dehydration and made a full recovery—thanks to her wits and her will to survive.

*   *   *

A SHARP BRAIN IS A PRODUCTIVE BRAIN

Mental acuity is essential to a healthy
life. So here's a simple brain exercise.

Start using your opposite hand to perform everyday tasks. If you're right handed, use your left hand, and vice versa. Begin with your computer mouse for a few minutes, then try the same with the TV remote control. At first, it will feel awkward, but keep with it. After a while, it will get easier.

What's happening is this: Your brain is going through the same processes it did when you were a young child learning to do life's tasks for the first time. As we get older and try new things, we seldom stray from our comfort zone. Using your opposite hand will cause your brain to work harder than it has in years. Not only will these exercises strengthen your neural connections, they will also create new ones. Result: You may find yourself becoming more skilled in some areas, less stressed, and better able to cope when new things come your way.

KID ACTIVISTS

"We cannot solve problems with the same thinking we used when we created them." —Albert Einstein

PROBLEM: In 1989, nine-year-old Melissa Poe saw an episode of the TV show *Highway to Heaven* that depicted an environmentally ravaged Earth 25 years in the future. All the trees were dead. She asked herself, "Is this what the world will be like if we don't help take care of the environment today?"

SOLUTION: Melissa founded Kids For A Clean Environment (Kids F.A.C.E.), a program that educates young people to adopt earth-friendly attitudes and practices, including planting trees. With more than 300,000 volunteers, Kids F.A.C.E. has planted a million trees all over the world.

PROBLEM: Leslie Burnside, a North Carolina social worker, told her 10-year-old sister, Aubyn, about how foster kids had to carry their belongings from temporary home to temporary home in garbage bags. It saddened Aubyn.

SOLUTION: In 1996 Aubyn started Suitcases for Kids, a program that distributes backpacks, duffel bags, and suitcases to foster children. In two years, Burnside personally collected over 1,700 bags. Suitcases for Kids is now an international operation that has distributed more than 30,000 suitcases.

PROBLEM: In 2001 young Anthony Leanna watched as his grandmother's hair fell out during chemotherapy treatments for breast cancer.

SOLUTION: The 10-year-old wanted to give comfort to cancer patients, so he started Heavenly Hats, an organization that collects and donates brand-new hats to cancer patients. Since it began, Leanna's organization has given away more than 75,000 hats.

PROBLEM: Three Victoria County, Texas, teenagers—Lacy Jones, Kate Klinkerman, and Barbara Brown—learned that farmers and ranchers disposed of old motor oil by using it as an herbicide. And it was leaking into the water supply.

SOLUTION: In 1997 the three formed Don't Be Crude. They petitioned the government to place five oil recycling sites in Victoria County so farmers could properly dispose of used motor oil. It's estimated they've kept 30,000 gallons of oil out of the local water supply.

PROBLEM: In 1996, 10-year-old Joshua Marcus noticed that some of his classmates didn't have the school supplies they needed because their parents couldn't afford them.

SOLUTION: Joseph founded Sack It To You!, a charity that gives backpacks filled with notebooks, pencils, and other school supplies to low-income children. Joshua has raised $250,000 and handed out over 8,500 bags in Boca Raton, Florida.

PROBLEM: Thirteen-year-old Charlie Shufeldt of Atlanta, Georgia, learned that 20 million computers were being thrown into landfills each year. There had to be a better way to dispose of them. Then he realized that cash-strapped charities and nonprofit organizations could use those computers.

SOLUTION: In 1993 Charlie and his friends Owen Boger and Josh Silfen formed Free Bytes. They collect used computer equipment from individuals and companies, refurbish and rebuild them, distribute them to charities, and train people how to use them. To date, they've donated roughly 7,500 computers.

SAVING A TURTLE

Here's a story that happened to BRI writer Jay Newman when he was 10 years old. It illustrates what a kid can accomplish with a little patience—and a lot of imagination.

INTREPID KID

As a boy, Jay was interested in herpetology—the study of reptiles and amphibians. He spent most of his summer days in the woods around his Fairfax, Virginia, home looking for snakes, frogs, salamanders, and his favorite: turtles. That's why he was so excited to find one on a sidewalk in his neighborhood.

But he noticed that something was wrong. The orange-and-brown box turtle—about the size of a softball—had a dent on the back of its shell, as if it had been hit by something hard. There was blood near the dent, and a small part of the shell was missing. The turtle seemed weak and couldn't lift its shell off the ground to crawl. As Jay carefully picked it up, he saw that it could move its front legs, but the back legs just dangled. That gave Jay an idea.

ON A ROLL

He took the turtle home and went into his dad's workroom. Above the workbench was a drawer labeled "spare cabinet wheels." In it, Jay found what he was looking for: a small black wheel connected to a flat metal plate about an inch long. Jay took the wheel, a roll of duct tape, and the turtle to his backyard patio. He taped the wheel to the rear of the turtle's shell, put the turtle on the concrete, and waited. After a few seconds, the turtle started walking, a bit wobbly at first. The back two legs still dangled, but the wheel was

192

turning and the turtle was able to move around a bit. Jay then cleaned the wound on the shell and used some tape to dress it.

PHYSICAL THERAPY

Jay kept the turtle in a fenced area in his backyard, and over the next few days he coaxed it to walk (and roll) by placing lettuce leaves just far enough from the turtle so it had to work to get to them. With each passing day, the back legs slowly started to move. On the fifth day, Jay took off the wheel. The turtle tried to walk but couldn't; its back legs were still too weak. So Jay reattached the wheel, but took it off each day to help the turtle exercise. On the tenth day, when Jay took the wheel off, the turtle walked a few steps on its own.

BORN FREE

Finally, after two weeks, the turtle was able to successfully negotiate its way around the backyard. Feeling proud, Jay went deep into the woods, let the little box turtle go, and watched it crawl away and disappear in the underbrush.

*   *   *

"When we draw inspiration from nature, we turn to a timeless source. Whether it comes in the cooing gurgles of an infant, the crash of a wave, or the soft beginnings of a sunrise, nature makes both her physical and spiritual presence known. Only when we have allowed ourselves to be dulled by nature is this source of inspiration lost to us. Getting it back, if lost, requires little more than simply paying attention."

—Henry David Thoreau

LIFE SAVERS

*Right when all seemed lost for these people,
somebody stepped in...just in time.*

REDIAL. In 1985 Kris Tamer, an office worker at a convalescent home, made a phone call, then quickly hung up when she realized she'd dialed the wrong number. But after she hung up, something felt wrong—she could have sworn she heard the person who'd picked up gasp "help." Tamer hit redial and discovered her instinct had been right—Alex Johnson, 81, was having a heart attack. Johnson managed to tell her his address. Tamer called paramedics, and Johnson's life was saved.

CALL FROM THE PAST. In 2005 Krisa Williams called the Omaha, Nebraska, Planning Commission on behalf of a friend on public assistance whose home had no heat. Mike Johnson took the call and after talking for a minute, recognized Williams' name—Johnson had saved her life when she was eight years old. She'd nearly died after being hit by a car, and Johnson administered CPR. They'd lost touch over the past 30 years but met up later that day.

CAUGHT ON CAMERA. Karin Jordal, 69, lives in California and keeps in touch with her two sons, Tore in the Philippines and Ole in Norway, via an Internet Web cam. In November 2005, Tore Jordal went online to see what his mother was up to, but couldn't see her at first. Then he saw her lying motionless on the floor. Karin is a diabetic, so he had to move fast. Tore called his brother Ole, who was able to get through to 911. The brothers watched on the Web cam—on the other side of the world—as paramedics arrived to take their mother to the hospital.

THE CUTTING
EDGE OF LITERACY

*Here's an unlikely community leader who combined
his love of books with a barber chair.*

SMALL TOWN ROOTS

Reuben Martinez grew up in the small mining town of Miami, Arizona. An avid reader as a child, he never lost his love of books. After graduating from high school, he moved to Los Angeles, where he worked as a grocery clerk and a crane operator until he saw an ad for barber school.

"I saw those white smocks they wore; it was the opposite of the dirt of the mining world," he says. "I wanted clean."

Martinez became a successful hairstylist and moved out of East Los Angeles to Santa Ana, a city with a large Hispanic population. It's there that he made his mark.

HIGHLIGHTING LITERATURE

Inspired by his own love of reading, Martinez made it his mission to raise the literacy rate among local Hispanics. He got the idea to open a Spanish-language bookstore inside his barbershop in 1993. The inspiration: Customers began borrowing from his personal collection of books, and some of his favorites—such as his autographed copy of Anthony Quinn's autobiography—started disappearing.

The bookstore took on a life of its own, expanding and moving to its present site as Libreria Martinez Books and Art Gallery in 1999. Martinez added a second location in 2001 and now plans to expand nationally. His goal is to open 25 stores by 2012…each with its own barber chair.

READING REWARDS

In September 2004, Martinez learned that he, along with 22 other Americans, would receive a MacArthur Foundation "genius grant," an award of $500,000. According to the MacArthur committee, he has "elevated bookselling from a business to a campaign in support of underserved populations." A National Endowment for the Arts survey has shown that although about 6 million Hispanic-Americans (of a population of 40 million) read literature, their actual reading level is half that of non-Hispanics.

"We've seen a 500% increase in sales of Spanish-language books in the past six years," says Carlos Azula of Random House's foreign division. "But Reuben isn't just selling books; he's selling reading."

"The award couldn't have gone to a better guy," says actor Edward James Olmos, who co-founded the Los Angeles Latino Book Festival with Martinez in 1997.

Martinez says he doesn't know what he'll do with the money, but adds, "This award belongs to all of us, our customers, our kids, our culture."

RECOMMENDED READING

Here are a few of the most popular selections in the Libreria Martinez Books and Art Gallery.

El Llano en Llamas
(*The Burning Plain*)
by Juan Rulfo

El Árbol Generoso
(*The Giving Tree*)
by Shel Silverstein

Amor en los Tiempos de Cólera
(*Love in the Time of Cholera*)
by Gabriel García Márquez

El Viejo y el Mar
(*The Old Man and the Sea*)
by Ernest Hemingway

IT'S ANT-SPIRATIONAL!

Being small doesn't make you insignificant.

BACKGROUND
There are more ants on Earth than any other creature. In fact, 10% of all animal matter on the planet... is ants. So next time you see a little ant, think of this:

• In 2005 biologists at UC Berkeley discovered a species of ant in the Peruvian rain forest that can glide, directing their flight from the tops of trees. They are the only wingless insect known to do this.

• In 2002 an interconnected string of ant colonies was discovered in Southern Europe... and it is more than 3,700 miles long. The "super colony" stretches from Northern Italy to Portugal, and it contains hundreds of billions of ants.

• Biologists observed ants in Southern England "teaching" other ants where to find food. The teacher ant ran ahead of the learner, which would sometimes stop and turn different directions—as if it were looking for landmarks. The teacher waited while it did this, and wouldn't go until the learner ant came up and tapped on the teacher's legs with its antennae. After learning, the learner became a teacher for other ants.

• Weaver ants from Africa to Australia "sew" leaves together to make their nests. And they cooperate to do it: Worker ants pull and hold the edges of two leaves together; other workers walk along the edge of leaves with larvae clutched in their jaws, binding the leaves together with strands of silk secreted from the larvae's salivary glands.

• In March 2006, scientists in Queensland, Australia, discovered a species of ant that voluntarily swim in water—and even underwater. It's the first ant species known to do so.

• Aphid-tending ants live off *honeydew*, a sweet substance secreted by various insects, especially aphids. Aphids themselves live on the juices they suck from plants. To allow the aphids to do that without being bothered, aphid-tending ants watch over them and protect them from predators, sometimes even building shelters around them. Worker ants stroke the aphids with their antennae to induce them to secrete the honeydew, which is transferred to other ants, who carry it back to the nest and share it with the colony.

•There are 10,000 trillion ants alive at any moment. The world human population is 6 billion. In other words, for every person, there are nearly two million ants on Earth.

• Tropical leafcutter ants have sharp outer jaws which they use to cut out chunks of leaves. They don't eat the leaves because they can't digest the cellulose—they take them back to their nests and chew them into a pulp. They use the pulp to make fungus gardens, which they harvest for food.

• Some ants secrete formic acid as a defense—that's what causes the intense sting of an ant bite. Some birds put ants in their feathers because the formic acid gets rid of parasites.

• A queen ant can live for up to 25 years but mates only once (worker ants live for about 60 days). After an incubation period of 2–3 weeks, she'll lay a few thousand eggs every day for a few months. Once the ants emerge from their cocoons, they immediately begin gathering food. From then on, the queen is taken care of and never works or breeds again.

IT'S AUNT-SPIRATIONAL!

BRI stalwart Rad Welles told us this story about his great Aunt Dorothy. But she's not his great-aunt— she's his "great" Aunt Dorothy.

A TWIST OF FATE

One day in 1960 Nolan McDougal (Rad's uncle) was driving in San Diego when he suffered an aneurysm... and died behind the wheel. His 1959 Lincoln Continental jumped the curb and headed straight toward a crowd of people standing outside a fast-food restaurant. Everybody scattered—except one man who froze. The big car struck him, making him the second casualty of the bizarre accident.

The man killed by Nolan McDougal's car was a schoolteacher and a father of three young children. His wife did not work, and they had no life insurance. She filed a claim with McDougal's insurance company, but—unbelievably—they turned it down. Reason: McDougal was already dead when he hit her husband, and therefore it was an "act of God." The grieving widow never contested the company's decision.

When McDougal's wife (Rad's Aunt Dorothy), now a widow herself, heard that the poor woman would not be getting any insurance money, she contacted her and offered to help in an unusual way. How? By sending her a check to cover the expenses of raising her children... every month until they graduated from high school. And when they graduated, she offered to pay for their college tuition (one child took the offer and went for four years and graduated). The story never made the news, and Rad himself never even knew about it until his aunt passed away in 1985. Ever since then, he says, he's called her "My Sainted Aunt Dorothy."

CURMUDGEON'S CORNER

Feeling over-inspired? You may draw a little extra inspiration from the fact that you're not one of these people.

• Two thieves in Austria took advantage of heavy snowfall to break into cars and steal 43 stereos in a single night. The police followed their footprints to their home.

• A woman in West Virginia asked police to remove a "Deer Crossing" sign from the road in front of her house. Too many deer were being hit there, she said, and they should cross somewhere else.

• A man in Pawtucket, Rhode Island, got his brother to act as a lookout as he robbed an apartment. Bad choice: his brother is legally blind. The owner showed up, and the brothers were arrested.

• A woman in Memphis, Tennessee, saw what she thought was a large bag of cocaine in her neighbors' refrigerator...and decided to steal it. First, she hired a hit man to kill the four men who lived there. Except it wasn't a hit man—it was an undercover cop. And it wasn't even cocaine—it was *queso fresco*, a type of Mexican cheese.

• In 2006 a man in Kewaskum, Wisconsin, was arrested for burglary after a woman found her house in disarray—and her computer on. The thief had checked his e-mail while robbing the place and had forgotten to log out of his account.

• In 2003 Bibhuti Bhushan Nayak of India fulfilled his life-long dream of entering the *Guinness Book of World Records*. How'd he do it? He had a friend smash three concrete blocks on his groin. (Ouch!)

ACCIDENTALLY EXCELLENT

Are you accident-prone? Don't worry—it could be a good thing.

FIRST GLASS

One day in 1903, French chemist Edouard Benedictus was working in his lab when he accidentally knocked an empty glass flask off his workbench. When he picked it up, he noticed something strange: The glass had shattered into many pieces, but they remained stuck together in the shape of the bottle. Upon investigation he found that the flask had been filled with collodion, a syrupy chemical solution that, when evaporated, leaves a clear film. The film had coated the inside of the glass and held the pieces together. (Collodion, though quite toxic, was used in those days to seal cuts after surgery.)

Although Benedictus thought this was interesting, he went back to his regular work. A few days later he read an article about a woman who had been killed by a broken windshield in a car accident. Benedictus rushed to his lab. By the next night he had invented the world's first safety glass, which can be found in virtually every car in the world today.

SUPERPRINTS

In 1977 Fuseo Matsumur, an examiner in a Japanese crime laboratory, was placing hairs on microscope slides during a murder investigation. Suddenly he noticed his own finger-prints developing on the glass slides. He mentioned it to his partner, Masato Soba, who asked what he had used to affix the hairs to the slides. Fuseo said he was using cyanoacrylate ester, better known as superglue. Soba began experimenting and soon discovered that superglue vapors are absorbed by the perspiration and oils left by fingerprints, turning them white. The use of cyanoacrylate fumes to reveal latent (hard-to-find) fingerprints became one of the biggest breakthroughs in the history of fingerprint forensics.

THAT'S JUST SILLY

In 1943 General Electric engineer James Wright was attempting to create artificial rubber, desperately needed for the war effort because the Japanese had invaded rubber-producing areas in Southeast Asia. In one experiment, Wright tried mixing boric acid with silicon oil. The substance that resulted was amazingly bouncy and could be stretched great distances. Those weren't very useful qualities, but the substance sure was fun. Wright's family members and friends—and even friends of friends—played with the "nutty putty" for years, until someone finally thought to market it. By the mid-1950s, Silly Putty was one of the most popular toys in the country.

THE NOBEL FOR ACCIDENTS GOES TO...

In 1928 Scottish scientist Alexander Fleming was experimenting with staphylococcus bacteria, the germs that cause staph infections, when he absent-mindedly left some petri dishes exposed. Mold grew on the bacteria—and killed them. It was determined to be penicillium mold, and Fleming named the active ingredient in the mold *penicillin*. He wasn't able to create a medicine from it, but 12 years later two other scientists at Oxford University, Howard Florey and Ernst Chain, succeeded. The accident-inspired invention came just in time: Penicillin was mass-produced during World War II and has saved millions of lives since then. In 1945 Fleming, Florey, and Chain were awarded the Nobel Prize in medicine.

MAUS

Cartoonist Art Spiegelman took his father's harsh memories of the Holocaust and turned them into a way to make a terrible tragedy accessible to thousands of readers. In the process, he finally connected with his distant father.

A SURVIVOR'S TALE

Vladek and Anja Spiegelman were survivors of the Auschwitz concentration camp. Their son, Arthur, attended art school in New York and became a graphic artist and cartoonist. After his mother committed suicide in 1968, Art Spiegelman decided to translate his tragedy into art in his comic book "Prisoner on the Hell Planet."

It was a watershed moment for Spiegelman. He realized he could tell real stories via comic books, traditionally not considered a very serious art form. That's also when he decided to tell his parents' harrowing tale of surviving the Holocaust. In 1972 Spiegelman published "Maus," a three-page comic strip in an obscure magazine called *Funny Animals*.

Spiegelman used a unique device to tell the story: he had seen 1930s Nazi propaganda that depicted Jewish people as rats, so he parodied it. In "Maus," Jews were mice and Nazis were cats.

BLEEDING HISTORY

In 1979 Spiegelman realized he needed to tell the entire story and he began to lengthen the work. For the next several years he spent months at a time interviewing his father. By hearing the stories in brutal detail, Spiegelman earned respect for his father, who was a difficult man to like—his wartime experience had left him hollow, distant, and cruel.

And working on *Maus* had another benefit: it gave Spiegelman a way to reconnect with his deceased mother.

A NOVEL IDEA

Spiegelman founded an avant garde comic magazine called *RAW* in 1980. Once a year, he ran a 10-page installment of *Maus*. By 1986 he had told the complete story of Vladek and Anja, from pre-war Poland evading the Nazis, to the Warsaw ghetto, to their entry into Auschwitz.

At that point Spiegelman decided to revise and expand the episodes so that they could be published as a single volume. But most publishers wanted nothing to do with it. They thought a comic book about concentration camps, played out by cats and mice, trivialized the Holocaust. Spiegelman thought it did just the opposite: it made nearly unthinkable events accessible, even to people who might not like to read. And by using animals, it made the events of World War II more accessible and—ironically—more human.

Pantheon Books agreed with Spiegelman and published *Maus I: A Survivor's Tale: My Father Bleeds History* in 1986. It was a surprise hit, selling 50,000 copies in its first month and eventually more than 300,000. It even made the *New York Times* bestseller list for three months.

Maus was the first successful "graphic novel," a novel told entirely in illustrated panels. It showed that comics could be literary works aimed at adults. Spiegelman continued his parents' story, documenting their time in Auschwitz in 1991's *Maus II: And Here My Troubles Began*. For the two volumes, Spiegelman won the Pulitzer Prize. And few readers thought *Maus* was trivial. The *Wall Street Journal* called it "the most effective and successful narrative ever done about the Holocaust."

BUILDING THE AL-CAN

Before 1942, people traveling to Alaska from the U.S. mainland had to go by ship or plane. But then a highway—built at a back-breaking pace to protect the nation during World War II—opened the Great North to the rest of the country.

AGAINST ALL ODDS

In 1942, 11,000 American soldiers dug and hacked their way through frozen and muddy wilderness to lay a road 1,500 miles long. And they did it in just eight months. Their goal: to build the first road connecting the continental United States with Alaska—The Al-Can Highway.

When the Japanese bombed Pearl Harbor on December 7, 1941, the U.S. government woke up to the fact that Alaska was closer to Japan than any other part of the United States. That made it a potential security threat; if the Japanese were to invade Alaska, it would become a staging point for attacks against the rest of North America.

STARTING POINT

Within two months of the bombing, the highway project was approved by both the American and Canadian governments, and troops started heading north. There were already decent roads well into British Columbia, so "mile zero" would be at Dawson Creek, about 500 miles north of the U.S. border. From there it was 1,522 miles though B.C. and the Yukon Territory to the final destination at Delta Junction, Alaska. There the road would connect with the Richardson Highway, just 100 miles from Fairbanks. One Army colonel called it "the biggest and hardest job since the Panama Canal."

The Army Corps of Engineers decided to begin construction at seven different points along the route. They would then push as hard as necessary to link up the seven sections and complete the road before the next winter set in.

PAINSTAKING PROGRESS

Work began on April 11, 1942. Soldiers with handsaws and bulldozers cut through forests and across mountain ranges 10 miles behind surveying teams. When they came to an insurmountable obstacle, they went around it. The crews camped where they worked, pitching tents in the snow as they waited for the northern spring to arrive.

The conditions the road builders faced weren't just uncomfortable—they were dangerous. The area was well-known for its cold weather, but 1942 turned out to be the coldest winter ever recorded. Temperatures hovered around -40° F. for weeks at a time in the northern sections of the road, even dropping as low as -79° F. Troops had to check each other daily for bits of frozen skin that required medical attention. (Most of the soldiers were from the South and had never experienced such cold. Many had never even seen snow.)

A SENSE OF URGENCY

As summer advanced, new problems arose. The road had to cross hundreds of miles of boggy, semifrozen marshland. Thick layers of decaying vegetation called *muskeg* swallowed bulldozers whole. The men were forced to build the roadway on top of a layer of logs—which they also had to cut...by hand—to prevent it from sinking. They called this "corduroying" the road.

During the Alaskan summer, the sun was out for more than 20 hours a day, so crews worked in shifts nearly around the clock, seven days a week. In early June, the pressure to

complete the project increased—Japanese soldiers invaded
Alaska's Aleutian Islands (the only time in modern history
that foreign invaders have landed on U.S. soil), so the crews
pushed even harder, battling their way through swarms of
mosquitoes and blackflies. By the end of July they were
halfway done, with 750 more miles to go.

And then they came to the permafrost—frozen ground
that immediately began to thaw and turn to mud as soon as it
was disturbed by road-building equipment. Work stopped for
six weeks while the engineers tried to figure out what to do.
Finally, they returned to the time-consuming work of corduroying. Because of the delay, the men were still working as
winter returned. Frostbite and hypothermia again became
threats.

SUCCESS

Yet in spite of all of the obstacles, the road was completed
and opened to military traffic on November 20, 1942. It took
the first truck convoys 210 hours (nearly nine days) to travel
the entire route. The road continued to be improved
throughout the war and was eventually opened to civilian
traffic in 1948.

The Al-Can Highway project was an amazing achievement at time of great national need. And it made Alaska
accessible to the rest of the country, changing life in the territory forever. By the time Alaska became a state in 1959, the
population had almost doubled. Many of the newcomers had
arrived by traveling the highway built by men from all across
the United States, working at soldiers' pay, in one of the most
impressive feats of engineering in modern history.

IT AIN'T OVER YET

One of the most dramatic finishes in baseball history.

BENCHWARMER
In Game 1 of the 1988 World Series, the Oakland
Athletics jumped to a 4–0 lead over the Los Angeles
Dodgers in the second inning. The Dodgers were without one
of their biggest stars, Kirk Gibson; he was sitting on the
bench with a knee injury and not expected to play.

The Dodgers managed to score three runs, but by the bot-
tom of the ninth inning they were trailing by a run...and run-
ning out of options. With Mike Davis at bat facing Oakland's
ace closing pitcher Dennis Eckersley, Dodgers manager
Tommy Lasorda sent Dave Anderson to the on-deck circle.
Perhaps Eckersley got distracted, figuring the free-swinging
Anderson would be an easy strikeout. In any case, he walked
Davis. But Anderson never came up to bat. Kirk Gibson did.

THE MOMENT OF TRUTH

Gibson took a couple of practice swings; the pain in his knee
was so bad that he nearly fainted. Still, he dug in. First pitch:
strike. Second pitch: strike. One more and the game would
be over. But Eckersley threw three balls. Then, with the
count full, he delivered the payoff pitch, high and down the
middle. Gibson, using only his upper-body strength, took a
huge swing...and hit the ball out of the park. Game over.
Dodgers win, 5–4.

Gibson hobbled around the bases, pumping his fists in triumph as his teammates stormed the field. It turned out to be
the pivotal moment in the World Series: Los Angeles went
on to win, four games to one.

WORD PEACE

If there was only one word we could learn in
every language, it just might be this one.

Albanian: Paqe
Armenian: Khanhaghutyun
Basque: Bake
Bengali: Shanti
Bosnian: Mír
Catalán: Pau
Chinese: Pingan
Cree: Wetaskiwin
Danish: Fred
Dutch: Vrede
Esperanto: Paco
Estonian: Rahu
Farsi: Ashtee
French: Paix
German: Frieden
Greek: Iri'ni
Haitian: Lapé
Hausa: Lùmana
Hawaiian: Maluhia

Hindi: Shanti
Hungarian: Béke
Igbo: Udo
Inuit: Tutkium
Irish Gaelic: Síocháin
Japanese: Heiwa
Javanese: Rukun
Khmer: Soksang
Kurdish: Hasîtî
Lao: 'Kwam Sa
Latin: Pax
Latvian: Miers
Maori: Rangima'arie
Navajo: K'é
Nepali: Saanti
Nez Perce: 'Éyewi
Pima: Dodolimdag
Pashto: Amniat
Polish: Pokój

Quechua: Sonqo Tiaykuy
Russian: Mír
Samoan: Filemu
Scots Gaelic: Fois
Sesotho: Khotso
Sioux: Wo'okeyeh
Slovak: Pokój
Somali: Nabad:Da
Spanish: Paz
Swahili: Amaní
Tagalog: Kapayapaan
Tahitian: Hau
Thai: Santipap
Turkish: Sulh
Urdu: Aman
Welsh: Hedd
Yiddish: Sholim
Yoruba: Alaáfía
Zulu: Ukuthula

NEVER SWAT A FLY

*Next time someone chides you for staying
in bed too long, tell them this story.*

THE "AHA!" MOMENT

French philosopher Rene Descartes (1596–1650) is probably best known today for his famous saying, "I think, therefore I am." But it was his groundbreaking work in mathematics that cemented his reputation as one of the great thinkers in modern history. Rene was a sickly child, so one of his teachers at the Jesuit school he attended allowed him to stay in bed in the morning as long as he wished, hoping it would build up his strength. It was a habit he continued for the rest of his life...and one he insisted brought him to his great insights.

One morning in 1637, Descartes was lounging in bed (as usual), watching a fly buzz on the ceiling. Mesmerized, he followed the fly's position as it wandered across the ceiling tiles. In a burst of insight, Descartes suddenly realized he'd found a method of mathematically describing the position of an object. He could plot the fly's position according to what ceiling tile it was on (like one square on a piece of graph paper). Descartes had created the x–y Cartesian coordinate system familiar to all geometry students. Later that year he published his discovery to great acclaim.

Its applications in math and science were profound. Cartesian geometry revolutionized navigation, and made possible any number of technological innovations, including space travel. For this reason, Descartes is commonly considered the father of modern mathematics—and all because of a fly and a curious man's tendency to stay in bed.

LOCAL HEROES

Few of us will ever encounter this kind of life-and-death situation, but if we do, here's hoping we can be as calm and collected as these folks were.

READING RETENTION

Ten-year-old Tilly Smith was vacationing with her family in Thailand in December 2004. Two weeks earlier, her geography class had studied tsunamis. One morning while walking on a beach on Phuket, she noticed that foam was bubbling on the water—a warning sign of an approaching tsunami. She immediately told her parents and the hotel staff. The beach was evacuated just minutes before the giant waves struck, and was one of the few in Phuket where no one was killed or injured. Tilly is credited with saving more than 100 lives.

CATCH OF THE DAY

Pregnant with triplets, Lanitta Lewis was on her way to a doctor's appointment in 2005. While waiting for a subway in Oakland, California, she felt the first telltale signs of labor and called out for help. Every commuter ignored her, except one: a high school teacher named Biko Eisen-Martin. He ran to a phone, called an ambulance, and returned just in time... the first triplet was coming. Eisen-Martin took his T-shirt off and used it to catch the three-pound baby girl.

HEAD ABOVE WATER

In September 2003, Frank Jackson, 19, was kayaking on the Potomac River near Washington, D.C. The turbulent water made for good kayaking—but bad swimming. Pavel Hruban,

17, went in to swim anyway. Immediately overcome by the current, he was carried downstream and fought to stay afloat. Jackson spotted Hruban and paddled frantically to reach him. The rough water overturned Jackson's kayak, but he managed to get close enough to Hruban for both of them to hang on to the boat and reach shore.

GARAGE FIRE

On New Year's Day 2004, Elnora Denmark of Dallas, Texas, was working as an in-home caregiver when a small airplane crashed into the patient's garage. The house quickly caught fire and filled with thick, black smoke. Neighbors shouted for Denmark to get out of the house, but she refused to leave without her patient, who had recently been incapacitated by several strokes. When she got to him, he was wrapped in a blanket and unconscious, so she threw him over her shoulder, and quickly carried him out of the house to safety.

REMAIN CALM

One morning in January 2006, Aaron McTavish-Tsuruda, 13, was napping in the rear seat of his school bus when the bus hit a patch of black ice, rolled twice, and crashed into a watery ditch. The vehicle was partially submerged as it balanced on a steep incline. The driver tried to calm the group of students, most of them under 10, but many were screaming in shock and fear. Aaron, however, had been in two other bus crashes in his life, so he knew exactly what to do. He took off his seat belt, popped open the rear emergency door, and started helping kids out as quickly as possible. Thanks to Aaron, nobody was hurt. (And he still takes the bus to school.)

EVERYDAY PEOPLE

We asked some of our BRI staffers to share their personal stories of inspiration. Here's what they told us.

Mana M: "Mean people inspire me to be a better person. When I see someone who doesn't care about the rest of humanity, I want to do something to fill the void they've created. A single act of kindness could make all the difference."

Ben L: "My high-school P.E. teacher told me to try out for the basketball team. I didn't make the team, but his words of encouragement inspired me to keep practicing and improving. I still play competitive league basketball today, and have even won several trophies."

Shannon K: "Mom's advice to me when I was in my teens: 'If you rely on others for your financial well-being, you may be disappointed. Be independent, and the rest will follow.'"

Jennifer T: "On my 16th birthday I got a bouquet of flowers from my aunt. I wasn't expecting anything from her, so it made the day seem really special. Because of that I try to do nice things for other people on their special occasions."

Laurel G: "My friend Kristi is a lot bolder than I am. So whenever I have to do something difficult, like ask a stranger for help or return something to a snooty store, I just pretend I'm Kristi... and usually I can do it."

Brian B: "After I told my mom I wanted to be a writer, every year during the 'best screenplay' part of the Academy Awards, she'd say, 'I just know I'm going to see you up there some day.' (She still phones me every year to say it.)"

NEVER TOO YOUNG

There's no reason to wait—whatever your dream is, start today.

• **Wolfgang Amadeus Mozart** performed across Europe…when he was 6.

• **Kirsen Wilhelm** biked across the U.S. in 66 days…at age 9.

• **Thomas Gregory** swam across the English Channel…at 11.

• **Carl Witte** earned a Ph.D. in mathematics in 1812…at age 12.

• **Stevie Wonder** recorded "Fingertips," a No. 1 hit… at 13.

• **Temba Tsheri** climbed Mt. Everest…at the age of 15.

• **Joseph-Armand Bombardier** invented the snowmobile…at age 15.

• **Arthur de Lulli** composed "Chopsticks"…at 16.

• **Pelé** led Brazil to the World Cup of soccer…at the age of 17.

• **Mary Shelley** wrote *Frankenstein*…at age 18.

• **Tommy Hilfiger** opened his first boutique… at age 18.

• **Bill Gates** started Microsoft…at the age of 19.

• **Magic Johnson** led the Los Angeles Lakers to an NBA title…at age 20.

• **Alexander the Great** became king of Macedonia …at the age of 20.

• **Nathaniel Palmer** discovered Antarctica…at age 21.

• **Tom Monaghan** started Domino's Pizza…at 23.

• **Daniel Rutherford** discovered nitrogen…at 23.

DJANGO

His is one of the most important names in the history of jazz. But without his dogged determination and will to succeed, the musical world would not be the same.

GYPSY CARAVAN

Jean Baptiste "Django" Reinhardt was a *Roma* (a Gypsy), born in 1910 in Belgium to a family of traveling musicians. Most of his childhood was spent in the Gypsy camps outside Paris, where he developed into a musical prodigy playing a six-string banjo tuned like a guitar.

In 1928 Django was an 18-year-old star on the rise, making a name for himself as a guitarist accompanying famous accordion players in the cafés and dance halls of Paris. Then tragedy struck: One night after a performance, Django's caravan caught fire in a freak accident. He escaped, barely, but was severely burned. He nearly lost his right leg and was bedridden for over a year. But the real tragedy was that Django's left hand—the one he used to play chords and solos on the fretboard—was permanently damaged.

STARTING OVER

The burns paralyzed Django's pinky and ring fingers. It looked like his playing days were over. He was destitute, but knew in his heart that couldn't give up on his lifelong dream. So even though he only had partial use of his index and middle fingers, Django began the long, painful process of relearning his instrument. Because he couldn't spread the two fingers apart, playing chords was out of the question. So instead he concentrated on melody lines, and in doing so helped pioneer a brand new style of music: lead guitar.

Django's playing steadily improved until he was once again dazzling audiences (and musicians) with solos that were as smooth as they were fast. Just six years after the fire, Django was starring with violinist Stéphane Grappelli in the famous Quintet of the Hot Club of France. By this time he had mastered his new style—a style that five-fingered guitarists have struggled to imitate ever since.

THE MUSICIAN'S MUSICIAN

How influential was Django? All of the greatest musicians of the Jazz Age wanted to play with him: Louis Armstrong, Coleman Hawkins, and Duke Ellington, to name a few.

And his influence doesn't stop there. Every notable guitarist since has cited Django as an inspiration—from Charlie Christian and Les Paul to Eddie Van Halen, Carlos Santana, and even Willie Nelson. Chet Atkins called Reinhardt "the single greatest guitar player of the 20th century."

Because Django refused to let a major setback derail him, he changed the face of popular music.

* * *

STOP AND SMELL THE LAUGHTER

"One day when I was little, and my parents were having a party, I went around to all the adults with a glass of water and said, 'Drink this, it's magic. It'll make you taller.' And they all drank it and said, 'How cute.' And then I snuck off into the room where they kept all the coats and hemmed everyone's sleeves an inch shorter."

—Steven Wright

LADY OF THE LOCKUP

Need proof that it's never too late to
answer a calling? Look no further.

SOUTH OF THE BORDER

In 1965 a Southern California housewife named Mary Brenner got a phone call from her local priest, Father Henry Vetter. Father Henry knew that Brenner did a lot of charity work in the Los Angeles area, so he invited her to join him on a trip to Tijuana, a Mexican city just south of San Diego. A few days later they filled a station wagon with donated medicine and other supplies, and headed south. After dropping off the medical supplies at various city hospitals, they made a stop at Tijuana's notorious La Mesa prison.

AN EYEFUL

There's a lot of poverty in Tijuana, and Mary, who grew up in Beverly Hills, must have been shocked at every stop they made. But it was the prisoners at La Mesa who moved her the most. Built in the 1950s to house 600, the prison now held more than 7,000 men and women in appalling conditions. It had a reputation as one of the most dangerous jails in Mexico.

Even though Mary was holding down two jobs and raising seven children, she resolved to return to La Mesa as often as she could. And over the next several years she managed to make the three-hour drive fairly regularly, bringing with her carloads—and sometimes even truckloads—of donated medical supplies, toiletries, used clothing, furniture, and fast food that restaurants saved for her instead of tossing into dumpsters at the end of the day. Yet after having accomplished so much, each time she left the prison she felt there was still more to do.

MAKING SOME CHANGES

When her second marriage ended in divorce in 1972, Brenner started thinking about what she wanted to do with the rest of her life. A devout Catholic, she thought about becoming a nun. But when she approached an order called the Maryknolls, they told her she was too old—only women aged 35 or younger were allowed to join. (Her two divorces didn't help her case, either.)

After talking it over with priests and nuns who knew of her work, she decided to take private vows and become a sort of "freelance" nun—one who didn't belong to any established religious order. She sewed her own habit and took the name Mother Antonia, in honor of Father Anthony Brouwers, a priest she admired. From then on the prisoners, the prison guards, and all their families would be her life's work.

GETTING STARTED

When the warden of La Mesa told Mary Brenner years earlier to come back anytime and stay as long as she liked, he probably never imagined that one day she'd show up at the front gate dressed as a nun, asking for permission to live in the prison. But he lived up to his offer and granted "Mother Antonia's" request; in March 1977 she took up residence in the women's block and began living at La Mesa full time.

Believing that every person has an innate capacity for good, Mother Antonia refused to judge the prisoners—she only wanted to help them. And her approach to serving the prison community was simple: if an inmate or guard needed anything, she'd do her best to get it for them. She focused on the most basic needs in the beginning—collecting and distributing food, blankets, toiletries, and medicine to the inmates, as well as caring for the sick and tending to the spiritual needs of both the inmates and the guards. But over time she became more ambitious:

• She recognized that bad or missing teeth were more than just a cosmetic problem: they were also a major barrier to parolees finding decent jobs and putting their criminal pasts behind them. So Mother Antonia recruited dentists to come to the prison and cap teeth and fit bridges and dentures for inmates and guards. The dentists donated their time; Mother Antonia paid for materials and other expenses out of charitable contributions she raised. It typically cost more than $200 to treat each case, yet so far Mother Antonia has managed to obtain treatment for 4,000 people.

• She also arranged for plastic surgeons to visit La Mesa to remove prison tattoos, repair cleft palates (the cause of some speech impediments), and perform other surgeries that improved the appearance of inmates and made it easier for them to reenter life outside the prison walls.

• Inmates were routinely being beaten when Mother Antonia arrived at La Mesa, something that she attributed to the guards' limited education, poor job training, and low pay. By befriending the guards and their families, she has been able to improve the treatment of inmates not just at La Mesa, but also at local police stations and jails. She is credited with ending three prison riots over the years.

• Many petty criminals were serving months or even years of hard time simply because they couldn't afford to pay fines— some as low as $25. Mother Antonia has used donated money to get thousands of nonviolent offenders out on bail or released from prison altogether.

STILL GOING STRONG

Mother Antonia, now 79, has spent 30 years at La Mesa prison. Advancing age has taken its toll: she suffers from heart trouble and sleeps with an oxygen tank next to her bed, but she insists on living at the prison. As word about her work has spread over the years, she has attracted other women to the cause. The Catholic Church officially recognized her work about a year after she started, and in 2003 she formed a new religious order called the Eudist Servants of the Eleventh Hour, which accepts women aged 45 to 65. In 2005 she was the subject of a bestselling book titled *The Prison Angel*.

Mother Antonia's work has made her one of the most famous and revered women in Mexico, but she says she has trouble seeing what all the fuss is about. "I don't understand why people are so amazed. To give help is easy," she says. "To ask for it is hard."

*   *   *

HELPING HER "MUM"

In 2005, 10-year-old Katie Morgan wrote to her local Member of Parliament in North Shropshire, England. Her mother had breast cancer. Doctors wanted to treat her with the new "wonder drug" Herceptin, but her local insurance program refused to pay for the drug—which cost £47,000 (about $80,000)—because her mother's cancer was "only" stage 2 and not severe enough. Katie ended her letter with "Please help us. We would like our mum to be here when we grow up." The letter somehow made it to the news media, and caught the eye of a mystery millionaire. The unknown benefactor paid for the drug.

FOSTERING LOVE

Doing good for others can be contagious...but somebody's got to get the ball rolling. Here's what happened to a community when one couple did just that.

THOSE LEFT BEHIND

The year 1997 was a sad one for Donna Martin, but it also changed her life. Her mother died, leaving her despondent, and she prayed for an answer to end her grief. One night, a single word popped into her head: "foster." She could take care of neglected kids. Inspired, Donna ran the idea by her husband, W.C. Martin, the reverend of Bennett Chapel, a black church in a small east Texas town called Possum Trot. He agreed and Donna went to work.

She started by taking state-run classes that license foster parents, where she learned some alarming information: More than 100,000 kids are awaiting adoption in the United States at any given time. And most of those are troubled or neglected older children from broken homes. The Martins' mission was clear: "We are adopting high-risk children, the ones who are hard to place. We believe that where there is life, there is hope."

IT TAKES A VILLAGE

The Martins shared their foster-parenting experience with their church congregation, and something amazing happened: other members of Bennett Chapel wanted to foster, too. Donna called Judy Bowman, a supervisor in the foster program, to give her the good news, and Bowman told her that if they could get 10 families to sign up, the classes could be held in their church, instead of Dallas (a 120-mile round trip). "We offer that to a lot of people," Bowman says. "But ten families is a lot." Not for Bennett Chapel: 23 families attended the first meeting. Ultimately, 18 children were placed with those families, and in most instances the children were permanently adopted.

For the small church, that was only the beginning. At last count, 42 families have been licensed to foster through classes at Bennett Chapel, and 70 kids have been placed in their care. And amazingly, more than 60 of these difficult-to-place children—all with backgrounds of abuse and neglect—have been adopted. Not only that, many of these children have siblings whom the families of Bennett Chapel are adopting, too.

CATCH THE VISION

The Martins have also developed a support network for the kids. If a parent is temporarily overwhelmed, the Martins will look after the children for a few days to give the parents a break. And other families are following their lead. They swap babysitting and parenting advice, and the children attend counseling sessions together.

The Martins hope that other communities will "catch the vision," and they regularly travel to churches to explain their system of fostering and adoption.

"You wouldn't believe the change that has occurred in our church," says Donna. "Before, if you came in on a Sunday morning, you'd find us friendly but a bit proper. These days—wow! There's a spirit of joy and energy in the place, and even the adults have become a lot more relaxed. There are kids, kids, just everywhere!"

A GREAT TEACHER

Mr. Clark showed underachieving kids that somebody really cared whether or not they succeeded. Result: they succeeded.

FIFTY-FIVE RULES
While working part-time as a teacher in North Carolina, self-styled adventurer Ron Clark saw a TV report about a school in Harlem that had smart students—but low test scores, because the school couldn't attract good teachers. So Clark moved to Harlem and got a job at an elementary school like the one he'd seen on TV. A few years later, Clark won a national award for Teacher of the Year.

How'd he do it? Clark has 55 rules his students must follow. Most are small but straightforward (make eye contact, respect others' opinions, be honest, do your homework every night), while others are designed to encourage students to aim high (stand up for what you believe in, be the best person you can be at all times, live life to the fullest). He highlights these ideas in lessons and makes it clear that the purpose of the rules is to let the kids know that he cares and that their actions matter.

Clark believes that enthusiasm is more important than discipline. He makes sure he gets noticeably excited when he's teaching a lesson. "It's important to show them the excitement you get from learning," he says. And Clark will do whatever it takes to earn his students' trust and respect. For example, when he first came to Harlem, double-Dutch jump roping was popular. So at every recess, Clark was on the playground jumping rope with the kids. It's all part of his plan to make his students become complete individuals and, as he puts it, "to love life."

THE PRIVY MAN

*Here is the story of a man who saw millions of people
suffering and made it his life's mission to help
them. How? By building a better toilet.*

CASTE-AWAYS

When Bindeshwar Pathak was a boy growing up in a
wealthy Indian family in the 1940s, he was punished
for breaking a cultural rule—he touched the arm of a family
servant. The punishment: Bindeshwar's grandfather forced
him to take a ritual bath in which every inch of his body was
painfully scrubbed clean, and then he had to swallow a
nugget of cow dung mixed with cow urine to "flush out the
filth from within."

The boy didn't understand why the punishment was so
severe, so his grandfather explained that the servants were
"untouchables"—people so filthy and dirty that they weren't
even given a place in one of India's four main castes. It was
their lifelong duty to clean up the waste of their masters, to
carry it away in buckets and dispose of it in holes. And they
had to live in small huts with no running water.

The lesson of that day stayed with Bindeshwar. He knew
in his heart that there had to be a better way for these people.
So he decided that he would use his stature and schooling to
help the untouchables live a better life. But first, he needed
a plan.

BUILDING A BETTER TOILET
After graduating from college with a degree in sociology, Dr.
Bindeshwar Pathak traveled throughout India and lived with
the poorest families to study them. He found that the worst

problem they had to deal with was sanitation. Of the 500 million people living in India at the time, nearly 75 percent either defecated in the open or used bucket latrines. And only a tiny fraction of India's 4,800 towns and cities even had sewers.

Bindeshwar saw that two things needed to happen: "First, every single house in India should have a proper toilet and adequate toilet facilities. Secondly, the untouchables in India should be adopted into mainstream lives."

He researched different plumbing systems and consulted with engineering experts around the world, and in 1970 came up with a simple but ingenious solution: the *sulabh shauchalaya*, a toilet consisting of two pits with a sealed cover. The *sulabh*'s benefits:

- It is very inexpensive, so every family can afford one.
- Waste can be cleaned without direct contact.
- It saves water by requiring only half a gallon for flushing instead of the usual four gallons needed for a bucket.
- It eliminates ground contamination by recycling human waste into fertilizer right there in the sealed pit.
- Because there are two pits, the toilets will never be out of service—one can be used while the other is being emptied.
- It eliminates the need for costly septic tanks, which use much more water and emit foul odors.

MAKING A DIFFERENCE

In the four decades since its introduction, the *sulabh* has drastically altered India's cultural landscape. Hundreds of thousands of former untouchables no longer have to be exposed to waste.

The second part of Pathak's plan—to rehabilitate

former untouchables into society—has been successful as well. In centuries past, no education or job training was available to these people. But now, thanks to the money that comes in from the public *sulabhs* (as well as some government funding), Pathak has set up vocational schools that train people in fields such as computer technology, typing and shorthand, electrical engineering, and other skilled trades.

There is still much work to be done. Although hundreds of thousands of lives have been improved, there are still millions of people in India whose job it is to clean toilets with their bare hands. And although the name "untouchable" has fallen into disuse in recent years, the stigma against them still exists, especially in rural areas.

But thanks to Bindeshwar Pathak, change has begun and continues to spread. "Let us save these people from squalid conditions," he says, "and in doing so we will be saving the national conscience."

*   *   *

WORDS OF WISDOM

For many people, religion is the primary source of inspiration. Here are some often-quoted passages from the world's holy texts:

The Bible (Christianity): "Do not resist an evil person. To him who strikes you on the right cheek, offer the other also."

The Koran (Islam): "Let there be no compulsion in religion; Truth stands out clearly from error."

Tao Te Ching (Taoism): "Those who know, don't speak. Those who speak, don't know."

The Talmud (Judaism): "Every blade of grass has its angel that bends over it and whispers, 'Grow, grow.'"

KEEP OUT: GENIUS AT WORK

Ever wonder what inspires brilliance? It may not be what you think.

LUDWIG VAN BEETHOVEN poured pitchers of cold water over his head to keep himself focused and awake as he composed from dusk until dawn.

ANTHONY TROLLOPE, a British novelist of the 1800s, wrote for three hours every day, from 5:30 AM to 8:30 AM. He kept a watch in front of him to make sure he wrote 250 words every 15 minutes. (He was so disciplined that if he finished a novel before 8:30, he took out fresh paper and started a new one.)

ALEXANDER GRAHAM BELL insisted on working all night long...and alone. He invented the telephone under the cloak of darkness. Bell said, "To take night from me is to rob me of my life."

CHARLES DICKENS couldn't begin to write until all the furniture in his house was in the proper arrangement. He always wrote in blue ink on blue-gray paper. Every morning he arose at 7 o'clock, bathed in cold water, and wrote two to four pages by lunchtime.

FELIX MENDELSSOHN composed entire symphonies completely in his head. When a friend came to visit and was about to excuse himself because Mendelssohn was working, Mendelssohn welcomed him into his room, saying he was only copying out. "But he was not copying," as the friend told it, "for there was no paper but that on which he was writing. The work whereupon he was busy was the Overture in C major. There was no looking forwards or backwards, no comparing, no humming over; the pen kept going steadily on, without pausing, and we never ceased talking. The copying out, therefore, as he called it, meant that the whole composition, to the last note, had been so worked out in his mind, that he beheld it there as though it had been actually lying before him."

THOMAS JEFFERSON and **VIRGINIA WOOLF** both wrote standing up.

RAYMOND CHANDLER typed his mystery novels on narrow slips of paper that were the width of a paperback novel turned on its side. This limited him to no more than 10 to 15 lines per page and forced him to put "a bit of magic"—an interesting image, funny quip, or clever bit of dialogue—on every piece of paper.

ALEX HALEY, the author of *Roots*, booked passage on a freighter at the beginning of each new project. He'd write the entire book at sea, with no distractions.

JENSON BUTTON, a Formula 1 race car driver, visualizes every race just before he starts it. He sits on an inflatable exercise ball and pretends to hold a steering wheel, then closes his eyes and pretends to drive a lap of the race, making all the engine sounds. His imaginary lap time is usually within a second of his real race time.

THREE TRUTHS

Don't be too timid and squeamish about your actions. All life is an experiment. The more experiments you make, the better. What if they are a little coarse, and you may get your coat soiled or torn? What if you do fail, and get fairly rolled in the dirt once or twice? Up again, you shall never be so afraid of a tumble.

—**Ralph Waldo Emerson**

The miraculous is not extraordinary—but the common mode of existence. It is our daily bread. Whoever really has considered the lilies of the field or the birds of the air and pondered the improbability of their existence in this warm world within the cold and empty stellar distances will hardly balk at the turning of water into wine—which was, after all, a very small miracle. We forget the greater and still continuing miracle by which water (with soil and sunlight) is turned into grapes.

—**Wendell Berry**

Everybody can be great, because everybody can serve. You don't have to have a college degree to serve. You don't have to make your subject and your verb agree. You don't have to know about Plato and Aristotle. You don't have to know Einstein's Theory of Relativity. You only need a heart full of grace, a soul generated by love, and you can become that servant."

—**Martin Luther King Jr.**

INSPIRED BY NATURE

Inventors have long known that solutions to complex problems are often hidden in plain sight—in nature. Science has a name for it: biomimicry. *Here are some famous examples.*

A GRIPPING STORY

Engineer Georges de Mestral was taking his dog for a walk in the Swiss woods in 1948 when he stopped to pull the cockleburs off his pants. He noticed that the burs had hooks that gripped the wool fabric of his trousers. That's when he realized that hooks and loops might make a terrific fastener. It took him almost a decade to perfect two nylon strips—one with hundreds of loops, the other with hundreds of hooks—but by 1951 he had patented his clever invention and named it...Velcro.

COTTON CLAWTH

Eighteenth-century inventor Eli Whitney was watching a cat swipe at a hen through the slats of a chicken coop. When the cat came up with just a pawful of feathers, that gave Whitney an idea. He'd been trying to find a new way of separating cotton fibers from their seedpods, a labor-intensive process that made cotton farming barely profitable. Whitney used small wire hooks to pull the cotton bolls through a wire screen, separating the fibers from the seedpods and making the process 50 times faster. On March 14, 1794, he was granted the patent on his cotton "gin" (short for "engine"), and cotton became king in the American South.

A THORNY SITUATION

Lumber for fencing was always in short supply on the plains, so 19th-century Texas ranchers planted hedges of Osage orange trees to corral their livestock. But it took five years for the thorny trees to grow into a "horse-high, bull-strong, and hog-tight" living fence. Besides, once they were in place, they couldn't be moved. While watching some ranchers plant the hedges, Texas entrepreneur Michael Kelly realized that a piece of wire, twisted around another length of wire and snipped just right, might emulate the thorny Osage hedges in a quick, easy, and inexpensive way. In 1868 Kelly took out a patent for his "thorny fence," which he called...barbed wire.

FLOORED

In 1995, textile designers Ray Anderson and David Oakey designed a carpet with a pattern that mimicked the randomness of a forest floor. But instead of a applying it to large roll of carpet, they put it on 12-inch-square carpet "tiles." The benefit: When any section of flooring became worn and had to be replaced, the diversity of color and pattern allowed the tiles to simply be switched at random—they always matched.

CHAIN REACTION

One crisp fall afternoon in 1946, a tiny beetle larva distracted Joseph Buford Cox from chopping firewood. The veteran logger watched in fascination as the bug chomped its way through a solid tree stump, just as easily across the grain as with the grain. Cox realized nature had just given him the answer to a problem loggers faced daily with the temperamental chains on their gas-powered saws. After studying the mandibles of the timber beetle larva, Cox created a chain that replicated the alternating action of their C-shaped jaws in the bits he used on his chain saw. In November 1947, he sold the first Cox Chipper Chain, the mother of all chainsaws used today.

GIVE UNTIL
<u>IT FEELS GOOD</u>

*If you became filthy rich, how would you spend
your money? Here are three suggestions.*

PHILANTHROPIC FORWARD

In 1998 Sergei Fedorov, hockey player for the NHL champion Detroit Red Wings, announced the opening of the Sergei Fedorov Foundation, a charitable organization to help abused and neglected children in Detroit. To get the foundation started, Fedorov made the initial donation...his entire salary for the upcoming hockey season. That was a bit more than $2 million.

THE "MORE" IN "MOORE"

Gordon E. Moore is a co-founder of Intel and one of the world's richest people. He's also one of the most generous. Between 2001 and 2005, he and his wife, Betty, gave $6.7 billion to support scientific research, conservation, and higher education. That's about two-thirds of their net worth.

EVERYBODY'S DEBT

In January 2006, Margaret Taylor died at the age of 98. She left her estate—$1.1 million—to the U.S. government. Why? To help pay down the U.S. national debt. When asked to explain the unusual bequest, her attorney, Tom Drake, told reporters, "It's not what I would have advised her to do with it, but she really wasn't interested in my opinion."

SAVING ANDY'S LEGACY

*A medical student with a rare form of cancer stunned
the medical world when he succeeded in culturing his
own cancer cells. But when Hurricane Katrina hit,
his work was at risk of being destroyed. Here's
Part 2 of the story. (Part 1 is on page 59.)*

STORM OF THE CENTURY

Shortly after 6 a.m. on August 29, 2005, Hurricane
Katrina made landfall 65 miles southeast of New
Orleans. It was the sixth-strongest Atlantic hurricane ever
recorded and caused an estimated $75 billion in damages,
making it the most costly in U.S. history.

The Tulane University Health Sciences Center was right
in the path of the storm. Tulane was where, a year before, a
med student named Andy Martin had succeed in culturing
the world's only living line of sinonasal undifferentiated carcinoma (SNUC) cancer cells before losing his own battle
with the disease. The hope had been that one day Andy's
cells might help scientists to find a cure. Now, as Katrina
bore down on New Orleans, it seemed like those hopes might
be dashed.

MEN OF THE HOUR

Most of the scientists at Tulane had played it safe and evacuated the city as the hurricane approached. Two who stayed
behind were Dr. Tyler Curiel, head of the cancer research center, and his colleague Dr. Michael Brumlik. Andy's cell line
was only a tiny part of many decades' worth of research in
danger of being destroyed, so Curiel and Brumlik wanted to
be on hand to salvage whatever they could if things got really

bad. In the hours before the storm hit, they prepared as best they could by moving all of the samples into four large freezers. Keeping the samples frozen was the key—if they thawed, precious scientific research would be lost forever.

RISING WATERS

Katrina hit the city hard, although the storm itself didn't do much damage to the labs at Tulane. The power was knocked out, but the emergency generators came on and the freezers kept humming. The real damage came when the levees that protected New Orleans from nearby Lake Pontchartrain failed and water poured into the city. Brumlik realized they were in trouble when he looked out his window and saw the streets below were flooded—and the water was rising fast.

The Health Sciences Center was designed to survive a hurricane and even some flooding. But not that much flooding—the emergency generators weren't high enough in the building to escape the floodwaters for long. And once they failed, there was no telling how many weeks or months might pass before power was restored. If the two doctors didn't do something fast, the samples in the freezer were going to thaw out and die.

MAKING THE MOVE

Knowing that the building next door had better emergency power than theirs, the first thing Curiel and Brumlik did was try to push the heavy freezers to it, but the doorways were too narrow. So they abandoned that plan and emptied the freezers instead, carrying boxes of samples next door and stuffing them into any freezer that had room. The process was exhausting: Curiel's lab was on the fifth floor, the freezers in the other building were on the seventh floor, and the elevators were out—so they had to climb up and down the stairs on each trip as they moved hundreds of boxes of samples from one building to the next.

PLAN B

The hard work bought Curiel and Brumlik a little time, but not enough. When they checked on the emergency generators in the new building, they saw that the floodwaters were within six inches of swamping them. When these generators failed, there would be only one place left where the samples would be safe: in some liquid nitrogen tanks back in the lab that they'd just finished emptying out. Those tanks would stay cold even after the power failed, and Curiel estimated that they'd keep the samples alive for about 10 days.

So, having just finished running the samples over to the new building, Curiel and Brumlik began moving them back again. The nitrogen tanks weren't nearly as large as the freezer, which meant they had to choose the handful of samples that were the most important, and let the others die. Many of the decisions were agonizing, but one in particular was not: "The number-one thing I knew we had to save was the Andy Martin SNUC cells," Curiel later explained to reporters.

GOTTA GO

Not long after the two men finished stuffing the three nitrogen tanks with as many samples as they could, they were ordered by armed National Guard soldiers to clear the building. They hopped into a canoe, paddled down the hallway and out of one of the exit doors to Charity Hospital, three blocks away. There they spent the next few days assisting in the care and evacuation of hundreds of stranded patients.

GOTTA GET BACK

It took three days to evacuate Charity Hospital, after which Curiel and Brumlik were themselves evacuated to Dallas. Knowing that, at best, the nitrogen would keep Andy Martin's SNUC cells and the other samples alive for another week, they immediately began e-mailing and telephoning anyone they could think of to help them get them back to New Orleans to rescue the samples. Finally, after lining up a corporate jet, 800 pounds of dry ice, and some insulated coolers, they flew back to New Orleans.

By now the temperature inside the building had climbed to over 90°F and the air was foul with the smell of rotting samples they hadn't been able to keep frozen. But what about the samples in the nitrogen tanks—had they survived? Curiel opened the lid on the first tank, reached in, and grabbed a box containing a sample. Amazingly, the first box he pulled out was labeled "SNUC"—Andy Martin's sample. And it was fine. "It was really cold. It was really white," Curiel said. "That's what it's supposed to look like."

So, thanks to the herculean efforts of two dedicated doctors, the samples were safe—and Andy's dream of finding a cure for the cancer that claimed his life is still alive and well.

*　　*　　*

"Hope is the thing with feathers
That perches in the soul
And sings the tune without the words
And never stops...at all."

—Emily Dickinson

HABITAT FOR HUMANITY

*Ever felt like something was missing from your life? Here are two
people who set out to find what was missing from theirs...
and ended up helping over a million people.*

BUILDING A BETTER LIFE

Millard Fuller knew there had to be a better way to live.
In 1965 he and his wife Linda seemed to be living the
American dream: He owned a successful marketing firm, and
the family was well provided for. Still, they felt unfulfilled. "I
worked all day," Millard said, "came home, had supper, went
to sleep, then back to work." So after some soul-searching,
they sold their house and moved to Koinonia Farm, a small
Christian community outside of Americus, Georgia, dedicated
to helping the poor. From the beginning, Millard and Linda
knew that homeless people needed more than money: they
needed education, inspiration, and a helping hand. Millard
and Linda decided to be that helping hand.

In 1968 they started "Fund for Humanity." The idea was
simple: Volunteers would work with charities to get donations toward affordable housing. Then they would work side
by side with the homeless to build the homes. One of the
main principles: The houses were not handouts. The families
who moved into them were given no-interest loans to cover
the costs, but were obligated to do 300 hours of construction
work themselves.

THE NEXT LEVEL

In 1973 the Fullers took their plan to Africa. They settled
in Mbandaka, Zaire, and spent the next three years helping
more than 2,000 people build adequate homes. Inspired by

237

their success, they returned to the United States in 1976 with plans to make the program worldwide. They named their organization Habitat for Humanity International.

STAR POWER

The next eight years saw slow but steady growth for HFHI, but it was still mostly unknown outside of the people who were associated with it. That all changed in 1984, when the press learned that former president Jimmy Carter had become involved, and was heading to New York City on his first Habitat assignment. The Jimmy Carter Work Project pushed HFHI into the national spotlight, and Carter became an unofficial spokesperson for the group. Result: New HFHI affiliates began to pop up around the world. By 1985, there were 14 chapters in the United States and 7 overseas.

Their mission can be summed up in a statement they released back in the early 1970s: "What the poor need is not charity but capital, not caseworkers but co-workers. And what the rich need is a wise, honorable, and just way of sharing their overabundance."

Today, Habitat for Humanity is still going strong. They've helped build more than 200,000 homes, providing shelter to more than a million people around the world.

*　*　*

"Action is a great restorer and builder of confidence. Inaction is not only the result, but the cause, of fear. Perhaps the action you take will be successful; perhaps different action or adjustments will have to follow. But any action is better than no action at all."

—Norman Vincent Peale

MEDICAL MIRACLES

Never give up hope.

THE ENERGIZER HEART

In October 2004, Lori Acoby went to the doctor with strep throat. But after running some tests, the 32-year-old mother of two was given grave news: Her aorta was about to rupture. They tried repairing it, but the operation didn't work and Lori was told that she needed a new heart—and soon—if she was going to survive. A few months later, an air bubble found its way to Acoby's brain and caused a massive stroke. She was removed from the heart transplant list and placed on life support. There she lay, nearly brain dead, her heart being kept alive by a machine. Her condition became so severe that doctors gave up any hope for recovery. The decision was made to remove Acoby from life support; two priests were called in to perform last rites. But when the plug was pulled, Acoby's heart didn't stop—it kept beating. And then she woke up.

Her heart came back. Her brain came back. Her smile came back. The doctors have no clue why Lori's heart didn't stop when the life support was turned off. But she and her family are convinced that a miracle kept her alive long enough for her body to heal itself.

THE DISAPPEARING TUMOR

Brandon Conner was born with a lump near his spinal cord. It was diagnosed as neuroblastoma, a childhood cancer from which few babies recover. In rare cases, the tumor will go away on its own by the end of the first year, which is what his doctors hoped for. Because it was located right next to the spinal column, removing it would probably leave Brandon paralyzed for life. But the tumor didn't go away; it kept growing and growing. By the time Brandon was two, the doctors had no choice but to remove the golf ball–size tumor. The Conners agreed—they'd rather have a paralyzed Brandon than no Brandon at all. But then a strange thing happened. On the day before the surgery, doctors scanned Brandon's back to pinpoint the tumor's location. And it was gone. Doctors were baffled—no tumor of that size had ever just… disappeared. Three years later, Brandon's cancer hasn't even hinted at returning.

THE MIRACLE KID

When Dayla Porter was a year old, she needed open-heart surgery to repair two serious defects that limited the flow of oxygen to her lungs. But something went wrong during the surgery and Dayla's heart stopped beating. Doctors were able to revive her, but not fast enough. The little girl was left deaf and blind, and her heart couldn't beat on its own. Placed on a machine that pumped her blood and breathed for her, Dayla's hope was fading.

Then, two months later, while lying in her bed at the Cincinnati Children's Hospital, Dayla looked up at her mom and smiled. Somehow, her sight and hearing had returned and her heart had started beating on its own again.

Dubbed the "Miracle Kid" by her doctors, Dayla went on to have a relatively normal childhood, until she got the news that her heart had done a lifetime's worth of work in nine years, and would need to be replaced. "She's so resilient," her father said. "We believe her when she tells us she's going to be just fine." A year later they found a donor. At last report, Dayla, the Miracle Kid, is doing just fine.

THE MAGIC TOUCH, PART 3

In Part 2 (page 125), Louis Braille took a soldier's system for reading at night and invented a practical alphabet for the blind. But getting it accepted wasn't easy. Here's the third and final part of the story.

BRAVE NEW WORLD

Six dots changed everything. Where once Louis Braille and his classmates had struggled to decipher every letter on a page, soon they were reading 120 words a minute using Braille's six-dot system. They also began to write—something that had never been possible before. Now any blind person with a piece of paper, a stencil (called a slate), and a poking tool (called a stylus) could learn how to write. For the first time, the students could take notes during class instead of having to memorize every detail as it was spoken aloud.

More importantly, they could express themselves: record their innermost thoughts in diaries, compose songs, write poetry and stories, and exchange letters and love notes. And they could do it without help. Thanks to the determination of one 15-year-old boy, the blind would never be shut out again.

THE REACTION

...Not that people wouldn't still try to shut them out. Even within the Institute's faculty, the system Braille had created—which, to Captain Barbier's disgust, was coming to be known as *braille*—had its opponents. A few years after Braille became the school's first blind teacher at the age of 19, he fell ill and took a six-month leave of absence in 1843. During this time the Institute got a new director, a man named P. Armand Dufau. Dufau was opposed to braille, because he thought it made blind people "too independent." With Braille conva-lescing in the countryside, Dufau quickly moved to ban his writing system, seizing every slate, stylus, and scrap of paper with braille on it and burning them all, along with every book in the library—including Valentin Haüy's original raised-letter books. Then he switched the school over to the Alston System, a new raised-letter system that had been invented in Scotland.

FLIP-FLOP

The new regime lasted only a few months. Going against the Institute's rules, students continued to use braille to read and write, using whatever implements they could get their hands on—pins, needles, nails, dinner knives—preferring to take beatings and go without meals rather than give it up.

Finally one of Dufau's assistants, Joseph Gaudet, pointed out that braille was catching on at every school for the blind in France, and was spreading to other parts of Europe. That reflected well on the institute where it had originated—and since Dufau was its head, it made him look good, too. So why not leave it alone?

That was all it took. Dufau lifted the ban, and became one of braille's biggest boosters.

MAKING IT OFFICIAL

But although schools and other institutions for the blind embraced braille rapidly, recognition by governments took longer, thanks in large part to the fear that while braille was liberating for the blind, it might also be isolating because sighted people couldn't easily read it. The search for a system that the blind and the sighted could use with equal ease continued, but none was ever found.

Sadly, Louis Braille didn't live to see his writing system implemented nationally even in his own country; he died from tuberculosis at the age of 43, two years before France recognized braille as the official communication system for the blind in 1854. The rest of Europe held out until 1878, and it wasn't until 1912 that braille was formally accepted in the United States. Today braille has been adapted to almost every major language in the world, and 40 million people have learned it—making it the most widely used medium of literacy for the blind. Pretty amazing, when you consider that it all started with a 12-year-old boy who wanted to read.

Perhaps the most lasting tribute to Braille's new language came from one of its most famous supporters, Helen Keller:

> Braille has been a most precious aid to me in many ways. It made my going to college possible—it was the only method by which I could take notes of lectures. All my examination papers were copied for me in this system. I use braille as a spider uses its web—to catch thoughts that flit across my mind for speeches, messages and manuscripts.

*   *   *

INVENTIVE INSPIRATION

• When Mark Gottlieb was a kid, he was playing in the driveway and his father ran into him because he couldn't see him. That was the inspiration that led Gottlieb to invent the Back-Up Alert—a regular taillight bulb that beeps to warn others when a car is backing up.

• Henry Heimlich, the developer of the Heimlich Maneuver, invented a valve for draining chest wounds. His inspiration for the slowly deflating device: the Whoopee Cushion.

RAGS TO RICHES

Some of the world's most successful people came from very humble—and sometimes painful—beginnings.

• **LAZAR MEIR** was born in Russia in 1885. While he was still a baby, his family fled the oppressive government and emigrated to Canada. Lazar grew up in poverty and was regularly abused by his father, but loved and supported by his mother, who urged him to follow his dreams. So when he was 19, he moved to Boston and changed his name to Louis B. Mayer. He sold scrap metal until he made enough money to buy a burlesque house. When movies became popular, Mayer converted it into a movie theater. After building a chain of theaters, he moved to Los Angeles in 1918. There, he partnered with Samuel Goldwyn and Marcus Loew (Metro Pictures) to create Metro-Goldwyn-Mayer—the biggest and most profitable studio of Hollywood's Golden Age.

• **OPRAH WINFREY** was born to unwed teenage parents who were so poor they had to send her to live with her grandmother. Oprah later moved back in with her mom, who was ill-equipped to care for her. From age 9 to 13, Oprah was molested by several male relatives, and at age 14, the confused and angry teenager gave birth to a stillborn baby. Not knowing what else to do, she moved in with her father, Vernon Winfrey, who had managed to turn his own life around and was now in a position to help his daughter. And that's what he did. Vernon made Oprah read a book every week and write a report on it. She earned good grades in school and got her first job as a reporter at 19. Today, Oprah is the "queen of the talk show" and one of the most successful women in American history.

THE PROVERBIAL TRUTH

Folk wisdom to inspire you from around the world.

No matter how long the night, the day is sure to come.
—Congo

One kind word can warm three winter months.
—Japan

One who asks a question is a fool for five minutes; one who does not ask a question remains a fool forever.
—China

Do not look where you fell, but where you slipped.
—Africa

He that can't endure the bad, will not live to see the good.
—Israel

You'll never plow a field by turning it over in your mind.
—Ireland

Hold a true friend with both hands.
—Nigeria

In every woman there is a queen. Speak to the queen and the queen will answer.
—Norway

More things grow in the garden than the gardener sows.
—Spain

Our first teacher is our own heart.
—Cheyenne

It is no longer good enough to cry peace, we must act peace.
—Shenandoah

Let the past drift away with the water.
—Japan

You must act as if it is impossible to fail.
—Ghana

A beautiful thing is never perfect.
—Egypt

TRASH LADY

When is trash disposal inspiring? When it creates
civic pride and new jobs for a city in trouble.

TOO MUCH GARBAGE

Back in the 1980s, the city of Lima, Peru, was in crisis. Its five million citizens were generating thousands of tons of garbage per day, but trash was only collected from wealthier neighborhoods, and only 60% of it was processed by city sanitation workers. The rest was thrown into the nearby Chillon River or dumped in vacant lots in the city's slums. One neighborhood, El Cono Norte, got the worst of it. In addition to the trash dumped there by the city, its one million residents were generating 600 tons of trash of their own every day. Result: The neighborhood was piled high in garbage, and the water supply was contaminated.

An industrial engineering student named Albina Ruiz decided to look for a solution. It didn't take long for her to discover one reason why the government sanitation program wasn't working: At El Cono Norte, the residents weren't paying the monthly garbage-removal fee. Why? They couldn't afford it.

JOBS AND CLEAN STREETS

Ruiz addressed both problems—trash and poverty—by starting an organization she called Ciudad Saludable (Healthy City). She recruited residents of El Cono Norte to be "micro-entrepreneurs," setting up small businesses to collect and process the garbage. They were also responsible for collecting a trash-removal fee from each household, which Ruiz insisted be affordable. The cost: $1.50 per month.

Unlike the municipal trash pickup, the Ciudad Saludable service was something the people of El Cono Norte were willing to pay for—it was their neighbors taking care of the trash, not the untrusted government. Result: The program beautified the neighborhood almost instantly and created dozens of new jobs, paying some people of the area a living wage for the first time.

So what did they do with all that trash? Some of it went to conventional landfills, but paper and other items were sorted out for recycling and sold to raw-goods processors. Food waste was converted to organic compost, which was then sold to the city to help grow plants and trees in parks.

INTERNACIONAL

The program was so successful that Ruiz expanded it. Now hundreds of people work in Ciudad Saludable programs in 20 cities throughout Peru. Even the federal governments of Peru, Venezuela, and El Salvador have asked Ruiz to oversee their waste-management programs. What's more, thanks to her lobbying efforts, legislation was passed in 2000 making recycling mandatory in Lima, Peru's largest city.

"What most people see as a problem," she says, "I see as a possibility."

*   *   *

JUST PUT ON YOUR SHOES!

"Wanting to reform the world without discovering one's true self is like trying to cover the world with leather to avoid the pain of walking on stones and thorns. It is much simpler to wear shoes."

—Sri Ramana Maharshi

WORDS TO LIVE BY

A few more of the best things ever said.

"It is not length of life, but depth of life."
　　—Ralph Waldo Emerson

"People rarely succeed unless they have fun in what they are doing."
　　　　—Dale Carnegie

"Never let the fear of striking out get in your way."
　　　　—Babe Ruth

"We must accept finite disappointment, but we must never lose infinite hope."
　　—Martin Luther King Jr.

"The key to happiness depends not on our circumstances, but on our dispositions."
　　—Martha Washington

"May you live all the days of your life."
　　　—Jonathan Swift

"He that does good for good's sake seeks neither paradise nor reward, but he is sure of both in the end."
　　　　—William Penn

"For myself, I am an optimist—it does not seem to be much use being anything else."
　　—Winston Churchill

"Real generosity toward the future lies in giving all to the present."
　　　—Albert Camus

"Not being able to do everything is no excuse for not doing everything you can."
　　—Ashleigh Brilliant

"The wisest mind has something yet to learn."
　　—George Santayana

THE GREAT POZO

Even if the cards are stacked against you,
you have to play the hand you were dealt.

HUMBLE BEGINNINGS

Born May 5, 1977, into an impoverished family in Ghana, Emmanuel Ofusu Yeboah seemed cursed. As soon as his father saw the boy's hopelessly deformed right leg (he was born without a shin bone), he thought it was a punishment from a deity and ran away. Neighbors advised Emmanuel's mother to "see him off," which in Ghanian tradition means to leave the child to die in the forest.

It would have been considered an acceptable choice. Two million people in the West African nation—about 10% of the population—are disabled and shunned by society, victims of centuries-old prejudice that considers them mistakes of nature and unfit to live. And if they survive childhood, the disabled in Ghana can look forward only to a life as beggars on the streets.

But Emmanuel's mother, Comfort Yeboah, refused to get rid of her child. Her faith in her first-born son was so great that she did the unthinkable: She enrolled him in school. In Ghana, as in many developing countries, education is so valuable that it is reserved for those children thought capable of using it to make a better future for their family. To send a disabled child to school was to waste a precious resource. But except for his leg, Emmanuel was perfectly abled—he was smart, strong, and physically fit. So Comfort persisted.

STUBBORN

Following his mother's lead, Emmanuel refused to resign

himself to being a beggar. Every day before school, he worked shining shoes for pennies a day. When his mother became sick and could no longer work, Emmanuel left school and worked full time, becoming the sole breadwinner of his family. It was hard, but he still refused to become a beggar.

In 1991, desperate to find better work, Emmanuel moved to Accra, Ghana's capital, 200 miles from his village. Alone and just 14, he witnessed for the first time the harsh reality of being disabled in Ghana. He saw that the disabled could earn as much as $10 a day if they would crawl through the filthy streets, begging for coins. But Emmanuel was determined to work for a living. He found a job making shoes that paid him $2 a day. He kept only what he needed to survive, and sent the rest back to his family.

Meanwhile, his mother grew weaker and weaker. During a phone call in 1997 she reminded him that his life was a gift and that "disability is not inability." She made him promise once again that he would never become a beggar. The next day, Comfort Yeboah died.

A NEW PATH

Strengthened by his mother's dying words, Emmanuel decided to do something for the disabled in Ghana. To raise public awareness, he would ride a bicycle across the country. He needed a special bike, which he got from the Challenged Athlete's Foundation in San Diego, California. "I want to ride a bicycle across Ghana," he wrote to them, "to create a brighter future for the disabled."

In July 2002, he made the trip, pedaling a mountain bike with one leg all the way across Ghana. Throughout his journey, he wore a shirt emblazoned with the words "The Pozo," slang for "The Cripple." "I want to send a message to change perceptions," he said. "The only way to do that is by example." His example worked. The Ghanian media covered his ride and dubbed him "the Great Pozo." Soon people all over Ghana were talking about the plight of the disabled and how perceptions had to change. Emmanuel had become a national hero.

Within a year, he become an international advocate for the disabled. He competed in two triathlons in the United States, received a prosthetic limb from Loma Linda University Medical Hospital (they amputated his bad leg below the knee), was the recipient of more than $50,000 in grant money to continue his work, and, in a world where mobility is paramount to success, distributed more than 250 wheelchairs to the disabled back home in Ghana. He continues to be an example, working to help others like him live their lives with dignity.

*   *   *

THE WRITE STUFF

What inspired these writers to produce their masterpieces?

- Marcel Proust wrote in a cork-lined room.
- Dame Edith Sitwell liked to lie in an open coffin before writing.
- Truman Capote wrote while lying down.
- T.S. Eliot believed he was more creative when he had a cold.
- Willa Cather read the Bible before writing.
- Colette picked fleas from her cat to focus her mind.
- D. H. Lawrence liked to get the creative juices flowing by climbing naked up mulberry trees.

BOOKS THAT ROCKED THE WORLD

Everyone's read a book that had a strong impact on them. But a few books are so powerful, they've had an impact on millions.

SILENT SPRING, by Rachel Carson (1962)

In 1945 a new pesticide came into widespread use in the United States—DDT. Unlike other pesticides, which could kill a few species of insects, DDT could kill hundreds. Many ecologists worried about its environmental and health effects. One, a biologist for the U.S. Fish and Wildlife Service named Rachel Carson, began writing anti-DDT articles—but no magazine would publish them, even though she was a best-selling author. By 1958, when birds in Massachusetts were dying from DDT exposure, Carson began work on her book *Silent Spring*. She detailed how DDT enters the food chain by accumulating in animal fat, and how after humans eat those animals, the DDT is stored in their bodies—leading to cancer and genetic damage.

Impact: *Silent Spring* became a bestseller. Although the chemical industry tried to discredit Carson, claiming that pesticides prevented the Earth from being overrun with diseased insects, President Kennedy ordered a federal investigation. Result: DDT was banned in 1972. The book also helped spawned the modern environmentalist movement.

THE COMMON SENSE BOOK OF BABY AND CHILD CARE, by Dr. Benjamin Spock (1946)

The conventional wisdom of parenting in the 1940s was that doctors knew all the answers, and there was only one way to do anything—their way. Benjamin Spock was a pediatrician, but he'd also studied psychology, which gave him a sense of the emotional aspects of childhood and parenting. His conclusion: The conventional wisdom was flawed; it was too harsh and not effective. Spock said that parents, not doctors, were the experts on their own children. He also downplayed the one-method approach, urging parents to be flexible and treat their children as individuals. He advocated picking up babies when they cried, contrary to the popular belief that this "spoiled" babies and prevented them from learning to be self-reliant. Most of all, Spock's book comforted parents, telling them, "you know more than you think you know." Why? Because common sense and instinct are strong when it comes to child-rearing.

Impact: In 60 years, the book has gone through seven editions, been translated into 39 languages, and has sold 50 million copies. (Ironically, Spock once commented that if he knew he was going to write the most influential parenting book of all time, he wouldn't have done it because he didn't think he knew enough.)

THE JUNGLE, by Upton Sinclair (1906)

After reading about a strike at a Chicago meat-packing plant, Sinclair spent two months observing the Chicago stockyards. He found sickening practices in the slaughterhouses, corrupt bosses, and underpaid immigrants working 12 hours a day and living in dilapidated tenements. Drawing from what he'd seen, Sinclair wrote *The Jungle*, the fictional story of Jurgis Rudkus, who hauls steer carcasses for a living, and then gets fired when he beats up his immoral boss. The book ends with workers unionizing. Five publishers refused to print the politically volatile book, but Doubleday accepted it in 1906.

Impact: *The Jungle* immediately caused public outrage over sordid meat-industry secrets: dead rats were tossed into sausage grinders, animal guts were swept off the floor and packaged as "potted meat," and inspectors were bribed to look the other way. President Theodore Roosevelt sent investigators to Chicago to see if Sinclair was right, and found that conditions were actually *worse*. Congress soon passed the Meat Inspection Act and the Pure Food and Drug Act of 1906. These formed the basis of the Food and Drug Administration, which today oversees safety of food and medicines in the United States.

COMMON SENSE, by Thomas Paine (1776)

American colonist Thomas Paine held political views that were radical at the time: he opposed monarchy and slavery, and advocated social security, minimum wage, and self-rule for the colonies. In January 1776 he published *Common Sense*, a pamphlet that laid out in simple terms why the colonies should be independent from Britain. Among his reasons: America comprised many cultures in addition to Britain's, the lag time on news between England and the colonies was too long, and the British Empire was likely to drag America into European wars.

Impact: More than 120,000 copies of *Common Sense* were distributed, and it soon led to widespread support of independent government. Thomas Jefferson used ideas from Payne's pamphlet in the Declaration of Independence, a cornerstone of the first modern democracy.

UNCLE TOM'S CABIN, by Harriet Beecher Stowe (1852)

In 1850 the United States was already politically split over slavery. But to appease pro-slavery states, Congress passed the

Fugitive Slave Act, imposing a $1,000 fine on anyone who assisted a runaway slave. In response, Ohio abolitionist Harriet Beecher Stowe angrily wrote *Uncle Tom's Cabin*, a novel about the evils of slavery. Stowe based the sprawling story of vicious slave owners, slave markets, families split up, and thwarted attempts at escape on information from former slaves.

Impact: When *Uncle Tom's Cabin* was published in 1852, it became the best-selling novel of the 19th century. It was also the second-best-selling book in the entire world (after the Bible), and was translated into 23 languages. But most importantly, *Uncle Tom's Cabin* helped fuel the growing anti-slavery sentiment in the northern states. This led to the Civil War in 1861, which eventually ended slavery.

*   *   *

STOP AND SMELL THE LAUGHTER

"Why is it you can measure distance by time—say, 'How far away is it?' 'Oh, about 20 minutes'—but it doesn't work the other way? 'When do you get off work?' 'Around 3 miles.'"

—**Jerry Seinfeld**

"I would imagine if you could understand Morse Code, a tap dancer would drive you crazy."

—**Mitch Hedberg**

"When I was born I was so surprised, I couldn't talk for a year and a half."

—**Gracie Allen**

IT AIN'T OVER YET

Another amazing sports comeback.

LIFE OF RILEY

The 1999 New York Knicks barely squeaked into the NBA playoffs. As the Eastern Conference's #8 seeded team, they'd have to play the #1 team, the Miami Heat in the first round. At the time, it was the league's most intense rivalry—former Knicks coach Pat Riley was now the Heat's head coach. Not only that, this was the third straight year the two teams were facing each other in the playoffs. In 1997 Miami beat New York four games to three in the semi-finals; in 1998 New York eliminated Miami in the first round.

This year, Miami was heavily favored to win, but New York battled hard and took the series all the way to a deciding Game 5. For most of the game, the score was close. With less than 10 seconds remaining in the 4th quarter, the Heat were leading 77–76. Would Miami hold on to the lead?

FINAL SECONDS

The Knicks' Latrell Sprewell had possession of the ball. Miami's Terry Porter tried to steal it, but knocked it out of bounds. Miami argued that Sprewell had touched the ball last, but the officials didn't agree. With 4.5 seconds to go, the Knicks inbounded the ball. Charlie Ward passed it to Allan Houston. Houston dribbled the ball, first around Miami's Dan Majerle and then around Tim Hardaway, and put up a 14-foot jump shot...with one hand...from the corner of the court. Time left: 0:00.8 (that's 8/10th of a second). The ball lingered on the rim for a fraction of a moment...and went in. Against all odds, the Knicks won the game, 78–77.

LONG HARD CLIMB

Don't let "minor setbacks" keep you from reaching your summit.

PEAK EXPERIENCES
Miriam Richards has climbed to the highest points in 49 of the 50 United States and has also scaled mountains in South America and Africa. That's not so unusual—lots of people have. But Miriam Richards isn't a typical mountain climber: She's completely deaf, she's heavy-set, and she has multiple sclerosis.

Born in 1965 in Vancouver, British Columbia, Richards has been deaf all her life. She began climbing in 1995 without any formal training, but that first year was almost her last. While trying to ascend Mt. Hood in Oregon, she fell 1,000 feet down a rocky slope, breaking her jaw, puncturing an eye, tearing off a kneecap, and shattering a shin. Then Richards had to wait six hours in the snow before she was rescued. But that didn't stop her. After a painful year-long rehabilitation, she went against her doctor's advice and returned to the mountains.

That year, Richards set a goal: "highpointing"—reaching the highest point in all 50 states. She wanted to be the first deaf person to do it. In 1999 she faced Mt. Hood again… and peaked it like a pro. In 2000, over a span of two days, Richards highpointed six states.

Currently, Richards is training to climb the 20,320 ft. Denali Peak in Alaska—the only state she hasn't highpointed. In addition to dealing with freezing temperatures and thin air, Richards will have to keep her stress level down to ward off symptoms of M.S. But it's a good bet that her positive attitude will get her to the top.

"Courage doesn't always roar. Sometimes courage is the little voice at the end of the day that says, 'I'll try again tomorrow.'"

—**Mary Anne Radmacher**

WORDS OF COURAGE

To find your way in this world, you have to be brave.
Here are a few pointers from some folks who know.

"Courage is what it takes to stand up and speak; courage is also what it takes to sit down and listen."

—**Winston Churchill**

"The best way out is always through."

—**Robert Frost**

"You gain strength, courage, and confidence by every experience in which you really stop to look fear in the face. You must do the thing which you think you cannot do."

—**Eleanor Roosevelt**

"To dare is to lose one's footing momentarily. To *not* dare is to lose oneself entirely."

—**Søren Kierkegaard**

"Courage is being scared to death—but saddling up anyway."

—**John Wayne**

"Whoever said anybody has a right to give up?"

—**Marian Wright Edelman**

"Courage is reckoned the greatest of all virtues; because, unless a man has that virtue, he has no security for preserving any other."

—**Samuel Johnson**

"Courage is being afraid but going on anyhow."

—**Dan Rather**

"Don't be afraid to take a big step if one is indicated. You cannot cross a chasm in two small jumps."

—**David Lloyd George**

"Life shrinks or expands in proportion to one's courage."

—**Anaïs Nin**

"Speak your mind, even if your voice shakes."

—**Maggie Kuhn**

THE HARLEM HELLFIGHTERS

The men of the 369th distinguished themselves as Americans, fighting for the French. Their acts of bravery inspired the world...and helped conquer segregation.

NO THANKS

In the months leading up to the U.S. entry into World War I in 1917, men living in the Harlem neighborhood of New York City—like so many men across the country—began volunteering for military service.

But the men of Harlem were black, and they were volunteering to fight in an army that didn't want them... at least not as fighters. The U.S. military was segregated, and the War Department didn't allow black soldiers to fight alongside white soldiers, when it allowed them to fight at all. Most blacks in the military ended up in labor battalions— they cooked, cleaned, loaded and unloaded ships, quarried stone, laid railroad tracks, cleaned stables, and worked on construction sites. If a job was demeaning or dangerous— such as recovering dead bodies from the battlefield—it was often left for black soldiers to do. They were shut out of the officer corps, too. Even the all-black 15th New York Infantry Regiment was headed by a white officer, Colonel William Hayward.

SELF-STARTERS

The men of Harlem were patriots—they wanted to fight, to strike a blow against Germany, which had been sinking American ships on the high seas. They also had a personal reason for fighting: They believed that if they proved their worth on the battlefield, they'd be proving their worth as Americans, and perhaps they could bring an end to discrimination at home.

But their first battle was just getting *to* the battlefield.

The 15th New York Regiment didn't have its own recruiting station, so it set one up in a cigar store. Harlem didn't have an armory (where troops would normally drill), so they drilled in vacant lots, on city streets, and in a local dance hall. The military didn't issue them uniforms, equipment, or weapons, so they hustled up what they could. Many drilled with broomsticks or wooden guns while wearing civilian clothes.

PERSHING'S SOLUTION

Finally, in December 1917, the 15th Infantry Regiment— now redesignated as the 369th Infantry Regiment—sailed for France. But they spent their first four months of active duty doing just what they'd hoped to avoid—they were assigned to labor service. Meanwhile, General John Pershing, commander of the American Expeditionary Forces, tried to figure out what to do with them and three other all-black regiments on their way to Europe.

By now the war had been raging for nearly three years, and the British and French had lost more than a million men in combat. The Germans had fought their way to within 60 miles of Paris, and the French army was near collapse. The French and the British wanted to use American soldiers as replacements in their own ranks, but Pershing wanted to keep them as an independent army serving under his command. The four all-black regiments provided the solution to both of Pershing's problems: By giving the "unworthy" black regiments to the French, he helped America's ally, while keeping white American soldiers under his own command.

The 369th was the first regiment to be reassigned to the French army. The men exchanged all their American gear for French equipment, keeping only their uniforms, which they wore with French helmets and French belts. Some adjustments were easier to make than others, but most important to the troops was the fact that the French army didn't practice segregation. The men of the 369th were being treated as equals—for the first time in their lives.

TOO EQUAL

The black troops were treated so fairly, in fact, that American officials became alarmed. If the soldiers got too used to being treated as equals on the battlefield, what would happen when they came home after the war?

Pershing's headquarters confronted the challenge head-on: A French officer was given the task of drafting a memo titled "Secret Information Concerning the Black American Troops." Its stated purpose was to give French officers "an exact idea of the position occupied by the Negro in the United States," and to instruct them on the proper treatment of black Americans under their command:

> We cannot deal with [black] officers on the same plane as with the white American officers without deeply wounding the latter. We must not eat with them, shake hands with them or seek to talk or meet with them outside of the requirements of military service. We must not commend too highly the black American troops, particularly in the presence of [white] Americans. It is all right to recognize their good qualities and their services, but only in moderate terms. Make a point of keeping the [French public] from "spoiling" the Negroes.

The French officers who received the memo ignored it and continued to give the black soldiers the respect they deserved.

A FIGHTING CHANCE

Most importantly, the French officers gave the men a chance to prove themselves in battle. Their first test came in the Argonne Forest west of Verdun.

One night in May 1918, two soldiers of the 369th, Sergeant Henry Johnson and Private Needham Roberts, were occupying an observation post forward of the front lines in the area known as "no-man's land," when they were suddenly attacked by a squad of German soldiers. Johnson and Roberts fought back with incredible ferocity: When they ran out of bullets, Roberts clubbed men with the butt of his rifle while Johnson fought with his bolo knife. Both men survived the fight, and when the battle was over, four Germans lay dead and 32 others were wounded. Johnson became the first American in the war to win the Croix de Guerre for bravery. (He didn't qualify for the Congressional Medal of Honor because only soldiers fighting in U.S. military units are eligible; even if he had been, Medals of Honor were never awarded to blacks.)

"RATTLESNAKE REGIMENT"

The rest of the 369th quickly earned a reputation as fierce fighters as well. They flushed the Germans out of an area called Belleau Wood, then saw action near Manancourt. The men spent an unheard-of 130 consecutive days on the front lines, received a week's leave, and went right back, serving as part of the left flank of General Pershing's advance through a heavily fortified section of the Argonne Forest. The fighting was savage—the men of the 369th clawed their way from one bomb crater to another, eventually capturing an important railroad junction at Sechault, where they took so many casualties that every man in the regiment was awarded the Croix de Guerre. They continued on from there, advancing more than 14 kilometers (nearly 9 miles) into heavily defended German-held territory. They fought so fiercely that the Germans nicknamed them *blutdurstig schwarze Männer*— "bloodthirsty black men"—and English-speaking soldiers called them the Harlem Hellfighters and the Rattlesnake Regiment.

DISTINGUISHED SERVICE

The men of the 369th went on to distinguish themselves as one of the toughest fighting regiments in U.S. history. They spent 191 days in front-line combat, more than any other American unit in the war, and received the most medals. Not one member of the regiment was ever taken prisoner, and they never gave up an inch of ground to the enemy. "My men never retire," Colonel Hayward explained to a French officer in the heat of battle, "they go forward or they die."

The U.S. Army would not be desegregated for another 30 years, when the Korean War finally brought full integration to the military. But the valiant service of the 369th Infantry Regiment influenced generations of African Americans who came after them.

*   *   *

A Happy Thought: According to a 1998 survey, Americans say happiness is the most important thing in life—even more important than money, moral goodness, or going to Heaven.

INTERNATIONAL FABLES

Here are some lesser-known fables from around the world.

THE BEAR AND THE TRAVELERS (Russia)

Two men were walking through the woods when they spotted a bear up ahead. One of the men quickly climbed into a tree and hid in some branches. The other, remembering that bears will not touch a dead body, dropped to the ground and held his breath. The bear came right up to him, sniffed at his "corpse," and whispered into the man's ear. Then the bear left. The other man quickly climbed down from the tree and asked his friend what the bear had said.

"He gave me some good advice," the man replied. "He said, 'Never travel with a friend who deserts you at the approach of danger.'"

THE WOLF AND THE DOG (France)

A wolf was nearly dead with hunger when he happened upon a very plump dog. The wolf asked the dog for some food, so the dog took him home, promising to share both his work and his food with the wolf. "Work?" asked the wolf.

"Yes," said the dog. "My master feeds me all I want, in exchange for a few chores." The wolf then noticed that the dog had a worn patch of hair around his neck and asked what it was. "Oh, nothing," said the dog. "That's where the collar is put on at night to keep me chained up."

The wolf politely said good-bye and left, for he knew that although he might be hungry, at least he had his freedom.

THE PITCHER OF NUTS (China)

A boy plunged his hand into a pitcher full of nuts and grabbed as many as he could fit in his fist. But when he tried to pull his hand out, he couldn't—it was stuck. The neck of the pitcher was so narrow that he couldn't get his bulging fist through it. Of course, he knew that if he dropped the nuts, his hand would easily slip out, but then he wouldn't have *any* nuts. Unwilling to drop the nuts, the boy burst into tears at his predicament. A kindly bystander saw him struggling and gave him this advice, "Don't be greedy. Be satisfied with half the quantity, and you will easily be able to withdraw your hand." And that's what he did.

THE BICKERING OXEN (Kenya)

A lion often prowled around a field where four oxen lived. He had tried to attack them many times, but whenever he approached, the oxen lined up in a formation to protect themselves. They turned their tails to one another, so that whichever way the lion tried to approach, he would always be met by the horns of an ox. One day, one of the oxen started to wonder whether this was the most effective method of holding the lion at bay. He expressed his doubt, and soon all the oxen began quarreling about the proper way to defend themselves. The lion sat patiently and watched as each of the oxen got angry and went, alone, to a separate corner of the field. That's when the lion attacked them one by one, and ate all four. The moral: Together we stand, divided we fall.

*   *   *

CRITICAL OBSERVATION

Finnish composer Jean Sibelius once told a young musician after a poorly received concert, "Remember, son, there is no city in the world where they have a statue of a critic."

OLD IS BEAUTIFUL

We're not sure how we ended up with three inspiring
tales about turtles in this book...but we did.

HOW OLD?
On November 15, 2005, the Australia Zoo on
Queensland's Sunshine Coast celebrated the birthday
of its oldest resident, Harriet the giant tortoise. How old was
she? Well, when she was born:

• There were only 24 states in the United States.

• Andrew Jackson was president.

• California, Texas, Arizona, Nevada, and Colorado were
all part of Mexico.

Harriet was 175 years old—the oldest known living creature on the planet—and still going strong. "It's amazing," says
keeper Kelly Jackson. "The second you tell people Harriet's
age, they just fall in love with her. When you look at Harriet,
you're looking at history."

AMAZING JOURNEY

According to the zoo, Harriet was brought to England in
1835 by none other than Charles Darwin. He had captured
her and two other tortoises on trips to the Galapagos Islands
aboard his famous ship, the HMS *Beagle*. The many different
species of giant tortoise that Darwin found on the islands
played a crucial role in formulating his theory of evolution.

But the cold English climate proved unhealthy for the
tortoises, so in 1841 one of Darwin's crewmembers took all
three to Australia, where they eventually found a home in the
Brisbane Botanical Gardens.

THE GOOD LIFE

It was at the Botanical Gardens that Harriet was first given a name: Harry, after the curator, Harry Oakman. But Oakman can be excused for his mistake; it's not easy to tell the sex of a tortoise. It wasn't until 1960—more than 100 years later—that staff members discovered "he" was actually a "she," and renamed her Harriet. (This is also the reason that Harriet has never mated; zookeepers were pairing her with other females.)

Harriet lived at the Gardens until they were closed in 1952. (The two other tortoises had long since died.) From there she was moved to another sanctuary in New South Wales, then in 1987 she was bought by the Australia Zoo, which is owned by "Crocodile Hunter" Steve Irwin.

Harriet, now a hefty 330 pounds, is the zoo's star attraction. When she's not dozing, which is fairly often, she's happy to get a scratch on the chin, accept a snack of zucchini, beans, parsley, or bok choy—or give children rides around the park on her back.

BIRTHDAY GIRL

On November 15, the day chosen to be Harriet's birthday, the staff makes a huge cake for zoo visitors and gives her a bag of her favorite food—hibiscus flowers—which she munches while everybody sings the birthday song. Irwin has promised that Harriet will spend the rest of her days at the park, and that could be a while. No one knows for sure how long giant tortoises can live, and Harriet's outlived most of the scientists who've studied her. So stock up on candles—there may be quite a few "happy birthdays" for Harriet yet to come.

DR. JOHN SNOW, EPIDEMIOLOGIST

A fascinating story about a man who figured out how to save thousands of lives...even though he couldn't get anyone to listen to him.

THE FIRST GLOBAL EPIDEMIC

When cholera struck London in 1831, anyone who was up on world affairs wasn't surprised. Cholera had been spreading along the world's trade routes for 14 years, devastating one city after another as it traveled around the globe. Any densely packed city along the way was vulnerable.

Cholera, a disease of the intestinal tract that causes severe diarrhea, can kill its victims in a matter of days with violent and painful dehydration. Today it is easy to treat—and even easier to prevent from spreading. But in London in 1831, it killed 30,000 people...and no one knew what to do.

THINK AGAIN

The conventional medical wisdom of the day was that cholera wasn't contagious, but was caused by an "atmospheric miasma" emanating from the poorer, more crowded parts of town. Civil authorities burned pitch and tar in the streets in an effort to ward off sickness by "purifying" the air. Meanwhile, doctors treated patient after patient without washing their hands or sterilizing surgical instruments.

John Snow was the most famous of a small group of doctors who thought differently. After treating victims during the first outbreak, and again when cholera returned to London in 1848 to kill another 50,000, he published a controversial pamphlet claiming that cholera was, in fact, contagious. The principal agent of its transmission: sewage-tainted water.

Today Snow's views seem obvious, but at the time, the medical community scoffed. Most doctors believed that environmental factors caused certain types of people to be susceptible to the atmospheric miasmas. They thought of cholera as a disease that primarily affected poor people, who were often alcoholics and lacked the moral fiber necessary to ward off cholera vapors, which could strike at any time.

When cholera struck Britain yet again in 1854, Snow was ready. He needed hard data to show that cities could prevent future outbreaks by building decent sewers and providing everyone with access to clean water. And the new epidemic gave him the numbers to prove his case.

THE BROAD STREET PUMP

The following year, Snow published his findings in his book *On the Mode of Communication of Cholera*, now considered a pioneering work in the field of epidemiology. The most famous study Snow presented concerned a public water pump on Broad Street in London. Neighborhood residents who drew their water from the Broad Street well had significantly higher cholera rates than those whose water came from other sources. A few examples stood out:

• The inmates of a nearby workhouse that had its own well were spared infection, as were workers at the Broad Street Brewery, who were given free beer and never drank water at work.

• Several individuals from uninfected neighborhoods became sick after visiting friends on Broad Street and drinking the water.

• One woman who had moved from the area died because she thought Broad Street water tasted so good she had it brought to her new neighborhood.

Another of Snow's studies documented the case of a landlord who received complaints that the contents of a cesspit were leaking into his tenants' well. He went to inspect, and

> On looking at the water and smelling it, he said
> that he could perceive nothing the matter with it.
> He was asked if he would taste it, and he drank a
> glass of it. This occurred on a Wednesday, he went
> home, was taken ill with the cholera, and died on
> the Saturday following, there being no cholera in
> his own neighbourhood at the time.

ACCEPTANCE

Snow turned out to be right about cholera. But it wasn't until 20 years later, when the cholera bacterium was finally identified under a microscope, that his views became fully accepted.

So the next time you flush your toilet, thank Dr. Snow for protecting your drinking water from sewage contamination. Though cholera still poses a threat to nations without proper water-treatment facilities, the disease has been virtually eliminated in industrialized nations—all because of one doctor's vision and persistence.

*   *   *

"In a room where people unanimously maintain a conspiracy of silence, one word of truth sounds like a pistol shot."
—Czeslaw Milosz

WELCOME TO DELANCEY STREET

They went from hardened criminals to productive members of society. How? Read on.

SELF-HELP

Would you hire a moving company or eat in a restaurant run by ex-convicts? You may think twice, but in San Francisco it's quite common these days.

It all began in 1971, when a woman named Mimi Silbert was overseeing a criminal-psychology clinic at the University of California, Berkeley. One afternoon a former thief and recovering alcoholic named John Maher approached her about starting a new kind of rehabilitation clinic: one in which ex-cons counseled and supported each other, instead of depending on social workers and professional staff. Silbert had been kicking around the same idea, so she agreed to work with Maher on setting up a program.

SOMETHING NEW

First, they came up with a list of organizing principles::

• The program would operate on an "each one teach one" principle—veterans of the program would be expected to teach what they'd learned to new arrivals. There would be no paid professional staff whatsoever; not even Silbert or Maher would receive a salary.

• It would be organized as a collective, free of charge to the clients—but they would also be expected to work to help support it.

• The program wouldn't accept any government funds. Silbert and Maher weren't necessarily worried about what kinds of strings would be attached; they just didn't want to set an example of solving problems by asking for government assistance. They would, however, accept donations from the public.

• Unlike other rehab programs that addressed a single issue, such as substance abuse or job training, this program would focus on teaching all the skills ex-cons needed to live honest, productive lives—academics, values, personal accountability, and even how to speak and dress properly. "We see ourselves as a kind of university that teaches them how to live," Silbert explains.

GETTING STARTED

Silbert, the child of Eastern European immigrants, believes the challenges convicts face in re-entering society are similar to what immigrants experience when they come to the United States. Immigrant communities are like giant extended families; everyone depends on everyone else. So she and Maher decided to name their program Delancey Street, after a famous immigrant neighborhood in New York's Lower East Side.

They borrowed $1,000 (from a loan shark) and used the money to rent an apartment for themselves and four ex-convicts. The early days weren't easy; the ex-cons had trouble identifying with Silbert, who came from a middle-class background and had never been in trouble with the law. Finally, one of them challenged her by asking, "What do you know about what we've gone through?" Silbert barked back, "I don't have to have shot dope. That's not a great talent. What I *do* know is how to live life successfully and decently, and if you keep your mouth shut long enough, I'll teach you that."

By the end of the first year, more than 100 ex-convicts and drug addicts were participating in the program. They pooled the money they made working odd jobs and used it to buy an old mansion in San Francisco's Pacific Heights neighborhood. By 1988 the program had grown to serve more than 350 residents living in three buildings.

DELANCEY STREET BASICS

Most new "immigrants," as Delancey Street calls them, enter the program as parolees, on probation, or serving an alternative to a prison sentence. The typical immigrant is functionally illiterate, has no job skills, has been in prison at least four times, and has spent more than a decade addicted to drugs.

• Immigrants are asked to commit to Delancey Street for a minimum of two years, although they're free to leave the program at any time.

• Each new immigrant receives a haircut, new clothing, an apartment within the complex, and a mentor. Each is also assigned an entry-level job in one of Delancey Street's businesses.

• Residents work a full eight-hour day, then spend evenings taking classes or attending meetings. Very little time is unstructured; the residents are kept occupied to prevent a relapse into substance abuse or criminal activity.

SURVIVAL SKILLS

Before they can "graduate" from Delancey Street, residents must master three different types of jobs: one involving physical labor, one in an office, and one that deals with the public. Delancey Street operates more than 20 different businesses, including a restaurant, a café, a catering company, a bookstore, and a very successful moving company. The businesses train the residents while also generating most of the income that allows Delancey Street to remain self-sufficient.

The average stay in the program is four years, but residents are free to stay for as long as they want. Some have lived at Delancey Street for more than 25 years. Residents who leave too early and slip back into criminal activity, alcoholism, or drug addiction can apply for readmission.

Life in Delancey Street is no walk in the park. For many residents it's the most difficult thing they've ever tried to do, and not everyone makes it. Even co-founder John Maher relapsed into alcoholism and left the program in 1985; he died from a heart attack in 1988. One in four participants in the program drops out, but of those who do graduate, an estimated 80% are completely rehabilitated and go on to lead productive lives.

GROWTH

By the late 1980s, Delancey Street was becoming a victim of its own success: Demand for the program was so great that 90% of the applicants had to be turned away for lack of space. As Silbert and the residents saw it, the only option was to grow. So Delancey Street leased a three-acre parcel of waterfront land and made plans to build a 370,000-square-foot complex—large enough to house 500. Residents did most of the building themselves, saving nearly $16 million in labor costs. (Before they received training from local construction unions, the most experienced "builder" at Delancey Street was an ex-convict who'd helped pour concrete for the handball court at San Quentin.)

STILL GOING STRONG

Over the years, Delancey Street has expanded to new locations in North Carolina, New Mexico, New York, and Los Angeles. To date, more than 14,000 residents of the program have succeeded in turning their lives around, at no cost to taxpayers. And yet, for all the organization's growth, some things have remained the same: Mimi Silbert, who raised her twin sons at Delancey Street, still lives there in a one-bedroom apartment and still receives no salary.

Silbert summed up her philosophy in a 2000 interview with the Institute for Social Entrepreneurs: "It is my choice in life to insist upon always believing in the best of everybody...because I've seen the most incredible people at the bottom rise to become that absolute best of themselves. I guess when you think about it, what happens here at Delancey Street is that I'm the role model for the residents when they first come here. Then, later, they become my role models."

*   *   *

THEORY OF INSPIRATION

"Contemplate an entangled bank, clothed with plants of many kinds, birds singing on the bushes, insects flitting about, and worms crawling through the damp earth, and reflect on these elaborately constructed forms, so different from each other, and dependent on each other in so complex a manner. There is grandeur in this view of life, with its powers, having been originally breathed into a few forms or into one; and that from so simple a beginning endless forms most beautiful and most wonderful have been, and are being, evolved."

—**Charles Darwin**

DIDI'S GOOD DEEDS

This teacher saw people in need of help, and gave it to them.

TRAIN OF THOUGHT

Every day the sight at the train stations was the same: dozens of destitute children begging for handouts. Inderjit Khurana of Orissa, India, wanted to do something to help, but she didn't have enough money or food for them all. Nearly all the children were homeless. They had no access to school, and most seemed destined to live lives of poverty.

But Inderjit (Didi to her friends) did have one very important gift to give them: knowledge. Didi was a teacher, and even though she couldn't bring all of those children to her school, she could bring the school to them. So in 1985 she started her first "Train Platform School." Armed with a modest assortment of school supplies, she chalked out a section of the train platform and invited kids to come and sit for a few minutes while she taught them the basics of reading and math. Khurana set up these small "classrooms" at each of the various stops on her daily commute. Every day, more kids would gather for her lessons. And then other teachers saw what was happening and followed Khurana's lead.

ROLLING ALONG

Today there are 35 platform schools in India that teach reading, math, health, and job training. Because of Khurana's idea and her devotion throughout the years, thousands of children have been given hope. "I measure success not in terms of awards and publications," she says humbly, "but in a child pulling on my sleeve and asking, 'Didi, when will I see you again?'"

A LITTLE GOOD NEWS

A few more unlikely stories—with happy endings.

PROPHETIC BULLET

In 2006 Donald Batsch was shot twice during a robbery of Chester Lane Market in Bakersfield, California. You'd think that was bad news, but when he had to have surgery for his gunshot wounds, a small tumor was discovered in his abdomen. Doctors said that if he hadn't been wounded, they wouldn't have found the tumor—it would have kept growing, and maybe even killed him. "It was like an act of God that he shot me," Batsch said.

KEEP YOUR PANTS ON

Researchers at the Regional Animal Protection Service in Spokane, Washington, made a funny discovery in 2005: They found that sometimes when dogs pant, they may actually be laughing. And apparently the laughter is contagious: When they played a recording of ordinary panting to a group of barking dogs, the dogs kept barking. But when they played the "laughing" pant—long, loud breath sounds—all of the dogs stopped barking within a minute. The researchers concluded that the doggy laugh had a "calming or soothing effect" on other dogs.

NINE LIVES (PLUS TWO YEARS)

In 2004 the Tighe family of Hallam, Nebraska, lost their home in a tornado. They also lost their eight-year-old cat, Harley. Almost two years later, their daughter spotted an orange-and-white tabby at the edge of their yard, and when she called to it, the cat ran up to her, meowing. It was Harley.

Mrs. Tighe was stunned. She was sure that if Harley had survived the tornado, nobody would have taken him in. "He isn't a very nice cat," she said. (But she was happy to have him back.)

IT WAS *THIS* BIG

In 2005 English angler Mark Everard set a new world record for the largest...minnow. At four-and-a-half inches long, it was more than double the size of an average minnow. He actually caught it with a rod and reel and a *really* tiny hook. "It fought with Hemingway proportions," he said, "but I managed to land it safely after a few seconds."

FROM THE MUCK

Two sanitation workers in Bellingham, Massachusetts, Randy Poirier and Dustin Ciccarelli, were clearing sludge from inside a manhole when they found a class ring in the muck. Poirier did some investigating and found out it was from local Milford High School, Class of 1961.

He looked in some old Milford yearbooks for anyone with the initials "M.C.," which were inscribed on the band. There was only one match: Margaret Calcagri. He made some phone calls and found Margaret's daughter, Angel Moll. Moll gave him some bad news: Her mother had died 19 years earlier.

Still, she was thrilled to get the ring. "He's like an angel to me," said Moll, who described her mother as her closest companion. "He found a piece of my mom's past, then went through all this so that I could have it."

"She doesn't have many things from her mom," Poirier said. "It felt really good to give her something that she could keep and cherish."

LIFE IN A JAR

One amazing woman in Poland—and four teens in
Kansas who tracked her down and told her story.

SENDLER'S LIST

In 1999 a teacher at Uniontown High School in Kansas encouraged four students to do a project for a national History Day contest. Norm Conard told his 9th-grade students —Elizabeth Cambers, Megan Stewart, and Janice Underwood, and 11th-grader Sabrina Coons—that the project should reflect the classroom motto, "He who changes one person, changes the world entire." The quote is from the Jewish holy book the Talmud, and Conard suggested basing the project on the Holocaust.

He showed them a 1994 news clipping about "other Schindlers," people who, like Oskar Schindler (made famous in the film *Schindler's List*), had saved Jews from the Nazis during World War II. One of the people mentioned was a Polish woman named Irena Sendler, who was said to have saved 2,500 Jewish children from the Warsaw ghetto. Schindler had saved about 1,100 people. "We thought this had to be a mistake or something," said Conard. "Maybe this Sendler saved 250, but not 2,500. I mean, nobody had ever heard of this woman."

SEARCHING FOR IRENA

"We became obsessed with finding out everything we could about Irena," said 15-year-old Elizabeth Cambers. And they soon found out that the number was right. But how Irena Sendler had saved the children was almost unbelievable.

Sendler was a social worker in Warsaw when the Nazis

invaded Poland in 1939. By 1940 they had created the
Warsaw ghetto: 400,000 Jews were confined to an area one
square mile in size. They were not allowed to leave, and conditions quickly became deplorable. Hundreds died every day
from starvation or disease, and soon more were being sent to
die in death camps. By 1942 more than 80,000 had perished.

Sendler, who was not Jewish, was sickened by what she
saw...so she made a plan. She forged a pass from the Warsaw
Epidemic Control Department and, starting in 1942, went
into the ghetto every day. There she would ask parents to do
the unthinkable: give their children to her so she could
smuggle them out. It meant that the parents would probably
never see them again, but for the children to stay, the strick-
en parents knew, was to let them die.

BURYING HOPE

At incredible risk to herself, Irena smuggled dozens of children out of the ghetto day after day. She took them right
past the guards, showing fake documents and saying they
were ill. Or she would put children in coffins, saying they
were dead. Once out, she gave the children phony papers
with new names and found Polish families to adopt them, or
she placed them in orphanages. Some she hid in churches
and convents.

But while she was saving the children, Sendler knew that
she was taking them from their families, and from their own
identities. So she made lists of all their real names and
addresses and their new locations—in code—and put the
lists into glass jars. Then she buried the jars beneath an
apple tree in a neighbor's backyard, hoping that one day she
could dig them up, find the children, and reunite them with
their families.

On October 20, 1943, Irena Sendler was found out by the Nazis. She was imprisoned—and, because she was the only one who knew the location of the children and the jars, she was tortured. Gestapo agents broke both her feet and both her legs, but Sendler refused to tell them anything. She spent three months in prison, then was sentenced to death.

The girls were so moved by Sendler's story that they wrote a play about it entitled *Life in a Jar*. Elizabeth Cambers played "Jolanta," Irena's code name and the only name by which the children knew her, and Megan Stewart played a mother who must give up her children. They performed the play at school, then in local clubs and churches. People in the community were so moved by Sendler's story that the school district, which didn't have a single Jewish student, declared an official Irena Sendler Day. On top of that, the girls' work won them first prize in the National History Day contest for the state of Kansas. But the best was yet to come.

FINDING IRENA
The girls kept looking for more clues about Irena's life. They contacted the Jewish Foundation for the Righteous, an organization that honors non-Jews who risked their lives to save Jews during the Holocaust, to ask if they knew the location of Irena's grave. They didn't, they said, but they had something else: her address. Irena Sendler was alive.

Elizabeth, Megan, Janice, and Sabrina immediately wrote to Irena in Warsaw and told her about their project and play. Six weeks later they got an enthusiastic reply. "Your performance and work," Irena wrote, "is continuing the effort I started over fifty years ago."

Sendler also told them the rest of her story: She had been brutally tortured and sentenced to death by the Nazis when she refused to tell them where the children were. But the Polish underground came to her rescue, securing Irena's release by bribing a guard. She spent the rest of the war a fugitive.

After the war ended, Sendler immediately went back to her neighbor's house, dug up the jars, and began tracking down the children, hoping to reunite as many as possible with their parents. She was able to find many, but hundreds she could not—and most of the parents were dead.

WARSAW

In 2001 the students' dream came true when they traveled to Poland to meet the subject of their long study. Irena Sendler, by then 89 years old, took the girls in like granddaughters. "We ran up and hugged her and cried," said Elizabeth Cambers. "We told her she is our hero, but she said she doesn't think of herself that way. 'Heroes do extraordinary things,' she told us. She just did what she had to do."

The group was even able to meet some of the children, now in their 50s, who were saved by Irena (and by others who helped her, Irena was always quick to point out). One was Elzbieta Ficowska, rescued by Irena when she was five months old by being carried out in a carpenter's toolbox. They also met a Polish poet who was saved by Irena, who called the young women "rescuers of the rescuer" for bringing Irena's amazing story to the public. And to the public it went. The story of the students' visit to Irena in Warsaw and of their performance of *Life in a Jar* spread. When they returned home, the four young women were interviewed on radio and TV, and in newspapers and magazines worldwide.

The four original students have all graduated, but the Sendler Project, as it is now known, continues today with Mr.

Conard and new students. *Life in a Jar* has been performed more than 170 times in the United States and Europe. They also have a Web site (irenasendler.org), through which they raise money for people like Sendler, who risked their lives to save others.

Irena Sendler, now 96, continues to correspond with the four girls (they've visited her twice more, the last time in 2005). She now lives in a nursing home in Warsaw and is being cared for, appropriately, by a woman she smuggled out of the Warsaw ghetto more than 60 years ago.

*   *   *

EVERYDAY PEOPLE

Some more personal inspiration from the BRI staff.

Connie V: "My dad always said, 'One for all and all for one.' Coming from a family of nine kids, it taught me that no matter how bad a situation gets, my family will always be there for me."

JoAnn P: "My first year in college was a revelation: I could stay out all night partying if I wanted to, but my grades really suffered. One day my parents told me, 'We know you're doing the best you can.' I was shocked that they thought I was so stupid. So I straightened up…and made the dean's list every quarter after that."

Jay N: "In elementary school, I had a lot of trouble paying attention, and was usually placed in the learning-disabled groups. But Mrs. Fitzhugh (5th grade) thought I was smarter than my grades showed, and challenged me by putting me at the 'smart' table. I excelled in her class, and discovered that I had a talent for writing."

HOPE FOR THE FUTURE

We leave you with a few reasons to remain optimistic.

"Most of the important things in the world have been accomplished by people who have kept on trying when there seemed to be no hope at all."
—**Dale Carnegie**

"We should not let our fears hold us back from pursuing our hopes."
—**John F. Kennedy**

"The very least you can do in your life is to figure out what you hope for. And the most you can do is live inside that hope. Not admire it from a distance but live right in it, under its roof."
—**Barbara Kingsolver**

"You must not lose faith in humanity. Humanity is an ocean; if a few drops of the ocean are dirty, the ocean does not become dirty."
—**Mohandas K. Gandhi**

"When you do nothing, you feel overwhelmed and powerless. But when you get involved, you feel the sense of hope and accomplishment that comes from knowing you are working to make things better."
—**Pauline R. Kezer**

"Your hopes, dreams, and aspirations are legitimate. They are trying to take you airborne, above the clouds, above the storms, if you only let them."
—**William James**

"Learn from yesterday, live for today, hope for tomorrow. The important thing is to not stop questioning."
—**Albert Einstein**

"Optimism is the faith that leads to achievement. Nothing can be done without hope."
—**Helen Keller**

UNCLE JOHN'S
BATHROOM READER
CLASSIC SERIES

Find these and other great titles from the *Uncle John's Bathroom Reader* Classic Series online at **www.bathroomreader.com**. Or contact us at:

Bathroom Readers' Institute • P.O. Box 1117 • Ashland, OR 97520

(888) 488-4642

E LAST PAGE

sitting along with us for *Uncle John's Tales to*
We hope it made you feel as good as the gang
BRI felt while putting it all together.

to take the plunge? Sit Down and Be Counted!
a member of the Bathroom Readers' Institute. Log
www.bathroomreader.com, or send a self-addressed,
ped, business-sized envelope to: BRI, PO Box 1117,
land, Oregon 97520. You'll receive your free membership
rd, get discounts when ordering directly through the BRI,
and earn a permanent spot on the BRI honor roll!

If you like reading our books...
VISIT THE BRI'S WEB SITE!
www.bathroomreader.com

- Visit "The Throne Room"—a great place to read!
- Receive our irregular newsletters via e-mail
- Order additional *Bathroom Readers*
- Become a BRI member

Go with the Flow...

Well, we're out of space, and when you've gotta go, you've gotta
go. Tanks for all your support. Hope to hear from you soon.
Meanwhile, remember:

Keep on flushin'!

THE LAST PAGE

Thanks for sitting along with us for *Uncle John's Tales to Inspire*. We hope it made you feel as good as the gang at the BRI felt while putting it all together.

Ready to take the plunge? Sit Down and Be Counted! Become a member of the Bathroom Readers' Institute. Log on to *www.bathroomreader.com*, or send a self-addressed, stamped, business-sized envelope to: BRI, PO Box 1117, Ashland, Oregon 97520. You'll receive your free membership card, get discounts when ordering directly through the BRI, and earn a permanent spot on the BRI honor roll!

If you like reading our books...

VISIT THE BRI'S WEB SITE!
www.bathroomreader.com

- Visit "The Throne Room"—a great place to read!
- Receive our irregular newsletters via e-mail
- Order additional *Bathroom Readers*
- Become a BRI member

Go with the Flow...

Well, we're out of space, and when you've gotta go, you've gotta go. Tanks for all your support. Hope to hear from you soon. Meanwhile, remember:

Keep on flushin'!